NEW PROCLAMATION

NEW PROCLAMATION

Year A, 2002

Easter through Pentecost

Warren Carter

Diane Jacobson

Carol J. Dempsey

John Paul Heil

FORTRESS PRESS

Minneapolis

NEW PROCLAMATION
Year A, 2002
Easter through Pentecost

Cover and book design: Joseph Bonyata

Illustrations: Tanya Butler, *Icon: Visual Images for Every Sunday,* copyright © 2000 Augsburg Fortress.

Library of Congress Cataloging-in-Publication Data

New proclamation year A, 2002 : Easter through Pentecost / Warren Carter . . . [et al.].
   p. cm.
  Includes bibliographical references.
  ISBN 0-8006-4246-5 (alk. paper)
   1. Lectionary preaching. 2. Common lectionary (1992) 3. Bible—Homiletical use.
 I. Carter, Warren

BS534.5 .N48 2001
251'.6—dc21

2001050136

The paper used in this publication meets the minimum requirements of the American National Standard for Information Sciences—Permanence of Paper for printed Library Materials, ANSI Z329.48-1984. ∞

Manufactured in the U.S.A.   AF 1-4246

06   05   04   03   02   1   2   3   4   5   6   7   8   9   10

CONTENTS

THE SEASON OF PENTECOST
CAROL J. DEMPSEY

THE SEASON OF PENTECOST
JOHN PAUL HEIL

PUBLISHER'S NOTE

New Proclamation continues the venerable Fortress Press tradition of offering a lectionary preaching resource that provides the best in biblical exegetical aids for a variety of lectionary traditions.

Thoroughly ecumenical and built around the three-year lectionary cycle, *New Proclamation* is focused on the biblical text, based on the conviction that those who are well equipped to understand a pericope in both its historical and liturgical contexts will be stimulated to preach engaging and effective sermons. For this reason, the most capable North American biblical scholars and homileticians are invited to contribute to *New Proclamation*.

New Proclamation is planned and designed to be user-friendly in a variety of ways:

- *New Proclamation* is published in two volumes per year, designed for convenience. The volume you are holding covers the lections for approximately the second half of the church year, Easter through Pentecost, which culminates in Christ the King Sunday.
- This two-volume format offers a larger, workbook-style page with a lay-flat binding and space for making notes.
- Each season of the church year is prefaced by an introduction that offers insight into the background and spiritual significance of the period.
- How the preacher can apply biblical texts to contemporary situations is a concern of each contributor. Exegetical work ("Interpreting the Text") is concise, and thoughts on how the text addresses today's world and our personal situations ("Responding to the Texts") have a prominent role.
- Although they are not usually used as preaching texts, brief comments on each assigned psalm ("Responsive Reading") are included so that the preacher can incorporate reflections also on these in the sermon.

- Boxed quotations in the margins help signal important themes in the texts for the day.
- The material for Series A is here dated specifically for the year 2002, for easier coordination with other dated lectionary materials.
- These materials can be adapted for uses other than for corporate worship on the day indicated. They are well suited for adult discussion groups or personal meditation and reflection.

We are grateful to our contributors, Warren Carter, Diane Jacobson, Carol J. Dempsey, and John Paul Heil, for their insights and for their commitment to effective Christian preaching. We hope that you find in this volume ideas, stimulation, and encouragement in your ministry of proclamation.

MARSHALL D. JOHNSON

THE SEASON
OF EASTER

WARREN
CARTER

"Good" Friday leaves a bad taste in the mouth. The good man Jesus is dead. The privileged and powerful elite—the Roman imperial regime and its allies, the Jerusalem leaders—seem to have triumphed. Privilege and power, sin and death, have won again.

But into this dismal scene bursts Easter, with new life, victory over sin and death, triumph, and hope.

At least that's how it is supposed to be.

But, as we know, it doesn't often happen like this. Various realities blunt Easter's impact: familiarity born of annual celebrations; the unchanged and apparently unchangeable ailments of our lives that seem impervious to Easter power and rhetoric; an unexamined Easter "joy" that knows some words ("He is risen") but little of their implications for daily life; the increasing secularization and consumerism that surround Easter with chocolate-coated distractions that have little connection to the barbarity of the cross and the miracle of the tomb; the incessant busy-ness that seems to distract or divert God's people.

Yet the lectionary's biblical texts urge us into this Easter season again to think deeply about what and who and why we are celebrating. What does it mean to be an Easter people in a society that has largely redefined the season in compatible secular terms? For some who gather in church, it is a day—or, more realistically, a morning or an hour. For the lectionary, it is a seven-week season. For the biblical texts assigned by the lectionary, it is a way of daily life that lasts forever. Easter is clearly much more complex than a few "He is risens" on Easter Sunday morning.

The lectionary texts shape an Easter people grounded in God's just, merciful, inclusive, and life-giving purposes. The texts form a people that share in the death and the resurrection of Jesus. The texts acknowledge that we live with the Risen One's presence and absence, in the process of being saved from all that subverts God's purposes. They point us to an eschatological horizon and a profound solidarity with all of God's creation. They envision a counter-cultural community that lives an agenda and distinctive practices that are often not shared by our larger society and that challenge its fundamental commitments, injustices, and idolatries.

And by the end of this Easter season, we know again that this identity is too hard for us without God's help. Easter leads us via the Ascension to Pentecost—and of course way beyond.

THE RESURRECTION OF OUR LORD—EASTER DAY

MARCH 31, 2002

REVISED COMMON	EPISCOPAL (BCP)	ROMAN CATHOLIC
Acts 10:34-43 or Jer. 31:1-6	Acts 10:34-43 or Exod. 14:10-14, 21-25; 15:20-21	Acts 10:34a, 37-43
Ps. 118:1-2, 14-24	Ps. 118:14-29 or 118:14-17, 22-24	Ps. 118:1-2, 16-17, 22-23 (24)
Col. 3:1-4 or Acts 10:34-43	Col. 3:1-4 or Acts 10:34-43	Col. 3:1-4 or 1 Cor. 5:6b-8
John 20:1-18 or Matt. 28:1-10	John 20:1-10 (11-18) or Matt. 28:1-10	John 20:1-9

THESE EASTER DAY TEXTS involve threatened and celebrating communities, Jews and Gentiles, men and women, gift and challenge. They present today's larger-than-usual congregations with a question: "Jesus is risen—so what?" Their answers won't reduce to a monolithic "comforting presence"/"Jesus is with me" approach, though that is one dimension. Other answers will disturb or transform. Some folks will welcome the possibilities and challenges of new life; others will elect not to return next week.

FIRST READING
ACTS 10:34-43 (RCL and BCP);
ACTS 10:34a, 37-43 (RC)

Interpreting the Text

Peter preaches to Cornelius, the Roman centurion, and his household. This narrative (10:1—11:18) demonstrates God's active intervention through numerous means (visions, angels, voices, the Spirit, circumstances) to accomplish God's purposes to bless all people (Gen. 12:1-3). Peter emphasizes the universal scope of God's blessing: "God shows no partiality" (10:34), "in every nation" (10:35), "Jesus Christ—he is Lord of all" (10:36); "everyone who believes" (10:43).

The supreme demonstration of God's universal blessing occurs in a particular intervention (10:36-39): a particular person (Jesus anointed [10:38] and ordained [10:42] by God) in a particular place (Judea, Galilee) with particular people (Israel) in particular actions (doing good, healing). A few witness God's raising of Jesus (10:40-41a). Has all the rest been forgotten? By no means! The few bear witness that others might experience God's forgiveness (10:41-43).

Responding to the Text

Why does Jesus' resurrection matter? What substance does it have beyond the all-too-common Easter fare of "Be happy—Jesus is your friend"? Peter's sermon indicates at least three dimensions. *Resurrection says something about God.* God works in the world for the new life of "forgiveness." The term means much more than personal renewal. It appears some fourteen times in Leviticus 25 (translated as "jubilee;" also Deut. 15:1-9; see Luke 4:18-19) to denote God's will that transforms destructive social and economic structures into a world accountable to God and marked by compassion and justice for all. *Resurrection says something about Jesus.* God vindicates him (10:42). Jesus' opponents do not have, nor will they ever have, the last word. The resurrection is God's seal of approval on Jesus' mission to create an inclusive world marked by universal justice and mercy (10:38) that challenges Rome's injustice, hierarchy, exploitation. *Resurrection says something about the church.* Empowered by the Spirit (10:38; chap. 2), we bear witness with life-giving words, actions, practices, and structures to this alternative world.

> PETER'S SERMON INDICATES AT LEAST THREE DIMENSIONS OF EASTER.

JEREMIAH 31:31:1-6 (RCL, alt.); EXODUS 14:10-14, 21-25; 15:20-21 (BCP, alt.)

Interpreting the Text

Jeremiah 30–31 forms "the Book of Consolation" as Jeremiah speaks to "Israel and Judah" (30:4). Assyria had overrun and exiled Israel in 722 B.C.E. Babylon was about to do the same to Judah (Jerusalem, 587). The prophet understands both catastrophes as punishment (30:14). But from this death, from this fatal woundedness (30:12-17), God promises healing and new life (30:17-24). There is grace in the wilderness, a new exodus, everlasting love, a display of God's covenant faithfulness, celebration, fertility, the successful completion of God's purposes that seemed to be in tatters (31:1-6)

The Exodus reading also celebrates God's power and mercy. Tyrannized by and fearful of the Egyptian powers, pursued by its military, and trapped by the sea, death is inevitable—apart from God's faithful, life-giving intervention and powerful deliverance.

Responding to the Text

Exodus . . . return from exile . . . resurrection—these big events in the biblical story critique "normative" human society and evidence God's alternative salvific purposes. Injustice, oppression, military might, imperialism, bullying, domination seem to reign supreme. But these narratives expose their lies and limits, and witness to God's different purposes for human interaction. In raising Jesus, God does it again. God's way of working, manifested long before, as well as in Jesus' resurrection, is to breathe life into every situation of death.

RESPONSIVE READING

PSALM 118:1-2, 14-24 (RCL); PSALM 118:14-29 or 118:14-17, 22-24 (BCP); PSALM 118:1-2, 16-17, 22-23 (24) (RC)

This psalm of thanksgiving centers on God's deliverance of an individual (representing the nation?) from a dangerous situation. As is typical of the Psalms, the danger is not clearly identified. Verses 10-12, 15-16 hint at a military danger, and the psalm belongs with other Passover psalms that celebrate deliverance from Egypt (cf. Exod. 15:2). But military threat and salvation from Egypt do not contain it. This imprecision enables the psalm to give voice to the thankfulness of worshipers (plural!) who have survived diverse threatening situations.

After the initial praise (118:1-4), the psalm testifies to God's saving power (118:14, 16, 21, 23) and to God's steadfast love demonstrated through such circumstances (118:29). The people entrust themselves to God's goodness that saves from the actively threatening power of death (118:17-19). Much later, the early church, wearing "Jesus" glasses, saw references to Jesus' crucifixion and resurrection (118:22, 26), "the Lord's doing . . . marvelous in our eyes . . . the day that the Lord has made." This day calls for rejoicing and celebration (118:23-24) and provides hope for participating in God's future salvation (118:25).

SECOND READING

COLOSSIANS 3:1-4 (RCL, BCP, RC)

Interpreting the Text

The author of Colossians (probably a disciple of Paul) upholds the central and supreme role of Christ in God's reconciling purposes that bless all, Jew and Gentile (1:15-29). In a context of false teaching (2:8-23), he exhorts the Colossians to "lead lives worthy of the Lord . . . as you bear fruit in every good work" (1:10; 1:9-14). This life participates in Jesus' resurrection, since believers "were also raised with him through faith in the power of God who raised him from the dead" (2:12). Jesus' resurrection is not his alone; it effects lived transformation for believers.

This emphasis on present participation in Jesus' resurrection differs from Paul's view. Paul sees believers being raised in the future completion of God's purposes (1 Cor. 15:20-28). Resurrection belongs to the "not yet" rather than the "now" of Christian existence. In Rom. 6:4-5, 8, Paul expresses this eschatological reserve with future tenses, "we *will* certainly be united" and "we *will* also live with him."

But in Col. 3:1-4, the author elaborates the present ethical and eschatological consequences of "having been raised with Christ." A new perspective, new focus, new priorities, and a new lifestyle result (3:2-4). The phrase, "the things that are above," has been seen to sanction detachment from or dismissal of all physical concerns and necessities like food, shelter, clothing, and to urge passive submission to and tolerance of sinful human structures. Nothing could be further from the truth. The author has already commended lives pleasing to God marked by "every good work" (1:12). In 3:5-17 he envisages the dismantling of greedy imperial society (3:5) and the abolition of fundamental social divisions (3:11). The end of impurity, greed, idolatry, and deceptive relationships means social transformation, whether in Rome's imperial world or twenty-first century capitalist society. He advocates an alternative human community (3:5-17) marked by personal (3:10) and social re-creation, new practices and relationships, and ruled by the peace ("wholeness") of Christ, not the military-based, economically exploiting, and socially oppressive peace of Rome or any other dominant power (3:15). Regrettably, the author does not follow through on this vision to replace hierarchical and patriarchal households (3:18—4:1). The transformation now under way as a display of resurrection life will be completed at the future glorious revelation of God's purposes (3:4).

Of what significance is resurrection? In this Colossians text, resurrection is not a litmus test of right words, not a celebration restricted to a particular day in the liturgical and ecclesial calendar, not a "feel good" moment. Rather, resurrection creates an alternative, counter-cultural way of life that confronts human injustice and displays God's cosmic, reconciling, re-creating purposes. It witnesses to Christ's resurrection as part of God's cosmic transformation, and anticipates its future completion. Believers live for personal and social transformation. They/we bear the suffering of present inequities and injustice (the "not yet"). They/we confront dominant social patterns and values: social exclusion and hierarchy, economic greed at the expense of enough, self-serving power, selfish consumerism, racial and sexual and gender prejudice. They/we anticipate God's coming just world.

> RESURRECTION CREATES AN ALTERNATIVE, COUNTERCULTURAL WAY OF LIFE THAT CONFRONTS HUMAN INJUSTICE AND DISPLAYS GOD'S COSMIC, RECONCILING, RE-CREATING PURPOSES.

ACTS 10:34-43 (RCL and BCP, alt.)

See First Reading, above.

1 CORINTHIANS 5:6b-8 (RC)

See below, Easter Evening, Second Reading.

THE GOSPEL
JOHN 20:1-18 (RC);
JOHN 10:1-10 (11-18) (BCP);
JOHN 20:1-9 (RC)

Interpreting the Text

John's Gospel concludes with two resurrection chapters (20–21). In this section, 20:1-18, it is, in typical Johannine fashion, a matter of what one sees. How does one interpret the sight of an empty tomb?

Mary visits the tomb in the dark, a time (3:2; 6:17) and metaphor (1:5; 8:12; 12:35, 46) of "not seeing" or unbelief. In the darkness, she sees a rolled away stone and an empty tomb. What does she make of this? She does not connect it with divine action or resurrection, even though Jesus has described himself as the resurrection (6:40; 11:25) and spoken of his own (2:19-22). Mary interprets the rolled away stone and empty tomb, plausibly, as theft: "They have taken the Lord." This explanation confirms her expectation of death. She does not know "where they have laid him" (20:2).

Peter, representative of disciples throughout, and another disciple, visit the tomb. They "see" the linen cloths and napkin (recall Lazarus in 11:44). Peter's response is not described. The other disciple interprets the tomb and garments as signs of God's action and believes (20:8; cf. 1:12). What does he believe? The empty tomb attests that Jesus defies the death-producing ways of the socioreligious and political elite. Their power is limited and not final. But the disciple's belief is imperfect. He is not yet informed by the scriptures (20:9). He has not met the risen Lord, nor is Jesus ascended (20:17), nor has the Spirit provided further instruction (14:26).

Mary reappears, still shrouded in grief, weeping (cf. 16:20-22), not believing. Seeing angels, she sees not signs of God's presence but company for her misery. In v. 13, she complains to them that she (not the "we" of 20:2) doesn't know where the dead Jesus is. In vv. 14-15 she sees Jesus but doesn't recognize him, "supposing him to be the gardener," mistaking the crucified for one of the crucifiers, and still honorably obsessed with his burial (20:15). He asks what she "seeks," a question that uses discipleship language (1:38) and recalls Jesus' self-giving (18:4-7).

JESUS COMMISSIONS MARY, THE FIRST WITNESS OF THE RISEN JESUS, TO BE THE FIRST PROCLAIMER OF THE RESURRECTION-ASCENSION GOSPEL AND OF ITS IMPLICATIONS FOR DISCIPLES.

Amazingly, belief happens! He speaks her name. She "hears" him as true sheep do (10:3, 27). She is blessed (20:29). She recognizes Jesus as "teacher" (20:16), then as Lord (20:18). He commissions this woman, the first witness of the risen Jesus, to be the first proclaimer of the resurrection-ascension gospel (20:17-18) and of its implications for disciples who share with God the same relationship and destiny that Jesus enjoys ("your Father . . . your God;" note "your" is plural; 14:1-3).

Responding to the Text

F. Moloney correctly points out that the first part of John is marked by faith journeys in which various characters respond to Jesus in different ways (Nicodemus, chap. 3; the Samaritan woman, chap. 4).[1] This passage offers three vignettes of responses that may interact with the responses of some who attend worship today.

Peter "sees" something but it is unspecified and vague. Does he "see" nothing? The presence of the burial linen described in detail in vv. 5-7 and reminiscent of Lazarus's raising (11:44) counts against Mary's conclusion of robbery. Peter's moment will come later, in chap. 21.

The other disciple sees and believes. He apparently interprets the empty tomb on the basis of what he knows about Jesus. Jesus has power over death, the power to judge those who judge him (5:21-22). He sees that demonstrated in the empty tomb.

Mary journeys to "see" both the tomb and Jesus. Her grief and unbelief give way to some faith as she recognizes Jesus as teacher, and then to greater faith as she names him Lord. But her journey is not over yet. The risen Jesus commissions her to proclaim, but her sermon topic is not resurrection! He points her beyond resurrection to his ascension (20:17). Why? His ascension (13:1-3), in which the crucifixion and resurrection are stages in his "lifting up" (8:28; 12:32), is crucial for the community of believers. It vindicates with God's seal Jesus' revelation as the will and words of God (14:10). It invites disciples to share now with God the loving relationship and common will that Jesus enjoys with God (1:12, 18; 5:19-24). It makes possible the gift of the Spirit to abide with and instruct disciples (14:16-17; 26) and to equip us to do "greater works" as a mission community (20:22) that attests God's life-giving purposes for the world (14:12). And it anticipates Jesus' return to incorporate believers into the very life and love of God that the Father and Son enjoy (14:1-3). That is, for Mary and for believers, Easter Day is not the final act. It points forward, ultimately to the time of the completion of God's purposes (6:35-51). Easter is gift and demand, grace and challenge, present and future.

MATTHEW 28:1-10 (RCL and BCP, alt.)

Interpreting the Text

Unlike John's Mary (John 20) and Mark's women (Mark 16), Matthew's women do not come to the tomb dominated by unbelief and grief. They bring no spices; they have no expectation of permanent death. They come to "see" the tomb, a verb that for Matthew denotes comprehension and belief (13:10-17; 20:29-34). Four times verbs of "seeing" denote encountering the risen Jesus (28:6, 7, 10, 17). That is what the women come to do, because they have "heard" Jesus teach that God will raise him (16:21; 17:22-23; 20:17-19). While the male disciples have chosen fear and flight (26:56), the women have remained faithful despite their fear (28:5, 8).[2]

God's presence and power, features of the eschatological in-breaking of God's empire, are evident in an earthquake and angel (28:2). Lightning, commonly associated with Jupiter, and with Rome's emperors as his agents, denotes here God's presence (Exod. 19:16; Ezek. 1:13). Rome's power, allied with the Jerusalem elite, has put Jesus to death, but Rome's power is revealed to be limited. Rome is viewed in part as God's agent in punishing the people (22:7, as imperial powers are often viewed in the biblical traditions; see Jer. 30:14). But ultimately, Rome is seen as the devil's agent, whose empire is under the devil's control (4:8). It has, along with the Jerusalem elite, crucified Jesus as a graphic display of its rejection of God's will (20:25-28; chaps. 26–27). In a nice touch, God's presence paralyzes the Roman guards (28:4). They become "like dead men" in this place of life, just as Rome's army, symbolized by its standard, the eagle, will become corpses in the eschatological battle of Jesus' return and the establishment of God's empire (24:27-31).[3]

The angel proclaims what the women expected to hear (28:6) and commissions them to proclaim this resurrection message (28:7). Joyfully and fearfully (28:8,10), they obey the divine will, only to encounter the risen Jesus (28:9) who in the midst of their worship renews their commission (28:10).

Responding to the Text

As with the Acts passage, these verses say something about God, Jesus, and discipleship. The women are at the tomb (without spices) because they have attended to Jesus' teaching and it has shaped their actions and expectations. They encounter the risen Lord and hear the commission to proclaim the resurrection message (twice for emphasis). Resurrection means worship, divine presence, faithfulness, power.

But it also means commission and risk. The women carry out their proclaiming task in a context of danger and fear. To associate with someone who was socially, politically, and religiously rejected in crucifixion is not smart. To proclaim that God has thwarted Roman power with resurrection in anticipation of establishing God's empire is downright seditious, as well as faithful and brave (16:24). Jesus' resurrection is the death knell for Rome's empire—and for any empire. It exposes the limits of its power, its pretensions to have sovereignty of the world, its evil in resisting God's anointed, its opposition to his vision of a just and merciful world. Preaching is threatening work. As always, the empire cannot tolerate such a challenge. It strikes back with its own untruthful propaganda and self-serving alternative story (28:11-15). But the women are faithful in a context of competing stories. They tell a counter-narrative that critiques the dominant cultural story, offers an alternative story for living, and anticipates God's future just world. Their faithfulness is attested by the disciples' gathering in 28:16, and perhaps by the fact that the risen Jesus risks committing the yet unfinished task to all disciples (28:18-20)!

EASTER EVENING

MARCH 31, 2002

REVISED COMMON	EPISCOPAL (BCP)	ROMAN CATHOLIC
Isa. 25:6-9	Acts 5:29a, 30-32 or Dan. 12:1-3	Acts 10:34a, 37-43
Psalm 114	Psalm 114 or Psalm 136 or Ps. 118:14-17, 22-24	Ps. 118:1-2, 16-17, 22-23
1 Cor. 5:6b-8	1 Cor. 5:6b-8 or Acts 5:29a, 30-32	Col. 3:1-4 or 1 Cor. 5:6-8
Luke 24:13-49	Luke 24:13-35	Luke 24:13-35

Food pervades these texts (Isa. 25:6; Ps. 136:25; 1 Cor. 5:6-7; Luke 24:30-32, 41-43). Too much food is quite a problem for many (not all) of us in the western world. But not so in the ancient world. These texts are shaped by imperial worlds and their realities of taxation and exploitation. Ninety-five percent of the population forcibly give up their food to support the extravagant lifestyle of the ruling 5 percent. Ezekiel 34 criticizes leaders for feeding themselves but not their people. Hunger, poor nutrition, hard work, and anxiety result. Imperial rule is hazardous to your health. So the biblical traditions, shaped by this world of want, frequently use abundant food and feasting to envision the coming of God's just world in which God's presence, life, and reign are established (Isa. 25:6; Matt. 22:1-10).[4] A meal with the risen Christ anticipates such a world, and reveals God bringing it into being, encountered in the sharing of food (Isa. 55:1-3).

FIRST READING
ISAIAH 25:6-9 (RCL);
DANIEL 12:1-3 (BCP, alt.)

Interpreting the Texts

Isaiah 24–27, probably postexilic additions to Isaiah, offers visions and promises about God's future. God—ironically in typical imperial style—will triumph over Israel's enemies, whether Assyria, Babylon, Persia, Moab (25:10-12). After judgment (Isaiah 24), God will establish God's reign of peace, justice, and compliance with God's will from Zion (24:23). The reading shows this reign as a feast of plenty "for all peoples" (25:6). It will be the death of death (25:7) and the end of suffering and disgrace (25:8). This is God's salvation.

Same song, second verse! Daniel 12:1-3 originates in the imperial tyranny of the Seleucid Antiochus IV Epiphanes (175–163 B.C.E.). Antiochus systematically dismantled Jewish covenant practices and worship in the Jerusalem temple (1 Maccabees 1). Daniel urges faithfulness, even to martyrdom, while promising God's rescue. This section completes Daniel's fourth vision, in which, after much anguish (12:1), Israel's angelic protector Michael, God's agent, delivers the people. The dead are raised for judgment, some (including faithful martyrs) to vindication, some to condemnation. Many see this passage as one of the earliest statements of resurrection faith in the canonical traditions (cf. Isa. 26:19).

Responding to the Texts

Both readings recall God's ultimate purposes, to reverse current inequities and establish God's sovereignty over the world, in place of those powers, imperial and diabolical, that illegitimately claim it as their own and order it unjustly. The fundamental question is as Ernst Käsemann once wrote, "To whom does the sovereignty of the world belong?"[5] The question is pressing for our own time. We know so well threats to our very future from ecological disasters; economic practices that ensure that the wealthy gain wealth and power while the poor accumulate debt, dependency, and desperation; wars over land; nuclear destruction; culture and ideological wars over competing visions of human society.

The biblical tradition styles the reigns of usurpers of God's sovereignty as the reign of death (Isa. 25:7). By contrast God's reign is often pictured as a reign of life marked by fertility and abundant food, and by just and harmonious social relations.

GOD'S REIGN IS OFTEN PICTURED AS A REIGN OF LIFE MARKED BY FERTILITY AND ABUNDANT FOOD, AND BY JUST AND HARMONIOUS SOCIAL RELATIONS.

These visions terrify and amaze. The establishment of God's perfect will on earth provokes hope and celebration. It provides the goal and the motivation for working against (not escaping from) all that resists God's purposes. But we must be cautious about expressing God's victory in imperialistic terms. The texts attribute to God what belongs to Caesar. God imitates the tyrants in forcibly and powerfully imposing God's will! Often God's reign is pictured benevolently, yet all tyrants view their reign as beneficial. Maintaining the good goal without violent means of imposition offers one way ahead.

What does this have to do with resurrection? In one sense Jesus' resurrection inaugurates this new era. But traditions like the exodus story attest that God has been at work for this sort of world for a long time! Even Jesus' pre-resurrection ministry of feeding the hungry (on a mountain no less, Matt. 15:29-39), shows

God's commitment to overcoming Rome's taxing rule that removed large quantities of food from peasant farmers, leaving them hungry and in poor health. The resurrection of Jesus further asserts God's sovereignty over death, decisively demonstrating that the crucifying powers do not control human destiny, and anticipating the completion of God's purposes.

ACTS 5:29a, 30–32 (BCP)

See below, Second Reading.

ACTS 10:34a, 37–43 (RC)

See above, First Lesson, Easter Day.

RESPONSIVE READING
PSALM 114 (RCL and BCP);
PSALM 136 (BCP, alt.)

Psalm 114 belongs to the group of Passover psalms (113–118). It celebrates, with minimal historical details, God's deliverance of the people from Egypt (114:1-6) and the establishment of the nation (114:2). All of this, like resurrection, is God's doing, a demonstration of God's presence (114:7-8). This presence is not gentle. It is powerful, transforming, frightening, and efficient in correcting a situation of captivity, in delivering on God's promise of a new land, and in maintaining life in the land (114:8).

Psalm 136 celebrates God's "forever" love. The introduction declares that theme (136:1-3) while the remaining four sections provide examples of it from creation (136:4-9), the exodus (136:10-16), occupying Canaan (136:17-22), and return from Babylonian exile (136:23-26). God's love is creative, redeeming, constant, powerful, active, faithful, resurrecting.

PSALM 118:14-17, 22-24 (BCP, alt.);
PSALM 118:1-2, 16-17, 22-23 (RC)

See Easter Day, Responsive Reading

SECOND READING

1 CORINTHIANS 5:6b-8 (RCL, BCP);
1 CORINTHIANS 5:6-8 (RC, alt.);
COLOSSIANS 3:1-4 (RC)

Interpreting the Texts

Paul is concerned in 1 Corinthians 5 to determine behavior appropriate to life shaped by the risen Christ. The Corinthians have, for whatever reason, ignored a man living with his stepmother (5:1-2, 6a). Paul argues that this individual's action and the community's tolerance are destructive. One rotten apple destroys the whole barrel (cf. 1 Cor. 12:1-13). Paul's argument, addressed to the community, is based in Christ's sacrifice, which is interpreted, in association with the Passover lamb (Exod. 12:1-13), not as removing sin but as giving new life. This new life is described as being "unleavened," free of the corrupting influence of leaven ("malice and evil") and marked by "sincerity and truth." This is Paul's indicative. He asserts the imperative in v. 7, "cleanse out the old leaven."

Responding to the Text

This difficult text assumes its readers' familiarity with the significance of leaven and of the paschal lamb, both of which are probably quite foreign for most contemporary congregations! Attempting to bridge this cultural gap with explanations might be useful. Or it may be more worthwhile this evening to focus instead on the striking communal nature of this text. This passage emphasizes, as does today's reading from Col. 3:1-4, that resurrection life is not particularly an individual matter but a communal existence. God is shaping a people. The implications of that thought are enormous for contemporary church communities so often riddled by pervasive cultural individualism and by the mistaken conviction that religious commitment can be but a small and private part of our lives.

ACTS 5:29a, 30-32 (BCP, alt.)

Interpreting the Text

Peter and the apostles have disobeyed the order not to preach (4:16-22; 5:25-26). Before the Jerusalem elite, they defend themselves and announce God's vindication of Jesus in his resurrection and exaltation (5:30-31). The significance of this assertion is threefold. It demands the elite's recognition and submission. Through it God offers repentance and renewing communal forgiveness (see the discussion of the First Reading for Easter Day). And God equips its human witnesses with the Spirit to continue Jesus' work (cf. 2:22). Peter's response and the trial's outcome establish that the inevitable opposition from the ruling elite will not quench God's work.

Responding to the Text

The story provides further testimony to God's action in raising Jesus, and to its impact on the courageous, undaunted proclamation of Peter. Regrettable in the scene is the very anti-Jewish statement of 5:30 that feeds stereotypes of Jews as Christ-killers. This verse may be reason enough to omit this text completely. If it is not omitted, preacher and congregation must understand unequivocally that Peter's accusation is not made against all Jews for all time, but against this particular group of the ruling elite. And both must understand that this Jewish socioreligious elite did not function in the Roman imperial world as exclusively "religious" leaders. They were social, economic, political functionaries in an imperial world. They were allies of Rome in enacting Rome's social vision and control. To denounce the "Jewish socioreligious leaders" is to denounce the imperial ruling elite for its opposition to God's ways.

THE GOSPEL
LUKE 24:13-49 (RCL);
LUKE 24:13-35 (BCP); LUKE 24:13-35 (RC)

Interpreting the Text

The reading begins with the Emmaus road and meal story (24:13-35), followed by Jesus' appearance to all the disciples and commissioning of them to worldwide mission for which the Spirit will empower them (24:36-49). The text moves from nonrecognition to recognition in the giving of the bread, from Jesus' absence to his undiscerned and then discerned presence and then to his absence, from the disciples' lamenting incomprehension (24:25) to their being entrusted with worldwide mission (24:47-49).

The narrative locates Emmaus in relation to Jerusalem. Jerusalem is the center of Luke's appearance stories (not Galilee as in Matthew, for example) and is the waiting place for disciples until the spirit comes at Pentecost (24:47-49; Acts 2). From here the mission spreads to the whole world. By contrast, Emmaus has not figured previously in the story and seems to have little special narrative significance. Nor have the two figures been named previously. The verb "talking" in "talking with each other," used in v. 14 in the imperfect, suggests a protracted conversation. Likewise the two "talking" verbs in v. 15a have the sense of examining or inquiring into. These disciples are trying to make sense of what has happened.

In vv. 15b-27 Jesus joins them. Readers know his identity but the two figures cannot recognize him. His opening question in v. 17 literally stops them in their tracks. In vv. 19-20 they rehearse as much of the Jesus story as they know, emphasizing classic Lukan themes: Jesus is a rejected prophet (4:24; 6:22-23; 7:16, 39; 13:33-34), he performed deeds of power (4:14, 36; 5:17; 6:19; 8:46; 9:1; 10:19; 19:37; Acts 2:22), he was crucified by the elite not the people (9:22, 44; 18:32; compare Acts 10:37-39). Their hope of Israel's redemption (24:21) continues this theme from the birth narrative (1:68; 2:38). Though they don't know it, God will accomplish this goal in triumph over Rome at Jesus' return.

Verses 22-24 summarize, with some changes in detail, the opening scene of chap. 24, proclaiming again the empty tomb and the appearance of the risen Jesus. Jesus laments and rebukes their unbelief and interprets the scriptures for them (24:25-27; note the importance of God's word in 24:44-47; cf. 1:38; 4:16-21). The necessity of his suffering indicates God's purposes being enacted (2:49; 4:43; 9:22; 13:14, 33; 17:25 21:9; 22:37; 24:7). Prophets (like Elijah, Isaiah, and Jeremiah) who confront the powerful elite are inevitably rejected. But through that suffering God works out God's purposes. Jesus will enter his glory, the establishment of God's rule (9:26).

The climax of the Emmaus scene comes in the meal (24:28-35). The language of v. 30 ("took bread," "blessed," "broke," "gave") is that of the feeding of the five thousand (9:16) and of the Last Supper (22:19a). Luke's Gospel contains numerous references to food. This is another meal scene, in line with many throughout the Gospel that reveal God's purposes, manifest God's presence through Jesus, and anticipate the future completion of God's will. The verb "give" is in the imperfect, suggesting that their eyes are opened while Jesus gives the bread. But then Jesus disappears! The recalling of his scripture interpretation (24:32, 26-27) emphasizes that these events are in accord with God's will, though again the narrative does not identify any specific scriptures.

They return to Jerusalem, hear news of an appearance to Simon, bear witness to what has happened, and Jesus appears to the assembled community (24:33-36). Despite the testimony, they do not respond well immediately to Jesus' initial proofs (24:37–39/41a). Eating again *seems* to help them believe (though the text does not give their response, 24:42). The scene closes with his commissioning them to worldwide mission, proclaiming repentance and the social transformation of forgiveness (see Easter Day, First Reading), and promising the Spirit's aid. These emphases anticipate crucial themes in Acts as Jesus' mission continues through the gathered and missional community.

Responding to the Text

This is a familiar and favorite story. It is wonderful in that disciples come to recognize the risen Lord but mysterious in a host of details. The story both reveals and conceals the risen Christ.

Why, for example, does it present as heroes two characters who haven't appeared previously in the Gospel? They are disciples, perhaps apostles ("of them," 24:13 and 11), but Cleopas doesn't appear on the list of disciples (6:13-16). Why not have two prominent disciples (Peter and John?) receive a personal appearance of the risen Lord and then be commissioned to proclaim it? And who is the other unnamed disciple (24:18)? Mrs. Cleopas? Friend of Cleopas? Cleopas Junior? How anonymous, how unimportant, can you get? Perhaps that's the point!

And why set the story on the way to Emmaus, of all places? What's so special about Emmaus? Nothing has happened there previously in the narrative. And why are they traveling? Are they returning home after the great disappointment (24:21)? Are they literally walking away in despair? Are they turning their backs on a lost scene? Are they escaping their troubles? And yet they walk straight into the risen Jesus in this nowhere place.

But they can't recognize him. What keeps their eyes from recognizing him (24:16)? They've heard reports that he was alive (24:22-23). Jesus has predicted it (9:22). They've heard his voice before. He explains the scriptures (24:25-27). Why don't they get it? What's so special about breaking bread?

And why do they claim afterwards that their "hearts burned within us" while he taught them on the road (24:32)? What did they think was happening? Out of shape on a modest walk? Twenty-twenty hindsight is a revealing thing.

Why does Jesus not specify which scriptures bear witness to him? If they so obviously speak about him, why don't these two, and many others, get it? Why does he rebuke them? It's a matter of perspective, isn't it? Revelation brings concealment.

Why, when they finally recognize him in giving the bread, does he suddenly disappear (24:31)? Present and absent. Revealing and mysterious.

Why do these two, who rush off to tell the other believers in Jerusalem what has just happened, have to listen to other reports before bearing witness (24:34-35)? Why is the Jerusalem group so convinced by Jesus' appearance to Simon, but not by his appearance to the women (24:11, 22-24)? What's that about? And why does Jesus suddenly authenticate the two travelers' story with an appearance (24:36), but not the testimony of the women? And how many times do they have to be told? And when he does appear, can't they do better than thinking they have seen a ghost (24:36-42)? Why does resurrection faith come so hard?

And why oh why would the risen Jesus commit to this lot the task of proclaiming God's forgiving, transforming purposes? Thank heavens for the Spirit (24:49).

Stories evoke stories. What, how, where do we encounter the presence of the risen Christ? What stories do we have to tell? How does he break into our distractedness, our grief and disappointment, our confusion, our walking away? Or do we have stories more often of nonrecognition than recognition, of absence than presence, of concealment not revelation? How do we put ourselves in the way of, make ourselves available to, make time for, focus on, God's working? Perhaps renewed attention in congregations to the daily practice of spiritual disciplines like Bible reading, prayer, and fasting would help our encounter if we make the time and cultivate the patience to practice them. Yet, as this story indicates, God won't be nailed down by any human structures—not for long!

> WHAT, HOW, WHERE DO WE ENCOUNTER THE PRESENCE OF THE RISEN CHRIST? WHAT STORIES DO WE HAVE TO TELL? OR DO WE HAVE STORIES MORE OFTEN OF NONRECOGNITION THAN RECOGNITION, OF ABSENCE THAN PRESENCE, OF CONCEALMENT NOT REVELATION?

And there is the matter of mission. We've heard for so long that actions speak louder than words and that many congregants have lost the ability—and nerve—to proclaim the gospel verbally. The "actions alone" approach arrogantly assumes our exclusive ownership of winsome virtue, a myth that declining numbers (not to mention our own sinfulness) should have put to rest ages ago. The text mandates that we train ourselves in contexts of authentic and caring relationships to speak the word of witness, nurtured by an inner and communal conviction that doing so matters profoundly.

SECOND SUNDAY OF EASTER

APRIL 7, 2002

REVISED COMMON	EPISCOPAL (BCP)	ROMAN CATHOLIC
Acts 2:14a, 22-32	Acts 2:14a, 22-32 or Gen. 8:6-16; 9:8-16	Acts 2:42-47
Psalm 16	Psalm 111 or 118:19-24	Ps. 118:2-4, 13-15, 22-24
1 Peter 1:3-9	1 Peter 1:3-9 or Acts 2:14a, 22-32	1 Peter 1:3-9
John 20:19-31	John 20:19-31	John 20:19-31

Jesus' resurrection shapes a life that is transitional, communal, and at odds with societal norms (Acts 2:22-32). God forms alternative communities such as Noah's death-bound community that witnesses the end of a sinful world and beginning of a new one. Acts 2:42-47 envisions a post-resurrection world of transformed economic practices. First Peter 1:3-9 locates its community in an alienating world but secure in God's uncompleted purposes. John 20 presents a community of presence and absence, mission and Spirit. Resurrection involves an ecclesiology of alternative communities.

FIRST READING
ACTS 2:14a, 22-32 (RCL, BCP)

See below, Second Reading.

GENESIS 8:6-16; 9:8-16 (BCP, alt.)

Interpreting the Text

The Noah story (Genesis 6–9) sounds one of the big themes of this Easter season. God brings new life from the death of God's judgment and destruction enacted in the flood (7:17-24). "But God remembered Noah and all the animals" (8:1). The passage highlights God's renewal of creation in a series of parallels to the creation story. God gathers the waters of chaos and ensures the emergence of the dry land in restoring creation's order (8:1-12; cf. 1:9-10). The dove's return with the olive branch and its subsequent nonreturn (8:10-12) attest the next stage of creation, the emergence of vegetation (1:11-13). The release of the animals (8:17, 19) and the humans (8:16, 18) parallels the creation sequence (1:20-25, 26-31). The reference to sons and wives echoes the command to multiply (cf. 1:28) and begins a new community of God's people. God makes a covenant never again to destroy the earth and promises to sustain life forever (9:8-16).

Responding to the Text

The themes of new creation, of God's commitment to life, of God's faithfulness, and of the formation of a people resonate richly with resurrection. Resurrection does not reveal things previously unknown about God. Rather it again demonstrates fundamental aspects of God's being previously displayed in creation, in this postflood re-creation, in exodus and exile. Nor does it reveal things unknown about God's people. We exist by God's grace as God's partners in caring for God's world and witnessing to God's purposes.

ACTS 2:42-47 (RC)

This scene (compared, say, to 1 Corinthians!) offers a somewhat idealized picture of the church shaped by the Spirit. In v. 42 the church is a community of learning, "common life" (fellowship, expanded in vv. 44-45), meals and worship, and prayers. God's presence and power are manifested in "signs and wonders," a continuation of Jesus' ministry. Verses 44-45 attest an economic structure of mutual caring that is antithetical and resistant to the hierarchical and acquisitive system of the empire that sustained huge inequalities of wealth and practiced the systematic exploitation of the many by the few through taxes. Such a community is winsome to some (2:47).

Responding to the Text

The scene asserts transformation in the face of despair and indifference. It counters the claim that nothing can change. God's power and human repentance form a potent combination. The new life takes shape in a community that is inclusive of all ("the promise is to you and to all those who are far off," 2:39) and marked by distinctive practices, including socioeconomic practices (2:42-47).

Where today does the church offer examples of the economic reordering of life? Do we have here some hopelessly naïve utopian fantasy or a radical critique of ancient imperial and contem-

THE SCRIPTURAL TRADITION CONSTANTLY PURSUES THE AGENDA OF JUSTICE AND ENVISIONS IN THE ESTABLISHMENT OF GOD'S REIGN THROUGH RESURRECTION A JUST WORLD IN WHICH THERE IS PLENTY FOR ALL.

porary capitalist structures and practices? Is the equitable distribution of resources and care for people a viable option to greed and incessant consumerism? Is our commitment to *enough* or to *more*?

Resurrection life, then, entails economic restructuring. Socioeconomic structures can embody resurrection life. The scriptural tradition is relentless in its critique of unjust ruling structures. It constantly pursues the agenda of justice and envisions in the establishment of God's reign through resurrection a just world in which there is plenty for all. For such a world we work, pray, and preach. The passage challenges us to be the church and to anticipate, to be a sign of, an embodiment of God's future empire. We have so much to lose in order to gain such a world.

RESPONSIVE READING
PSALM 16 (RCL)

The psalmist entrusts his life and future to God as "my Lord" (16:2) who provides protection and "good" for the psalmist. This trusting commitment is uncompromised in that the psalmist does not cover other bases "just in case" (16:3-4). Using the language that Joshua employs to describe the occupation of the land, the psalmist locates himself in a tradition of God's covenant faithfulness (16:5-6). Covenant brings responsibilities to live according to God's will (16:7-8). The psalmist's trust means God will not banish him from God's presence in which there is life and joy. Verse 10 appears in Acts 2:24-32 and 13:35 in relation to God's resurrection of Jesus as a demonstration of the "path of life" that passes even through death (see comments on the Second Reading).

PSALM 111 (BCP)

This psalm praises God's active and powerful faithfulness to the covenant (111:5, 9), especially in the exodus and occupation of the land (111:4-6). This faithfulness or righteousness (111:3, 7) exemplifies God's mercy or grace. The initial "I" blends with the community to celebrate God's dealings with a people. Such faithfulness sustains "fear of the Lord" or faithful attentiveness to God's will (111:10).

PSALM 118:19-24 (BCP, alt.);
PSALM 118:2-4, 13-15, 22-24 (RC)

See the Responsive Reading for Easter Day.

SECOND READING
1 PETER 1:3-9

Interpreting the Text

First Peter is written to mixed Jewish-Gentile communities of Christians in Asia Minor (1:1) that are experiencing some local hostility (2:12; 3:16; 4:4, 14) and social alienation or displacement as "visiting strangers/exiles" (1:17) and "resident aliens" (2:11). The letter exhorts them to stand fast in God's grace (5:12) and to live their distinctive lives (4:3-4). They are not to abandon their society and in some ways, such as maintaining patriarchal households (2:18-3:7), they assimilate to it. The letter sets their socially ambivalent existence in the context of their certain and sure acceptance by God (as here in 1:3-9) and in the community of God's people.

Hence the reading begins with an emphasis on God's foundational call and mercy (1:1-2) and on their certain eschatological destiny effected through the resurrection and guaranteed by God's power encountered through hope and faith (1:3-5). Christian existence begins with a new birth that establishes a new family/community and lives in hope toward this future salvation yet to be revealed (1:5, 7). In the meantime, suffering, especially from being out-of-step with the surrounding society's commitments, is normative as subsequent lectionary selections will address. Faith, testing, love, and rejoicing mark this existence (1:6-9).

> CHRISTIAN EXISTENCE BEGINS WITH A NEW BIRTH THAT ESTABLISHES A NEW FAMILY/COMMUNITY, AND LIVES IN HOPE TOWARD THIS FUTURE SALVATION YET TO BE REVEALED (1:5, 7). IN THE MEANTIME, SUFFERING IS NORMATIVE.

Responding to the Text

The reading sets out a classic "already and not yet" understanding of Christian existence in which God's mercy and new birth are known but God's saving purposes are not yet completed. Resurrection initiates a beginning and guarantees the end. This "now and not yet" perspective, often lost in mainline denominations because of embarrassment over some fundamentalist scenarios of Jesus' return, places the present in the context of the future. The present is a conflicted and paradoxical existence evidenced here in suffering (because the world is not as God wants it and resents challenges to its claimed autonomy and [in]vested interests) and rejoicing (because God is at work and the future is sure). So much for a health and wealth gospel! This future orientation is often, wrongly, understood to mandate ethical passivity or societal escape ("to hell with the rest of the world"). But hope, faith, and love are never passive in the biblical tradition. They constitute an engaged way of life marked by the struggle of resurrection life against all forms of death, in anticipation of God's future.

ACTS 2:14a, 22-32 (bcp, alt.)

Interpreting the Text

The context is Peter's Pentecost sermon; the focus is on adducing scriptural, especially Davidic, testimony for Jesus' resurrection as the basis for Pentecost (2:33). Peter quickly traverses God's action in Jesus' life (2:22), his crucifixion (2:23; cf. Luke 22:2; 23:32), and resurrection (2:24). Verses 25–31 utilize Ps. 16:8-11 to confirm and interpret God's action summarized in v. 32.

Peter makes several key assumptions in his midrash. (1) David writes the Psalms (about half are ascribed to David); (2) David is God's "anointed" or "christed" one; (3) God has promised David an eternal line and reign; (4) what applies to David in the Psalms can also apply to his descendants, others who are anointed or "christed"; (5) David is a prophet; (6) Jesus is a descendant of David (Luke 1:27). So in vv. 25–28 Acts reads Ps. 16:8-11 in relation to Jesus, the Christ / Messiah. It cannot apply to David who is buried (2:29), but must refer to his descendant (2:30). Peter interprets Ps. 16:10 to refer to the resurrection of the Messiah. Verse 32 completes the identification with Jesus. God's action is in accord with the scripture and witnessed by "us."

Responding to the Text

The risk of anti-Jewish rhetoric is present in three ways. (1) The prophetic use of Psalm 16 can emphasize discontinuities and Christian supersessionism. A more appropriate line would be to emphasize continuities in God's purposes. For all the talk of newness in this Easter season, there is something very "old" about God continuing to bring life out of death (see comments on Genesis 8, above). (2) Verse 23 will feed stereotypes of Jews as Christ-killers (see comments on Acts 5:30, Second Reading for Easter Evening). (3) The Christian reading of Psalm 16 seems so obvious if one starts, as most contemporary congregations do, with the affirmation of resurrection (2:32). By implication, Jews seem so willfully resistant! Preachers must supply an alternative reading. One might dare to imagine that congregations could be helped to understand the psalm in *several* ways, without giving up a Christian reading but recognizing it is precisely that. If multiple readings are impossible, or preferably tackled in a Christian education setting, it is best not to include this reading.

THE GOSPEL
JOHN 20:19-31

Interpreting the Text

This reading continues the Easter Day account in John 20. After Mary has seen the risen Lord (20:11-18), Jesus appears to the disciples (20:19-23) and then to Thomas (20:24-29).

The setting of the first scene is Sunday evening (20:19a) in a locked house (20:19b). The participants are "disciples," a term not restricted in John to the eleven or twelve. The pervasive atmosphere of fear, deriving from association with a crucified person, indicates they have not given much weight to Mary's testimony (20:18). The phrase "the Jews" commonly denotes the Jerusalem elite who, allied with Rome, have crucified Jesus (1:19; 2:18; 18:12). The term also seems to reflect the bitter dispute between John's community and a synagogue (9:22; 12:42: 16:2), a situation that greatly influences this Gospel's story and theology.

Jesus appears in a context of fear and skepticism. He greets them with "Peace," a conventional but hugely significant greeting that means not "peace of mind" but suggests the wholeness and right relatedness of God's world marked by justice and righteousness (Psalm 72). Jesus has promised this "peace" as his gift to a community hated by the world (14:27; 15:18-25) in anticipation of the completion of God's purposes. Jesus reveals himself by his scars, and the disciples are convinced and rejoice (20:20; so 16:20-22).

Jesus then commissions them for mission and empowers them with the Spirit (20:21-22; also promised in 14:25-26; 15:26-27; 16:13-14). The exact nature of this mission is difficult. It is addressed to the whole community, not a few select leaders. It emphasizes the work of forgiveness (20:23). Throughout, sins have to do with rejecting God's will, particularly Jesus whom God has sent (3:19-21; 8:21-24; 9:39-41; 15:22-24). To accept Jesus means welcoming his revelation and passing from death to life (5:24). Forgiveness, then, is not only a personal matter, but a cosmic and social transfer (20:23; Lev. 25; Deut. 15:1-9). The promised Spirit is to be at work convicting the world of sin (16:8-9). This imparting of the Spirit, linked to Jesus' glorification (7:37-39), is clearly different from Luke's Pentecost timetable of fifty days later, the timing observed in the ecclesial calendar. The act of breathing recalls God's work in creation (Gen. 2:7) and in restoring exiled Israel (Ezek. 37:9). Jesus continues to form a new community.

The second appearance concerns Thomas (20:24-29). Not present for the previous appearance, he cannot believe the proclamation (20:25a). He wants to see what the others have seen, Jesus' scars, in order to believe (20:25b). That is, Thomas, so often separated from the other disciples as one who has a particular problem with doubts, is no more or less doubting than the rest! Jesus obliges. He challenges Thomas to believe (20:27b), addressing him not in terms of doubt, a term that does not appear in the Greek text despite omnipresent references to "doubting Thomas," but as one who, like the other disciples previously, does not believe. He is "faithless," without belief (20:27, preferable to NRSV's "do not doubt"), until Jesus' demonstration. Thomas's confession may be directed to Jesus, or to God whose words and work he encounters in Jesus (20:28; 14:7-9). "Seeing" is one way to faith. But Jesus also blesses those who believe the proclamation offered by the Gospel narrative.

Verses 30-31 make that point. Through the gospel narrative, people can know, and be sustained in knowing, Jesus when he is absent. Faith has content. Jesus is believed in as God's Son. The Son-Father relational metaphor is central to the gospel. Son indicates that Jesus is God's agent, commissioned by God to manifest life with God enjoyed in intimate relationship with God (1:1-18; 10:30). "Son" commonly denotes kings (Ps. 2:7), the people Israel (Hos. 11:1), and the wise person (Wisd. of Sol. 2) as God's human agents. In Jesus is revealed life or "life of the age" (eternal life) marked by quantity (unbroken by sin) and quality (intimate fellowship with God in God's just world; 5:24; 17:3).

Responding to the Text

Members of contemporary churches know daily the pervasive pressures of living in a society that politely acknowledges God's existence, consumes God's blessings, but passionately ignores the implications and responsibilities of that consumption. John's narrative addresses a postresurrection community, like the contemporary church, located in a world that denies its central claims: dead men don't walk; God doesn't intervene or care or hold anyone accountable; God doesn't challenge the status quo but benignly, supportively, blesses its success; God is not relevant or important.

How does an out-of-step community live in such a context? How does it maintain focus, passion, commitment, priorities?

Resurrection life is lived in the Spirit. Jesus' crucifixion-resurrection-ascension, his "lifting up" (3:14; 8:28; 12:32-34), his glorification (13:1-3), constitute one event that means his return to the Father and the giving of the Spirit (7:37-39). Through the Spirit, Jesus in his absence remains present

RESURRECTION LIFE IS LIVED IN THE SPIRIT. JESUS' CRUCIFIXION-RESURRECTION-ASCENSION, HIS "LIFTING UP," HIS GLORIFICATION CONSTITUTE ONE EVENT THAT MEANS HIS RETURN TO THE FATHER AND THE GIVING OF THE SPIRIT.

with the church. The Easter season provides an important opportunity to explore that absence-presence dynamic. In an age apparently yearning for spiritual encounter, why is the church so often a desert for some? This narrative is alive with surprising, unpredictable, convincing divine presence. What do we need to *do* by way of spiritual disciplines, schedules, priorities, and time management, and what do we need to *be* as people to put ourselves in the way of God's elusive presence? Of course there is no place for manipulation or instant formulae, nor for forgetting that presence *and* absence form the dynamic.

The giving of the Spirit also means mission. Resurrection life is missional existence. Empowered by the Spirit, the church does not exist for itself but continues Jesus' work against sin, revealing God's loving purposes for the world and enabling people to know life lived in fellowship with God. For John, this mission is conducted in a world that more often than not rejects its creator (1:10-11), is hostile to God's agents (15:18), and is ruled by Satan (14:30). That is, the missional community is counter-cultural in demonstrating God's transforming love but dogged in its persevering faithfulness. Mission requires people of focus and passion who can speak of God and do God's loving work in the fearful and hostile world beyond the security of locked doors and compatible company. The narrative encourages our suspicion of a lack of tension between church and society.

Jesus' appearance to Thomas, as with Mary and the disciples in the locked room, displays grace or, as this Gospel prefers, love. Jesus does not rebuke or scold Thomas but actively elicits his faith. The blessing of 20:29b and the promise of 20:30-31—not a slam against Thomas but a promise for subsequent generations—enacts the same grace. Those who were not there are not excluded from God's purposes. The gospel continues those purposes, making God's presence and life available to readers/hearers. Telling these stories, carefully, thoughtfully, prayerfully, matters enormously, especially in a secularized world that would rather pursue wealth, power, self-satisfaction. . . .

THIRD SUNDAY OF EASTER

APRIL 14, 2002

REVISED COMMON	EPISCOPAL (BCP)	ROMAN CATHOLIC
Acts 2:14a, 36–41	Acts 2:14a, 36–47 or Isa. 43:1–12	Acts 2:14, 22–33
Ps. 116:1-4, 12-19	Psalm 116 or 116:10-17	Ps. 16:1-2, 5, 7-8, 9-10, 11
1 Peter 1:17-23	1 Peter 1:17-23 or Acts 2:14a, 36-47	1 Peter 1:17-21
Luke 24:13-35	Luke 24:13-35	Luke 24:13-35

How do we embody God's resurrecting work? This Sunday's texts provide their readers (the plural is so important) with contours for and dimensions of transformed lives. They name repentance, new socioeconomic structures and relationships, worship, and learning (Acts 2:36-47). They attest conversion, confession, praise, testimony, and committed lives (Psalm 116; 1 Peter 1:17-23). They envision worlds marked by love (1 Peter 1), where God's presence is recognized and enjoyed (Luke 24). They celebrate God's faithful, powerful, gracious saving work in freeing the exiled from their oppressive captors in Babylon (Isa. 43:1-12).

Such visions employ broad brushstrokes that require us to do the hard, communal work of identifying their implications and practicalities in local communities of faith. But their power can be readily tamed by not teasing out the generalities and by a skepticism that doubts that any change is possible. But even in the quiet despair of our various Emmaus journeys, the risen Christ might be encountered.

FIRST READING

ACTS 2:14a, 36–41 (RCL);
ACTS 2:14a, 36–47 (BCP)

Interpreting the Texts

This reading focuses on the effect of Peter's Pentecost sermon (see the Second Reading for the Second Sunday of Easter). Peter has interpreted speaking in tongues as a sign of the Spirit's presence (2:14-21) and has proclaimed Jesus' resurrection, in accord with the scriptures, as the basis for the Pentecost event (2:22-36). He finishes his sermon by declaring God's work and Jesus' identity (2:36), and fields a question about the appropriate response (2:37-40) that is described in vv. 41-47.

Verses 14 and 36 bracket this sermon addressed to "all the house of Israel," God's covenant people (Ps. 98:3). God has not broken the covenant and abandoned Israel. The crucified one is, by God's act, "Lord and Christ/Messiah." Verse 37 describes a twofold response. First they are "cut to the heart." The verb expresses a range of intense emotions not easily expressed in one English phrase. It means "to be sorrowful or remorseful" (Gen. 27:38), "silenced" (Lev. 10:3; Isa. 47:5), "humbled" (1 Kings 20:27-29). Second, realizing some action is necessary, they ask the group of apostles (cf. 2:14) what constitutes an appropriate response (cf. Luke 3:10).

Peter names repentance, a changed way of life marked by forgiveness, and baptism (2:38-41). Two of the three, repentance and forgiveness, are named by the risen Jesus in Luke 24:47 as instructions for the church's mission. Both demands are common throughout Luke-Acts. Peter is faithful to the divine commission. Forgiveness (as I have noted in the First Reading for Easter Sunday) does not only mean personal renewal but points to a social renewal with actions of societal restructuring and economic justice. These realities will be demonstrated in 2:44-45. And in these responses, the promised gift of the Spirit is received (10:44-45; 11:17).

ISAIAH 43:1-12 (BCP, alt.)

Interpreting the Text

Deutero-Isaiah addresses the sixth-century community in exile in Babylon with a proclamation of God's redeeming purposes (43:1-7) and of Israel's role as a witness to the nations (43:8-13). The time of Israel's punishment is over (cf. Isa. 6:9-10). God who created Israel (cf. 41:8-13) redeems the people and enjoys an intimate relationship with them (43:1). The language of v. 2 of a journey through water recalls the Egyptian exodus and so indicates the nature of God's redeeming work. God will save the people by leading them home. They will know God's presence and protection (43:2). Subsequently we learn that the agent of this redemption is God's anointed ("christed"), the Persian king Cyrus (44:28; 45:1). He will capture other nations in order to let Israel go. God's motive is love and covenant faithfulness (Exod. 19:5; Deut. 7:6-11). God will gather the scattered people (43:6-7).

This redemption brings about a changed role for the people (43:8). They become witnesses to the nations that this God is the only God (43:10-12). Israel is chosen not to enjoy a privileged relationship with God alone, nor to indicate that others are rejected. Rather Israel is chosen as God's servant (43:10) to bear witness to God's redeeming deeds.

Responding to the Text

Exile, like creation, the exodus, and resurrection, is one of the big events in the biblical story that exhibits fundamental qualities of God's ways of working and of the people of God. God's love, faithfulness, saving initiative or grace, power, partnership with the people, and exclusive sovereignty over the world are on display. God enters the situation of brokenness, suffering, humiliation, defeat, death, to bring new life and a new future. God also calls the people to be faithful to their role, to bear witness to the nations. God's purposes are inclusive and universal. The remaining readings indicate numerous parallels to the resurrection.

ACTS 2:14, 22-33 (RC)

See the Second Reading for the Second Sunday of Easter

Responsive Reading

PSALM 116:1-4, 12-19 (RCL);
PSALM 116 or 116:10-17 (BCP);
PSALM 16:1-2, 5, 7-8, 9-10, 11 (RC)

Psalm 116 gives thanks for God's deliverance from a situation of great distress. The situation is not specified, though in vv. 3, 8, and 15, the Psalmist feels close to death, and vv. 10-11 suggest some sort of social alienation or hostility. The lack of clarity allows others to utilize it as a means of thanksgiving for rescue from similar situations. It is located in the group of Psalms 113–118 associated with the exodus as a supreme example of God's deliverance of the people from affliction and anguish.

The opening two verses express the basic dynamic of God's salvation. The psalmist is in trouble. He calls out or prays to God. God responds with saving power. The psalmist expresses love for God and promises in gratitude to serve God as long as he lives. The rest of the psalm elaborates these elements: the trouble (116:3, 8-11), the psalmist's turning to God (116:4), acknowledgment of God's saving response (116:5-7), and the psalmist's thankful response as he enjoys God's salvation (116:12-19). This response is motivated by God's goodness

(116:12) and takes the form of worship with prayers, sacrifices, and vows in the Jerusalem temple (116:12-19). The psalm is very much a love poem addressed to the Lord, yet is also public confession that encourages others to trust God.

Second Reading
1 PETER 1:17-23 (RCL, BCP);
1 PETER 1:17-21 (RC)

Interpreting the Text

On the situation of social alienation and ambivalence addressed by 1 Peter, see the second reading for the Second Sunday of Easter.

The readers live in "exile" (1:17), a term that denotes social outsiders, those who live with few rights as sociocultural and political "resident aliens" in a place that is not their own land or area. Their existence is shaped not only by this reality but also, as vv. 17-23 emphasize, by their location in God's purposes. This latter context requires and exhorts their faithful living. As children of God (1:14), they live in relation to God who judges all impartially according to their deeds (1:17). That future accountability awaits all people and "fear" of it alternately solicits and bullies compliance. The indicative implies imperatives.

Yet their life is also shaped by the past. Christ's death has ransomed or set free these (Gentile) readers from "futile" lives not focused on God (1:18-19; cf. 1:14). The image of ransom indicates freeing slaves and prisoners of war. But it also denotes God's saving of the people from the tyrants of Egypt in the exodus (Deut. 7:8) and from Babylonian imperialism in the exile (Isa. 43:1). Christ's sacrificial death, in which sin is understood to be transferred onto the sacrificial victim and life and purity (1:22) are transferred to those whom the sacrifice represents, secures the setting free. Verse 20 attests God's purposes at work in this death for the benefit of the readers. God's raising of Jesus from the dead elicits their trust and hope for the present and future.

Verses 21-22 provide two further images of their past conversion and its present ethical and ecclesial consequences. In vv. 21-22 their soteriological identification with Christ is described as "purifying your souls," a moral transformation hinted at in 1:14 and elaborated in 1:18 as a change of direction and commitment. That new direction comprises "obedience to the truth" (cf. 1:2) and is expressed in practical love for one another. That is, their conversion constitutes a new community. Relationships of love sustain their faithful discipleship and provide a secure "home" in a difficult social environment.

Second, the writer returns to the image of new birth, first used in 1:3 to indicate God's active and merciful work (1:23). That birth comes about by God's word, the proclamation of the good news (1:12, 25). Just as God spoke and creation came into being (Gen. 1), just as God spoke the word of redemption from Egypt and Babylonian exile (Isa. 40:6-8 quoted in 1:24), so God's word has brought freedom for these believers from futile lives (1:18) to live in a new community of love. That word is, for these social aliens, imperishable, living and enduring. It will sustain them in a difficult and transient situation.

Responding to the Text

The text attests various dimensions of transforming resurrection. God's mercy and power turn lives around. Those former lives are described in 1:18 (1:14) as "futile." They are not desperately wicked, but they are misguided or godless in their commitments. One can think of numerous ways in which contemporary people invest themselves and miss life lived in relation to God. The transformative dimension of the passage mandates prophetic evaluation of contemporary values and societal practices and values.

But the passage is also clear that to be "born again" does not leave room for going back. Their living is now accountable to God. So their commitment to the gospel does not lead into an easy cultural accommodation but into tension with the status quo, into exile. Someone has said that to be well adjusted in a sick society means big problems! In a time in which we seem to know little about Christian distinctiveness in perspectives and practices, this passage and its insistence that resurrection life is a counter-cultural, "resident alien" lifestyle should trouble us and challenge our ready cultural compliance.

An alternative way of life is difficult. So the passage insists on committed and practical relationships of love to sustain one another in this against-the-grain existence. I heard a radio announcer comment this morning on the popularity of "gladiator" schools since the movie *Gladiator* appeared. The announcer commented disapprovingly, lamenting that people were so keen to learn violence and wondering where they might go to learn to love one another. The church did not seem to come to her mind! But the church of 1 Peter is a "love survival" community in which believers mediate God's love to one another and sustain faithful discipleship in an alien world that does not, by and large, actively or eagerly consent to the good news of the gospel. Such love cannot be talk. One cannot love without economic justice and social inclusion. The letter's subsequent endorsement of conventional patriarchal households (3:1-8) unfortunately indicates a lack of follow-through on its vision.

THE CHURCH OF 1 PETER IS A "LOVE SURVIVAL" COMMUNITY IN WHICH BELIEVERS MEDIATE GOD'S LOVE TO ONE ANOTHER AND SUSTAIN FAITHFUL DISCIPLESHIP IN AN ALIEN WORLD THAT DOES NOT, BY AND LARGE, ACTIVELY OR EAGERLY CONSENT TO THE GOOD NEWS OF THE GOSPEL.

ACTS 2:14a, 36–47 (BCP)

See above, First Reading.

THE GOSPEL

Luke 24:13-35

The reading of this appearance story will remind folks that Easter is not a day but a season, a way of life, a community. See the comments on the Gospel for Easter Evening, above.

FOURTH SUNDAY OF EASTER

APRIL 21, 2002

REVISED COMMON	EPISCOPAL (BCP)	ROMAN CATHOLIC
Acts 2:42-47	Acts 6:1-9; 7:2a, 51-60 or Neh. 9:6-15	Acts 2:1, 4a, 36-41
Psalm 23	Psalm 23	Ps. 23:1-3a, 3b-4, 5, 6
1 Peter 2:19-25	1 Peter 2:19-25 or Acts 6:1-9; 7:2a, 51-60	1 Peter 2:20b-25
John 10:1-10	John 10:1-10	John 10:1-10

In these texts, the relationship of shepherd and sheep provides a common metaphor. Psalm 23 and John 10 develop it at length, while 1 Peter 2:24-25 employs it. The metaphor highlights the relationship between shepherd and sheep, though it must be noted that "sheep" is plural and communal ("sheeps"). Resurrection life takes form in a community that renounces the hostility and violence rendered to its shepherd by the dominant society. Contemporary congregations will need help to understand that the metaphor of "shepherd" is a common political, as well as pastoral, one.

FIRST READING

ACTS 2:42-47 (RCL)

See the First Reading for the Second Sunday of Easter, above.

ACTS 2:1, 4a, 36-41 (RC)

See the First Reading for the Third Sunday of Easter, above.

ACTS 6:1-9; 7:2a, 51-60 (BCP)

Interpreting the Text

These selections cover huge (and dangerous) territory. Acts 6 details the solving of a significant problem. There is bias in the distribution of support for widows (cf. 2:44-45). The distinction between "Hellenists" and "Hebrews" refers to linguistic not ethnic differences between the two groups (for the use of the term "Hebrew" in Luke-Acts, see Acts 21:40; 22:2; 26:14; for ethnic distinctions, 14:1; 16:1; 19:17; 21:19). The Gentile mission is not yet underway. Hebrew widows are Aramaic-speaking Jews; Hellenist widows are Greek-speaking Jews. But the apostles are busy preaching and cannot add the task of distribution (6:3-4). Seven men are chosen (6:5-6), and the preaching ministry continues (6:7).

That much seems clear. But there are some rough edges. The seven have Greek names. Are they to look after the Hebrew widows also? More importantly, the seven include Stephen and Philip who will be prominent through chap. 8, not in administering the distribution for which they are chosen, but in prophetic activity and preaching, the task of the apostles! It seems that the initial distinction of function disappears once these legitimate leaders have been chosen.

The focus in 6:8-9 moves to Stephen who, with the phrase "full of grace and power," continues the work of Jesus and the Spirit (Luke 4:14; Acts 1:8; 2:22). His Jerusalem sermon (7:2-53) ends with a stern condemnation of the Jerusalem leadership (6:12; 7:1) for rejecting Jesus, God's prophet. (7:51-53). This leadership, the Sanhedrin, also rejected the apostles in chaps. 4–5. Now it rejects Stephen (7:54, 57-60). Stephen's vision in 7:55-56 of the ascended Jesus (2:33) underlines his prophetic identity and link with Jesus. There are significant similarities between Stephen's death and that of Jesus: out of the city (Luke 23:32; Acts 7:58), garments (Luke 23:34; Acts 7:58), giving up his spirit (Luke 23:46; Acts 7:59), forgiveness (Luke 23:34; Acts 7:60), burial by faithful people (Luke 23:50-55; Acts 8:2). In sharing the fate of the prophets that he has just preached about, Stephen embodies his own sermon. This time they do kill the messenger. The Jerusalem elite, part of the imperial power structure, reject God's purposes.

Stephen's death is highly significant. The related persecution provides the catalyst for further Judean and Samaritan mission, enabling, not hindering the will of the risen Jesus (1:8). And the introduction of Saul in 7:58 prepares for the next step in the church's expansion, the Gentile mission. Saul's conversion will follow in chap. 9.

Responding to the Text

The first part of the reading (6:1-7) exemplifies the church as an inclusive community that responds flexibly to its context. Differences of color, appearance, sound, custom, sexual orientation, and belief are realities in every community of faith. So too are covert or overt barriers. The resurrection life shapes open, inclusive, responsive, flexible communities. Addressing the issue in a positive, relational, and dialogical manner that results in appropriate actions can have a significant impact.

The second part of the reading (7:51-60) raises a difficulty present in several other Acts readings. The harsh condemnation of 7:51-53 and the vivid death scene can easily confirm "Christian" anti-Jewish prejudices and stereotypes. If it cannot be made absolutely clear that the condemnation is not of all Jews for all time (the larger narrative context is mission in Jerusalem), it is best to leave the passage alone. If it cannot be clearly understood that Stephen's attack is against the Jerusalem leadership (who as allies of Rome in an imperial society are not exclusively "religious"), it is best to leave it unread. But if it can be clearly stated and understood that Stephen's attack is on the resistant powerful (among whom are some of our congregants), go ahead.

THE RESURRECTION LIFE SHAPES OPEN, INCLUSIVE, RESPONSIVE, FLEXIBLE COMMUNITIES.

NEHEMIAH 9:6-15 (BCP, alt.)

Under Persian control, Nehemiah was governor of Judea first from 445 to 433 B.C.E. (2:1-8; 5:14), with a later second term (13:6-7). He reinforces a distinctive Jewish identity by encircling Jerusalem with a wall and removing foreigners.

This text comprises part of Ezra's prayer offered on a day of penitence, only for Israelites (9:2), following the Festival of Booths (Tabernacles) (8:13-18). In this reading, Ezra rehearses a version of Israel's salvation history, setting up the confession's basic dynamic "you (God) have dealt faithfully and we have acted wickedly" (9:33). Verse 6 begins with creation, vv. 7-8 continue with Abraham, and vv. 9-15 the Exodus and Sinai covenant.

This text section accentuates God's faithfulness, power, and gracious provision for the people, and rehearses big parts of the salvation history story. Such memory that human faithlessness does not negate God's faithfulness (Rom. 3:1-8) shapes our identity and provokes our own communal witness-bearing to the experience of God in our midst.

RESPONSIVE READING
PSALM 23 (RCL, BCP);
PSALM 23:1-3a, 3b-4, 5, 6, (RC)

The psalm expresses confidence in God. Verse 4 attests some distress but—typically—it is not specified. The shepherd metaphor is partly pastoral (though comparing the people of God to a flock of sheep, not the brightest of animals, may not be complimentary)! The shepherd provides for the sheep

(23:1-2), guides them (23:3) and protects them from harm (23:4). But the image is also one of political leadership. David the king is God's shepherd (Ps. 78:70-72). False kings and leaders or shepherds are condemned in Jer. 23:1-4 and Ezek. 34. Hence the psalm expresses loyalty to God as the people's faithful leader.

SECOND READING:

1 PETER 2:19-25 (RCL, BCP);
1 PETER 2:20B-25 (RC)

Interpreting the Text

The middle section of 1 Peter (2:11—4:11) is concerned with appropriate conduct for these Christians who because of their commitment to Christ live in tension with and alienation from their hostile cultural context ("exile," 1:17). Christians are not to withdraw but nor are they to provoke conflict. Instead, they are to be submissive (2:11-3:7) to the governing authorities (2:13-17) and within households (2:18-3:7). Christian slaves are to endure unjust suffering and understand it as a sign of God's approval (2:19-20). Moreover, such suffering imitates Christ's footsteps and example (2:21-23). Christ's patient endurance of such suffering as the suffering servant who absorbs imperial violence (2:22; Isa. 53:9) has the additional benefit of redeeming the believers (2:24-25).

Enduring suffering imitates Christ but it has another advantage. God has vindicated Jesus in the resurrection and ascension to share the very power and rule of God (3:21-22). To share in Christ's suffering means the encouraging certainty of sharing in his vindication (5:10).

Responding to the Text

This text assumes experiences that our contemporary congregations know little about and, accordingly, advocates behaviors that in some contemporary situations are not desirable. The passage is addressed to slaves and deals with responses to harsh and unjustified beatings (2:18-20). We no longer have this social structure and we live in a mass-media society with representative government where, given resources, good will, and public opinion, some social evils can be rectified rather than endured. *No such option existed around slavery in the first century.* Furthermore, the text's teaching addresses a larger situation in which Christians are in tension with, at odds with, and alienated from their society because of their Christian identity and practices, hardly the everyday experience of our culturally compromised and over-accommodated congregations.

Given these significant differences between the text's first-century context and contemporary realities, we must be very careful with it. And, given commitments to forming inclusive communities of faith, we don't want to uphold a text that can be understood to support slavery or to endorse the passive endurance of household/domestic violence.

But that is not to say that the text has nothing useful to say. Verses 21-23 instruct the slave to do what every Christian should do (1:6-7; 3:13-22). With no instruction for masters, the whole community is viewed as a household of slaves (2:16), indeed an alternative, egalitarian, countercultural community. These verses, then, could cause us to think about appropriate responses to the tyrannies that always mark dominant structures on micro and macro levels, or about responses to other contemporary enslaving realities such as rampant materialism, violence, racism, etc. How might one resist? Fight? Flight? Or with active nonviolence, an alternative way of life that attests a clearly different way of living (e.g., Matt. 5:38-42)?

> THE WHOLE COMMUNITY IS VIEWED AS A HOUSEHOLD OF SLAVES (2:16), INDEED AN ALTERNATIVE, EGALITARIAN, COUNTERCULTURAL COMMUNITY.

Verses 24-25 outline Christ's suffering that benefited others, and who now as our shepherd finds the straying and comforts the vulnerable. Other texts can perform these same functions without the risks of this one. And without sustained interpretation and discussion, this text is perhaps best not read in worship.

ACTS 6:1-9; 7:2a, 51-60 (BCP, alt.)

See First Reading above

THE GOSPEL

John 10:1-10

From 9:40 Jesus continues to address the Pharisees. In chap. 9 he healed the "blind man" who now sees physically (9:7), socially (he resists the elite, 9:24-34), and spiritually (9:35-38). The chapter has artfully explored different responses to Jesus including the Jerusalem leaders' opposition. These leaders perhaps represent the synagogue from which John's community has separated because of its confession of Jesus as the "anointed one" sent by God (9:22). They cannot see how blind they are (9:40-42)! They do not know who Jesus is, where he originates, or that he determines eschatological destiny. They do not recognize that response to him accomplishes their judgment (9:39).

Jesus tries to help them see with a "figure of speech" (10:6). Verses 1-6 focus on the shepherd and his relationship with the sheep. In vv. 7-10 Jesus identifies himself as the gate to the sheepfold and in vv. 11-16 as the good shepherd.

As noted in the comments on Psalm 23 above, the shepherd image draws on well-known pastoral practices. It also commonly denotes God (Ps. 23:1; Isa.

40:11) and political leadership. David the king is God's shepherd (Ps. 78:70-72). False kings and leaders, imaged as shepherds, are condemned in Jer. 23:1-4 and Ezek. 34. The emperor Tiberius is reported to have rebuked a provincial governor intent on levying very harsh taxes by saying it was the part of "a good shepherd to shear his flock, not skin it" (Suetonius, *Tiberius* 32). Dio Chrysostom tells the emperor Trajan that the emperor as "shepherd of peoples" is to "oversee, guard, and protect flocks, not . . . to slaughter, butcher, and skin them" (*Fourth Kingship Oration* 43-44).

As the good shepherd, Jesus reveals God's rule among this community of disciples. The passage is theological, christological, soteriological, eschatological, ecclesiological, and ethical. As is typical in John, to believe in Jesus is to encounter God and to be cosmically, soteriologically, and socially relocated: from darkness to light, from death to life, from synagogue to "church" (9:22).

THE PASSAGE IS THEOLOGICAL, CHRISTOLOGICAL, SOTERIOLOGICAL, ESCHATOLOGICAL, ECCLESIOLOGICAL, AND ETHICAL.

In 10:1-6, one's relationship to the shepherd determines whether a person enters the sheepfold. Directed to the Pharisees who are disciples of Moses (9:28), the tone is polemical. Verses 1 and 2 create a double contrast. They contrast one legitimate way to enter the sheepfold ('by the gate") with an illegitimate means of entry ("climbing in"). And it contrasts the people who do so. Those who enter illegitimately are "a thief and a bandit." The latter term can refer to leaders of peasant-based movements who often present themselves as kingly or messianic figures and employ violence to carve out their own "empire" by attacking the wealthy and political elite. In Jeremiah 7 it refers to those who mislead and exploit the people. By contrast, the shepherd enters through the gate that a gatekeeper opens (10:3).

Verses 3b-5 dwell on the relationship of shepherd and sheep. Verses 3-4 identify two dimensions. One element comprises the shepherd's voice to express a reciprocating relationship. He calls them by name. They recognize his voice. The second element comprises his leading and their following or obedience. Verse 5 highlights the two elements of this intimate and reciprocal relationship with a contrast. The sheep do not know the voice of a stranger. They do not follow a stranger but run from him.

The Pharisees, though, cannot understand the figure (10:6). The figure assumes Jesus as the shepherd, so this element of non-understanding identifies the Pharisees as "bandits and thieves." The sheep in the sheepfold do not listen to their voice. They do not follow them. They are not legitimate leaders as far as this gospel is concerned.

Jesus develops the pastoral, political, and religious "figure of speech" in vv. 7-18 by elaborating its elements. Verses 7-10 identify the gate and the thieves and bandits, and by implication the sheep and shepherd. (1) Jesus declares himself to be the gate (10:7, 9). In Ps. 118:19-20, to enter the gate is a metaphor for finding salvation. He is the gate "for the sheep." That is, their entry to the sheepfold, their membership of the flock, is determined by recognizing him as the gate, as the one who reveals and provides access to God's saving work and to the community that follows him. Some commentators suggest that it was customary for shepherds to sleep across the doorway of a sheepfold to be both shepherd and door.

(2) By contrast, the "thieves and bandits" are other leaders who lay claim to the sheep but are illegitimate leaders. In immediate context, these include the Pharisees, but the language is by no means restricted to them. Other religious leaders and political (Roman) rulers who exercise control as their allies are included.

(3) The obvious implication is that the sheep, often an image for God's people (Psalm 100), are Jesus' disciples. They listen (5:24). They find pasture (10:9; recall Ps. 23:2; Ezek. 34:14). They are "saved," a verb that denotes belief in Jesus that effects cosmic and social transfer (3:16-21). The destructive rule of others is contrasted in 10:10 with Jesus' mission of bringing life. "Life," a key Johannine term, denotes, as Jesus explains it in 17:3, an existence marked by knowing God and Jesus. "Life" means that believers share in the very life of God and in the relationship between God and Jesus (10:14-15). This life belongs to the new age ("eternal life" is "life of the age") not limited by death, sin, or judgment (5:24; 6:51; 11:25).

Responding to the Text

This is a rich and wonderful passage for proclamation. With its christological, soteriological, eschatological, and ecclesiological material built on the previous nine chapters of the Gospel, it asserts fundamental aspects of Christian identity and existence in the Johannine worldview. Jesus is God's anointed, sent from God to reveal God's loving salvation (3:16) by laying down his life for the sheep (10:15). To so believe allows one to enter "life" now. To do so is to become part of a people, a community, centered on and founded by Jesus.

These dimensions are interconnected. To discern Jesus' identity is to discern one's own identity, but in communal not individual terms, a challenging corrective to the rampant and often selfish individualism of our society. That community shares God's life. Such understandings bring challenge and questions. In what appropriate ways is the church to live out this life? There are no divisions

> TO DISCERN JESUS' IDENTITY IS TO DISCERN ONE'S OWN IDENTITY, BUT IN COMMUNAL NOT INDIVIDUAL TERMS, A CHALLENGING CORRECTIVE TO THE RAMPANT AND OFTEN SELFISH INDIVIDUALISM OF OUR SOCIETY.

among the sheep; there are plenty among us. Only one criterion is identified for entering the sheepfold and belonging to the sheep. How many criteria operate in contemporary faith communities to exclude? Ethics, then, is a crucial part of the ecclesiology.

It should also be noted that the passage accomplishes this significant and complex self-definition in polemical terms. It includes and affirms (and challenges) its Christian readers by excluding and disqualifying the Jerusalem, temple-based, leadership. The passage's clear affirmations emerge, at least in part, from a context of bitter dispute, antagonism, and separation that existed in the late first century between John's community and a synagogue and Roman-ruled society. One can understand the historical and sociological reasons for that dispute, and the need, once it had happened, to engage in the polemic and self-assertion and definition that mark this passage. But it raises a question. Does this "over-against" dimension vis-à-vis Judaism have to continue to be a defining mark of Christian identity? Do we have to continue to assert our own inclusion at the price of others' exclusion? It would seem clear that after two thousand years of Christian history that has often been marked by antagonism toward Jews that the time has come in this multi-religious world to repent of such anti-Judaism. That does not stop us upholding and asserting the very important Christian affirmations found in this passage that are so crucial for our identity and way of life. In fact it requires us to do so. But it does encourage us to do so without hate and without claiming to determine the destiny of all others. Jesus has other sheep not of this fold (10:16).

FIFTH SUNDAY OF EASTER

APRIL 28, 2002

REVISED COMMON	EPISCOPAL (BCP)	ROMAN CATHOLIC
Acts 7:55-60	Acts 17:1-15 or Deut. 6:20-25	Acts 6:1-7
Ps. 31:1-5, 15-16	Ps. 66:1-11 or 66:1-8	Ps. 33:1-2, 4-5, 18-19
1 Peter 2:2-10	1 Peter 2:1-10 or Acts 17:1-15	1 Peter 2:4-9
John 14:1-14	John 14:1-14	John 14:1-12

Issues of identity, experiences of faithfulness, and the paradox of divine presence and absence provide common links in this Sunday's readings. The God who faithfully frees people from Egypt, and who raises the Lord Jesus from the dead continues to do saving, life-giving work. An Easter people serves this God with words that recognize (Psalms 31, 66), and actions that faithfully embody, the divine purposes.

But things do not always go smoothly. Stephen, like Paul and Silas, boldly proclaims God's purposes, only to be met with hostility and violence. Stephen's death is Christ-like, and grotesquely violent! Where is the faithful God of resurrection? The psalmist in desperation calls out for help and finds it. The reading from 1 Peter celebrates God's faithfulness and the wonderful identity and mission entrusted to believers, but recognizes that faithfulness is hindered by our ever-present sinfulness and vulnerability in a hostile society. John's Jesus addresses a situation of absence and locates signs of God's presence. Easter demonstrates God's faithfulness, promises new life, challenges us to faithful living, causes conflict with the status quo, and guarantees a future not yet completed.

FIRST READING

ACTS 7:55-60 (RCL)

See First Reading, Fourth Sunday of Easter

ACTS 6:1-7 (RC)

See First Reading, Fourth Sunday of Easter.

DEUTERONOMY 6:20-25 (BCP, alt.)

Moses addresses the people for a second time (Deuteronomy 1–4; 5–28) as they camp to the east of the promised land, Canaan. The passage instructs its hearers to rehearse for their children God's mighty acts in delivering the people from Egypt (6:20-23a), in making covenant (6:23b), and in requiring the people to obey God's will revealed at Sinai in order to know God's blessing (6:24-25).

Contemporary concerns with the church's identity and role are very old. This reading reminds folks in difficult transition situations (whether historically in the Babylonian exile, or narratively after the exodus wilderness wanderings) that the people of God take their bearings from key events. The exodus, wilderness wanderings, and Sinai covenant and revelation reveal God's purposes. An Easter people belong in this long tradition of God's liberating and missional work. God forms people to witness in its actions and words to God's life-giving purposes for the world.

ACTS 17:1-15 (BCP)

In Thessalonica, Paul and Silas have been faithful missionaries, testifying to God's resurrecting work with some positive results (17:1-4), though others are upset (17:5-9). In Beroea they receive a positive response from both Jews and Gentiles (17:10-12). But some from the synagogue in Thessalonica cause a disturbance. Paul escapes to Athens while Silas and Timothy stay behind (why?).

The incidents in Thessalonica and Beroea demonstrate the theological agenda of Acts. The mission to Jews continues as Paul and Silas preach the resurrection message in the synagogue. A division takes place. Some Jews believe. Verses 11-12 develop a related theme, the continuity of God's purposes declared in the scriptures. The Jewish believers exhibit a model commitment to God's word (17:11). Others do not believe and actively oppose the preaching. The preaching confronts Rome's proclamations of control over the world (17:7). Faithful mission provokes opposition. But as intense as the opposition, more intense is the believing. Some Gentiles hear the message and believe. God's purposes are faithful and inclusive, for the benefit of all people.

RESPONSIVE READING
PSALM 31:1-5, 15-16 (RCL)

The psalmist is in deep distress from enemies (31:1, 15). He appeals for God to "deliver," "rescue," or "save" him. The appeal is to God's "righteousness" (31:1), a term that denotes faithful, powerful actions that express God's covenant commitments, to God's "steadfast love" (31:16b), a similar covenant commitment, and to God's "shining face," an image of God's presence and favor (31:16a; cf. Num. 6:22-26). God's response is deemed to be "redemption" because the Lord is a "faithful God" (31:5). To such a God the psalmist commits his life as God's servant (31:5, 15-16).

PSALM 66:1-11 or 66:1-8 (BCP)

Psalm 66 celebrates God's power and care. The psalmist exhorts all the earth (66:1, 4) to express praise for God's "deeds . . . and power" (66:3-5), especially the exodus from Egypt and control over the nations (66:6-7, 8-12).

PSALM 33:1-2, 4-5, 18-19 (RC)

SECOND READING
1 PETER 2:2-10 (RCL);
1 PETER 2:1-10 (BCP);
1 PETER 2:4-9 (RC)

Interpreting the Text

This passage closes the opening section of 1 Peter (on its sociohistorical context see the comments on the Second Reading for the Fourth Sunday of Easter). These verses richly intertwine imperatives and indicatives, affirm the special place of this community of socioeconomic and cultural marginals in God's purposes, and challenge it to grow toward salvation (2:2) and to be faithful to its identity and mission as God's chosen people brought into existence by God's mercy (2:9-10).

The first three verses develop from 1:23 the image of being "born anew." These "newborn infants" live a new life free from practices that undermine love for one another (2:1; 1:22). Their status as a minority and countercultural community requires considerable mutual support and a steady focus on or "longing for" the milk of God's word (cf. 1:23-25) that leads to salvation. The *now* of God's grace (2:3, citing Ps 34:8) and the *not yet* of its eschatological goal of salvation at Jesus' return (1:5, 13; 4:5-7) frame their existence.

The transition to a different image of "stones" in vv. 4-8 is abrupt, but the theme of being God's people through Christ continues (2:9-10). In fact, vv. 4-5 announce that theme with a contrast between those who reject Christ, God's chosen stone, and those like the readers who, in accepting him, become living stones in a new community. Those who reject may be Jerusalem's religious and political elite who crucified Jesus, or may refer to the readers' own time and experience marked by rejection and cultural hostility (1:6, 17; 2:11). The believing "living stones" constitute a house under the Spirit's control, or more likely, with the references to priesthood and sacrifices, a new temple (2:5) in which God's presence is encountered. But they are also people (2:9; cf. Isa. 28:16). The image of priesthood, applied to the whole community not a particular group, highlights not individual direct access to God but lives of service acceptable to God. These lives include love for one another (1:22), moral integrity (2:1), a constant and faithful journey to salvation (2:2), and mission (2:9). The experience of acceptance and rejection accords with God's purposes announced in scripture (2:6-8). The passage ends by affirming God's election of the community (2:9-10; see Exod. 19:6 and Isa. 43:20-21). This election results from God's election of Christ (2:4), expresses God's mercy (2:10), is experienced in a world that more often than not is hostile to God's purposes and faithful people (2:4, 7-8), and mandates public testimony to God's grace (2:9).

Responding to the Text

This strong affirmation of the church's identity and mission, appropriately unpacked, may both affirm and challenge the contemporary church that so often seems to lose its way, unsure of its identity both as a recipient of and witness to God's mercy. The affirmations encourage and challenge us not to be religious imitations of our culture, but a distinctive, faithful, and out-of-step presence and voice in its midst. As cultural changes continue in our society, often marked by indifference or hostility to communities of faith,

THIS STRONG AFFIRMATION OF THE CHURCH'S IDENTITY AND MISSION, APPROPRIATELY UNPACKED, MAY BOTH AFFIRM AND CHALLENGE THE CONTEMPORARY CHURCH THAT SO OFTEN SEEMS TO LOSE ITS WAY, UNSURE OF ITS IDENTITY BOTH AS A RECIPIENT OF AND WITNESS TO GOD'S MERCY.

and as we become increasingly marginalized and suffering communities—like 1 Peter's audience—perhaps we will value such affirmations much more highly.

The appeal of 2:1-3 names not only the goal of salvation and the beginning of the journey ("the kindness of the Lord") but also the continuing reality of sin. It recognizes that we are always "growing up to salvation," always capable of terribly destructive words and actions, always capable of not living faithfully to the mandate of love. So we must always extend "the kindness of the Lord" not only to ourselves but to one another.

The passage also offers two quite different though connected ecclesial metaphors. (1) The newborn children form an extended family marked by love. (2) As living stones, they comprise a temple in God's service. The first emphasizes social relationships and a style of church and worship that is informal, welcoming, inclusive. The second image points in a quite different direction, to the sacred and awe-ful, to mystery, to priestly service, to sacred space. The two images suggest quite different practices and understandings of spirituality. So often we see the two as alternatives. First Peter presents both as necessary for the church to be faithful (not successful) in its worship, mission, and transformative service.

ACTS 17:1-15 (BCP, alt.)

See the First Reading for today, above.

THE GOSPEL
JOHN 14:1-14 (RCL; BCP);
JOHN 14:1-12 (RC)

Interpreting the Text

This reading is part of Jesus' Farewell Discourse or testament (chaps. 13–17). Following the footwashing (chap. 13), Jesus asserts his departure, outlines its consequences, and equips disciples to live in his absence. In 14:1-14, Jesus assures the disciples that his departure to his father by the cross, resurrection, and ascension (13:1-3; his "lifting up," 12:32) means their continuing communion with him and with God (14:1-7). He asserts again his claim to be the one who reveals God (14:8-11), and points to the disciples' task of manifesting God's works (14:12-14).

Chapter 13 closes with talk of Jesus' death and departure (13:31-35) and his assertion that the disciples could not go with him now but would do so later (13:36-38). Verse 1 of chap. 14 addresses their possible distress in viewing his death/departure (12:23-33; 13:26-28) as the apparent victory of the Jerusalem and Roman elite in Jesus' crucifixion and their anxiety about living in his absence. Jesus' exhortation to the disciples to "believe in" God and Jesus asserts the unity of the two (10:30), and invites them to see Jesus' death/departure as revealing God's salvific and life-giving work.

In vv. 2-4, Jesus uses the metaphor of his "Father's house" (Ps. 123:1) and "rooms" (a cognate of the verb "abide" in John 15) to denote the intimate relationship with God that he shares (1:1, 18; 14:10) and makes available to disciples (15:1-11). Jesus' departure means that this relationship is not broken. Moreover, "I will come again" (14:3) points to its eschatological completion (cf. 6:35-51) when Jesus returns to take believers to share in a relationship with God that is not bound by death but lasts forever (3:16; 17:3; 20:30-31). Thomas's question in v. 5 seems to focus more on geography than on understanding the relationships Jesus has been describing. So in v. 6 Jesus elaborates the relationships with another "I am" saying that reveals God's purposes at work in him. This "I am" formula of God's self-revelation occurs in Exod. 3:13 and commonly in Deutero-Isaiah (e.g., Isa. 43) to proclaim God's salvation from opponents.

To be "the way" picks up a biblical image that depicts life lived in union with God's purposes (Ps. 119:1-5). Jesus is the way to the Father (14:6b), a way of self-giving and life-giving death (13:1; 10:16-18) that reveals God's loving purposes (3:16) and that is to become the disciples' way of life (13:15, 34-35). Jesus' way is explicated as "truth." In the biblical tradition, "truth" denotes trustworthiness and reliability. God is true in acting faithfully and reliably in making covenant (Exod. 34:6) and saving the people (2 Chron. 15:3-4). In Jesus' death/departure as well as in his life, God's truthfulness or faithfulness in carrying out God's revealing, saving, and life-giving purposes is demonstrated (1:14; 8:31-32; 17:3). So Jesus again claims to be "life" (11:25), the one who manifests God's life that is not destroyed by sin and death (5:24). "Eternal life," or "life of the age," means a union with God (17:3) of intimate quality and never-ending quantity. If truth and life, God's faithfulness and intimate relationship with God, are known in Jesus, it follows that one "knows" and "sees" or encounters God's purposes in Jesus (14:7).[6]

> "ETERNAL LIFE," OR "LIFE OF THE AGE," MEANS A UNION WITH GOD (17:3) OF INTIMATE QUALITY AND NEVER-ENDING QUANTITY.

As often happens in this Gospel, Philip's request in 14:8 enables Jesus to develop important material. Jesus' response does not offer new "proofs" but reviews his ministry (14:9). He claims (14:10), as he has throughout, that his words (5:24; 8:38) and works (5:19-23; 10:32) reveal God's presence and will (5:19-30; 8:19, 38; 10:37-38). People, though, must decide to believe (three times in 14:10-11) that the Father and Jesus are one, that Jesus reveals the Father (14:11). If they do, believers will manifest God's works and purposes in their lives (14:12). In Jesus' absence, the community of believers, the church, becomes the continuing revelation of God's saving and life-giving presence. Yet paradoxically, though Jesus is absent, they will encounter him in prayer and in his life-giving responses to their prayer (14:13-14).

Responding to the Text

One vital thing that preachers can do with this passage, as with any Johannine material, is unpack John's specialized theological vocabulary and worldview. No doubt it was familiar to the Gospel's original audience, but it is often a riddle for contemporary congregations. Attention to John's realized and future eschatology, the use of space to denote relationships ("Father's house," "room"), the language of "way," "truth," "life," "know," "see," "believe," the relationship between God as Father and Jesus as Son, is required. The text's literary context or connection with chap. 13 is important, as is the passage's address to the anxiety of absence.

The eschatology of 14:2-5 presents a challenge. Because these verses are commonly used in funeral services, many understand them to refer to Jesus' presence as the destiny of the loved one who has died. Texts are often polyvalent and interpreters make multiple meanings from them, so I do not disqualify that reading. But I don't think it is a particularly sustainable reading in its Johannine context. A reading related to John's context (my interpretation above) brings a different issue to the surface, namely, understanding the imminence of Jesus' death and the challenge of discipleship in his absence.

This issue has much relevance. Perhaps the fundamental question in this Farewell Discourse (chaps. 13–17) concerns how people live in Jesus' absence. For John's generation living when Jesus is physically absent, and at a point in history when most if not all eyewitnesses have died, this is a pressing issue. The Gospel's basic response is to recognize Jesus' absence but to assert his presence in various ways: through the telling of the stories (20:30-31), his blessing on believing without seeing (20:29), through various everyday symbols (bread), through promises of his future return (14:3), and here, a promise that in "believing" disciples enter into permanent, intimate relationship with God in which God's powerful presence is demonstrated through various works (14:11-14).

> PERHAPS THE FUNDAMENTAL QUESTION IN THE FAREWELL DISCOURSE (CHAPS. 13–17) CONCERNS HOW PEOPLE LIVE IN JESUS' ABSENCE.

This dilemma of absence and presence seems very contemporary. Some have argued that contemporary interest in angels, in "new age" spirituality, and in the current fad of "spirituality" (so vaguely defined that it often seems to refer to nothing more than a little emotion) attests to a spiritual hunger to experience and encounter God (though usually in benign, certainly not demanding ways). That people often do not look to mainline churches for an encounter with God is a tragic commentary. So too are the blank stares and silence I sometimes get from church folks (including seminarians) when in various Bible study and class contexts I ask them to name ways in which they know God's presence or the presence of the risen Christ in their lives. Exploring this Johannine dynamic might offer folks some resources and disciplines to encourage such encounters.

Finally, a note on John 14:6 is warranted. In one sense, this marvelous text sums up the heart of John's pastoral theology, that God's faithful and life-giving revelation is encountered in Jesus. This affirmation was crucial in sustaining and confirming John's small, "out-of-step" community, which was rejected and suffered for such an affirmation. Originally this text was a claim made in the tumult of post-70 C.E. Jewish religious debates, within a tradition that John's community shared with various groups including the synagogue from which it had separated (9:22; 12:42; 16:2). It was their answer to the question with which numerous post-70 Jewish groups were faithfully struggling, "How/where is God known?" It located them in this debate by expressing a distinctive Christian claim. It did not deny that God had been revealed through other figures, even though it questioned the adequacy and focus of those revelations (Moses; John; 5:41-47).

But it does not for one moment offer a verdict on all religious experience and traditions. Its contemporary address lies not in stimulating us to celebrate our inclusion at the expense of others, but, rather, in challenging contemporary believers to wrestle with what distinctive and faithful Christian identity—verbalized and lived—looks like in a pluralistic world and in a society where the church seems so often compromised by pervasive cultural aspirations and worldviews. What does it mean to live as an Easter people?

SIXTH SUNDAY OF EASTER

MAY 5, 2002

REVISED COMMON	EPISCOPAL (BCP)	ROMAN CATHOLIC
Acts 17:22-31	Acts 17:22-31 or Isa. 41:17-20	Acts 8:5-8, 14-17
Ps. 66:8-20	Psalm 148 or 148:7-14	Ps. 66:1-3, 4-5, 6-7, 16, 20
1 Peter 3:13-22	1 Peter 3:8-18 or Acts 17:22-31	1 Peter 3:15-18
John 14:15-21	John 15:1-8	John 14:15-21

The mysterious, multifaceted experiences of God's presence and absence provide one focal point for these texts. A second focus on the interaction between the believing community (the church) and the world offers another point of reflection on resurrection life. In Acts 17 Paul skillfully affirms and builds on aspects of his contemporary culture in announcing good news that both critiques and challenges the status quo. In Isaiah 41 God's gracious but powerful salvation of the people from oppressive exile is demonstrated in such a way that "all may see and know" (41:20; so also the Holy Spirit in Acts 8). Psalm 66 invites "all the earth" to hear about God's "awesome deeds" (66:3). In 1 Peter the minority community suffers from verbal opposition and is offered the presence of the resurrected and ascended Jesus to strengthen it in its faithful responses including proclamation. The readings from John's Gospel continue to work with a situation in which Jesus is absent yet present with believers (through the Paraclete) to shape obedient lives of loving and fruitful actions that manifest God's presence and purposes. His absence/presence means not a vacation from its task but God's equipping for the faithful living of its vocation among those who often do not share its fundamental commitments.

FIRST READING

ACTS 17:22-31 (RCL, BCP)

Interpreting the Text

Paul, the itinerant Jewish-Christian preacher is questioned in cultured Athens by "some Epicurean and Stoic philosophers" (17:18-21). In a highly crafted speech he proclaims God's activity and being. Paul develops rather than condemns his audience's religious sensibilities as he points his audience to the God who has raised Jesus from the dead and to appropriate human responses.

The speech divides into three sections. In vv. 22-23, Paul acknowledges the religiosity of his audience, its seeking for the "unknown god," and promises a revelation. Verses 24-28 offer the revelation: God is creator (17:24a). This God does not live in shrines or depend on human help (17:24b-25). God gives life to all including humans (17:26). God also gives humans a desire to seek for God (17:27), who is accessible as a parent to children (17:28-29). Third, vv. 29-31 outline some implications of being God's offspring. While idols are futile (17:29), there is accountability to God who requires repentance (17:30-31a). God has appointed "a man" to enact judgment. God's resurrecting of Jesus guarantees both the present demand for repentance and future accountability (17:31).

> PAUL DEVELOPS RATHER THAN CONDEMNS HIS AUDIENCE'S RELIGIOUS SENSIBILITIES.

Responding to the Text

In this meeting between Jerusalem and Athens, the text balances a valuing of and a critique of contemporary culture. Paul recognizes worthwhile qualities: awareness of life's religious dimensions, the testimony of the created order and human experience to some fundamental realities about God the search for God. But the gospel reveals the status quo's limitations by disclosing further realities about God (God's active involvement, God's closeness) and about humans (the demand to repent; accountability to God). The challenge for contemporary readers and preachers is to engage in similar cultural valuing and critique knowing that some will reject a Christian perspective, while others will welcome it (see 17:32-34).

ISAIAH 41:17-20 (BCP, alt.)

This wonderful passage foreshadows the return of the people from Babylonian exile in 539 B.C.E. instigated by the Persian ruler Cyrus, God's "anointed" or "christed" one (44:28; 45:1). God sees the desperation of the people in exile expressed in the metaphor of being "parched with thirst" (41:17). Verses 18-20 extravagantly describe God's response in terms of abundant provision of water, life, and fertility in the wilderness (echoes of the exodus from Egypt). God's response attests God's saving power in bringing the people home, a deed that demonstrates to all God's power and mercy (Isa. 41:17-20).

ACTS 8:5-8, 14-17 (RC)

God's presence is evident through the Holy Spirit's activity in the church's mission. Philip enacts God's will revealed by the risen Jesus and goes to Samaria (1:8). His proclamation is confirmed by exorcisms and healings, demonstrations of God's power over all oppressive forces (see 1 Peter 3). These actions are understood to be the work of the Holy Spirit active now among Samaritans. God's blessing and presence demolish traditional ethnic divisions and hostilities. Where and how is the Spirit at work in the contemporary church?

RESPONSIVE READING
PSALM 66:8-20 (RCL);
PSALM 66:1-3, 4-5, 6-7, 16, 20 (RC)

Verses 1-7 call "all the earth" (66:1, 4) to worship God in response to God's "awesome deeds" (66:3, 5), particularly for the deliverance of the exodus (66:6-7). Verses 8-12 continue this invitation with a further rehearsal of God's saving power. The language of testing like silver suggests that Babylonian exile and return to the land are in mind (cf. Isa. 48:10). In vv. 13-15 a representative figure offers abundant offerings in the temple as thanksgiving to God. In 16-20 this figure further testifies to God's actions on behalf of the people. God has heard their prayers and demonstrated faithful, steadfast (covenant) love. Blessed be God.

PSALM 148 or 148:7-14 (BCP)

With echoes of the creation story of Genesis 1:1—2:4, all creation, heaven and earth, is invited repeatedly to "praise the Lord." Verses 1-5a solicit praise from the heavenly regions and occupants, while vv. 5b-6 provide the reason, namely God's creative work through God's authoritative word. Verses 7-13 take up the invitation again, directing it this time to the earth. A special place is reserved for God's people to express God's praise (148:14).

Second Reading

1 PETER 3:13-22 (rcl);
1 PETER 3:8-18 (bcp);
1 PETER 3:15-18 (rc)

Interpreting the Text

This reading continues to sustain 1 Peter's readers in faithful living as a minority community in a somewhat hostile social context of Asia Minor (see comments on the Second Lesson for the previous Sundays). The suffering consists predominantly of verbal harassment or abuse (2:12; 3:16) that expresses an intolerance and/or fear of a distinctive and alternative existence. This reading places their suffering in the cosmic and eschatological context of Christ's triumphant ascension and victory over all powers.

THIS READING PLACES THE READERS' SUFFERING IN THE COSMIC AND ESCHATOLOGICAL CONTEXT OF CHRIST'S TRIUMPHANT ASCENSION AND VICTORY OVER ALL POWERS.

The passage begins with its basic claim that harm cannot come to the believer who does God's will (3:13). The assertion seems strange for several reasons. All readers of this letter know from their/our own experience that suffering does result from doing God's will. The letter writer has already said as much (1:6; 2:19-20; cf. 4:14-19). Christian readers know the story of Jesus who suffered in this way. Rhetorically the statement functions to surprise and to stimulate interest as we anticipate its explanation.

Verse 14 begins that explanation by reframing the meaning of suffering "on account of righteousness" or "for doing what is right" (NRSV). Those who suffer *because of faithfully doing God's will* are blessed, not cursed or abandoned by God. They know God's favor. Five admonitions follow that outline appropriate behavior when experiencing this suffering (3:14b-16): have no fear, do not be troubled, revere Christ, be able to explain your "hope" or faith, have a clear conscience. Verse 17 essentially repeats the claim that suffering for doing right is a blessed state (God's will). Believers must stand firm in their loyalty to Christ during this verbal harassment and pressure to conform culturally.

Verses 18-22, very difficult verses,[7] offer a christological foundation for the claim that suffering for doing right does not harm a believer (3:13, 17). Christ's death, the death of a righteous person, benefited others, including the readers, by "bringing *us* to God" (3:18) through baptism (3:21). His suffering was also, at least in part, an opportunity for proclamation (so also for believers in 3:15) to the imprisoned evil angels from the flood. But there is a difference and further significance in that his "preaching" announced their judgment in contrast to the "eight persons" who were saved (3:20). That is, Christ demonstrated to the imprisoned evil powers the triumph that he has over all "angels, authorities, and powers subject to him" (3:22) through his resurrection and ascension "into heaven." This further aspect of Christ's suffering encourages his followers' fearless confession in the face of suffering. Through their baptism, they share his triumph over all the powers including those who oppose them in situations of social animosity. Participation in his triumph means that God's purposes will be accomplished, that their hope is secure, and that their suffering is a blessing, not a source of harm (3:13-14).

Responding to the Text

Talk of "the benefits of suffering" can be cheap and is always dangerous. It can seem so facile and heartless in the face of the very destructive terrors of pain, suffering, and loss. I sat through a sermon recently in which a departing minister tried to assure the congregation that there were "No Sad Goodbyes!" The unreality of that title should have been self-evident (from trips to the airport or from conducting funerals), but it was graphically exposed by the loud sobs of the woman three rows behind me who had buried her mother three days previously! It is crucial, then, that this reading not be understood in terms of general human suffering. It is not a general theodicy. It concerns the challenges of a particular form of suffering (verbal and social harassment for doing God's will) that these Christians are facing as Christians, and it places their suffering in God's eschatological purposes. It is not about the vicissitudes of daily human existence,

The passage forces us to think about this experience of verbal opposition. Certainly it, and much worse, is familiar to some brothers and sisters in parts of the world. Some Christian kids trying to live faithfully in school and college situations know the reality of being ridiculed, as do some adults in difficult work situations. It makes us contemplate what comprises our Christian witness and distinctiveness. To what do we bear witness with our lives? And at what cost, if any? And how do we respond—by retreat, retaliation, or continued faithful witness? Communities of faith must train our members to be able verbally to "account for the hope that is in you." Of course that assumes a "hope" (a conviction and expectation of God's completed purposes, not wishful thinking) integral to who we are and how we live as Easter people.

ACTS 17:22-31 (BCP, alt.)

See above, First Reading.

THE GOSPEL

JOHN 14:15-21 (RCL and RC)

Interpreting the Text

As with last Sunday's reading, this passage comes from Jesus' Farewell Discourse (John 13–17). Jesus continues to provide reassurance and direction for the small community of "trouble-hearted" believers (14:1, 5, 8, 22) that understands itself to be oppressed and that struggles to live faithfully in his absence (14:1-3, 18-19). Two emphases mark these verses: love for Jesus means obeying his teaching, and God's presence remains with disciples through the Spirit after Jesus' absence.

Though he has spoken of the Father's love for the world (3:16) and for himself (10:17), and his own love for people (11:5; 13:1), only once prior to chap. 14 has Jesus used "love" to define the relationship of disciples with himself (8:42). To love Jesus is to believe him (14:1, 10-12), to know him (14:7), and here to obey him (also 14:21). Jesus' commandments (14:15) or words (14:23-24) reveal God, including God's will that disciples relationally embody the very love that Father and Son share (13:34-35; 15:9). Disciples are to live his words. They are to love by doing his works (14:12-14).

In this community of love, God's presence is encountered through the Spirit (14:16-17) called here for the first time, "Paraclete" (14:26; 15:26; 16:8-11, 12-15). The noun has multiple meanings and translations (exhorter, comforter, helper, advocate, counselor). Its background is perhaps forensic (advocate), though its origin in relation to heavenly intercessors cannot be ruled out given the adjective "another" and the reference to prayer in 14:13-14 (Jesus is "paraclete" in 1 John 2:1). The Paraclete manifests God's presence (14:16b) and continues Jesus' work in manifesting truth (14:6), namely God's faithfulness (14:17a). The Paraclete also maintains the boundary between disciples and "the world" that rejects God's purposes and Jesus' mission (1:10-11). The world does not see or know Jesus or the Paraclete (14:17; 15:18). But the community of believers is assured twice in 14:17b, repeating the assurance of 14:16 that the Paraclete's presence is with them.

God's presence encountered through the Paraclete means that Jesus' departure does not leave them "orphaned" (14:18-20). His death (13:36-38) is not their abandonment. But the timing of this promised presence is not clear. Some have suggested it indicates the resurrection on the basis of verse 19's references to "seeing me" and "I live." But while that is true (chaps. 20–21), it is not adequate because Jesus will then depart in the ascension. Several factors also point to an eschatological appearance: the eschatological phrases "I am coming to you" (14:18b) and "on that day" (14:20), and the sequence in which Jesus' coming is placed after the Paraclete's presence. On that day, the unity of Father and Son, and of son and disciples, already experienced, will be fully demonstrated. In the meantime (14:21), love for Jesus means obedience to his teaching. In that context, God's love and Jesus' revelation are encountered.

Responding to the Text

The text challenges us to continue to wrestle with the mysteries of divine absence and presence. What do we make of the repeated affirmations of divine presence (4 times in 14:16, 17 [twice], 18) when so often God seems absent or asleep or oblivious to the struggles, conflicts, and desperation of many on planet earth? What do we make of these promises in ever-comfortable suburban lives lived amidst plenty, comfort, and self-reliance? What do

> WHAT DO WE MAKE OF THE REPEATED AFFIRMA-
> TIONS OF DIVINE PRESENCE WHEN SO OFTEN GOD
> SEEMS ABSENT OR ASLEEP OR OBLIVIOUS TO THE
> STRUGGLES, CONFLICTS, AND DESPERATION OF MANY
> ON PLANET EARTH?

we make of them amidst regular and predictable church routines and activities that more often than not entertain rather than disciple, and that are usually not marked by a desperate search for divine presence and reassurance?

The text also posits an integral connection between the presence of divine love and active human obedience. Our acts of service or works of obedience are one locus in which we are to know God's presence and through which we manifest God's love in the "world." That word reminds us that the experiences of divine presence and love and of the Paraclete are part of what distinguishes the church from the world. The world cannot discern the Paraclete, cannot share this primary emphasis on knowing God's presence, cannot value the gift of God's love because it has not chosen to live life in relationship to God. Talk of the church's privileged identity often disturbs us because of so many abuses and claims of elitism. But for communities like John's, small and culturally out-of-step and knowing rejection, such talk is life-giving and life-sustaining. The passage challenges us to think again about our cultural accommodation, about the ever-sharpening lines being drawn in our secular society, about what matters to us as communities of "faith," about our experiences of God's presence, and especially about the church's difficult tasks of being faithful and being in mission as an Easter people.

JOHN 15:1-8 (BCP)

Interpreting the Text

Despite inviting the disciples to depart with him (14:31), Jesus continues to teach, comfort, and challenge. The metaphor of the vine and the branches depicts the relationship of Jesus (the vine, 15:5) and his followers (the branches, 15:5).

Verses 1 and 5 contain the Gospel's final "I am" saying. It seems to draw on the common biblical use of the "vine" to symbolize God's people (Isa. 5:1-7). But it reinterprets the image in terms of Jesus' relationships, first with God (15:1), and then with the community of disciples (15:5). Jesus "connects" God and the community. The focus in vv. 2-4 concerns the production of fruit by the branches. "Fruit" in the context of chap. 14 refers to the works of loving obedience required of Jesus' followers (14:12, 15, 21). Disciples are warned that they must faithfully live Jesus' teaching. Judgment awaits the non-fruitful followers (15:2), but fruit will follow if believers "abide" or "remain" or live in close relationship with Jesus (15:4). This point is so important that it is repeated in 15:5, restated in terms of the dreadful consequences of not abiding (15:6, judgment), asserted again positively in 15:7 with an emphasis on prayer (cf. 14:13-14), and repeated in 15:8 in terms of honoring the Father as a continuation of Jesus' work (14:13) and as a demonstration of being a disciple.

Responding to the Text

The passage provides an image of the church marked by mutual interrelationship with God and Jesus. Such an image calls contemporary faith communities to faithful and fruitful acts of love, to spiritual disciplines that nourish such intimacy with God, and to relationships with one another as the basic means of belonging (committee assignments!). There is no room for individual and private retreat. Nor given that all followers are branches is there any place for hierarchical structures and privileged positions. All exist in loving relationships.

THE ASCENSION OF OUR LORD

MAY 9, 2002

REVISED COMMON	EPISCOPAL (BCP)	ROMAN CATHOLIC
Acts 1:1-11	Acts 1:1-11 or Dan. 7:9-14	Acts 1:1-11
Psalm 47 or Psalm 93	Psalm 47 or 110:1-5	Ps. 47:1-2, 5-6, 7-8 (Heb. Bible 47:2-3, 6-7, 8-9)
Eph. 1:15-23	Eph. 1:15-23 or Acts 1:1-11	Eph. 1:17-23
Luke 24:44-53	Luke 24:49-53 or Mark 16:9-15, 19-20	Matt. 28:16-20

Easter, for all its affirmations of divine intervention and presence, struggles with the very acute reality of divine absence. Though risen, Jesus did not stay here. What happened to him? Where is he? Why is he no longer present with the church as in the Easter appearance stories? The ascension references address these questions by affirming Jesus' departure to God and his continuing activity of partaking in God's rule over

> ASCENSION INDICATES THAT LIFE WITH GOD, NOT RESURRECTION, IS JESUS' DESTINY.

the church and the world, and through the coming of the Spirit, until Jesus returns. Ascension indicates that life with God, not resurrection, is Jesus' destiny.

Jesus' elevation draws on older traditions of the elevation of kings to the throne as a display of their ruling power, a symbol applied to God to depict God's sovereignty over the earth (Psalms 47; 93; 110). The Roman world employed a similar motif of "ascending" in elevating (apotheosis or deification) a founder figure like Romulus and emperors at their death (mocked by Seneca in his satirical work on Claudius, *Apocolocyntosis*, the "Pumpkinification" of Claudius). The ascended Jesus, then, has not disappeared into disinterested obscurity. Approved and exalted by God, the crucified and risen Jesus now shares in the rule and purposes of God (Matt. 28:18), manifested on earth through the church. The ascension references render the absent Jesus, ascended into heaven to rule with God, very present to believers as one who participates in God's rule. But the church's task to manifest that rule is, of course, very difficult in a world that more often than not fails to recognize its creator. Jesus' ascension prepares the way for God to give the Holy Spirit to the church to empower (Luke) and guide (John) it in this very difficult task until he returns. Eschatology, Christology, and ecclesiology interact for the latter's benefit.

The ascension readings utilize images of power and domination in depicting God's reign in which Jesus shares. This image, influenced by various kingly and imperial systems including Rome's, ironically seems to trade one ruling power for another. The readings encourage us to affirm God's sovereign reign, a rule that is life-giving and graciously beneficent. But we should not lose sight of the observation that some do not experience God's reign in this way, and that the church has used this metaphor to oppress and terrorize. Nor can we overlook the observation that in our society kingly rule is not normative or desired. In our celebrations we need to tread humbly while engaging the quest for metaphors that re-present God's work and ultimate purposes.

FIRST READING

ACTS 1:1-11

See the First Reading for the Seventh Sunday of Easter.

DANIEL 7:9-14 (BCP, alt.)

Interpreting the Text

After six chapters exhorting faithful loyalty to God in difficult situations, the book of Daniel now looks to God's future action in establishing God's reign and vindicating the righteous. This reading is part of King Belshazzar's dream vision of four kingdoms (7:1-8): Babylon, the Medes, Persia, the Greeks, including Antiochus Epiphanes (7:8) who in the 160s B.C.E., the time of reference for Daniel, overthrows the Jerusalem cult and forbids Jewish observance of Torah (see 1 Maccabees 1). Then in the vision, in vv. 9-14, God the "Ancient One" appears in judgment (7:9-10). God is seated on a fiery throne (resembling Ezekiel's vision of God's throne in Ezek 1:15-28) and surrounded by the heavenly court (compare Micaiah's vision in 1 Kings 22:19 and Isaiah's in Isa. 6:1-2). Verses 11-12 describe judgment on Antiochus Epiphanes. The mighty tyrant who had created such havoc for the community/ies addressed by this document is/are destroyed by God's judging power that establishes God's reign on the earth. Then a new ruler emerges, one "like a human being" or "like a son of man," to whom God entrusts power over all creation. This figure may well be the archangel Michael

(10:13, 21; 12:1), patron angel of the Jewish nation and representative of faithful Jews, though it is also akin to a heavenly ruler in 1 Enoch 46–48; 62 who is also identified as "son of man." The Christian tradition subsequently adjusted the time periods and referents (the fourth beast becomes Rome in Revelation 13) and read the figure in relation to Jesus, triumphant over Rome (cf. Matt. 26:64).

Responding to the Text

This first reading establishes the day's emphasis on God's power and reign triumphant over all that opposes God's purposes. Its use on Ascension Day encourages a christological reading that detaches it from its mid-second-century context (160s B.C.E.). That is a pity, because faithful attention to the text's function in that historical context alerts us to the pastoral power of this image in giving encouragement and hope for those trying to live faithfully and at the risk of their lives in desperately oppressive circumstances. Such visions of power, and such scenarios of utmost confidence in God's purposes are born not out of comfort and self-assurance, but desperation and life-giving conviction.

RESPONSIVE READING
PSALM 47 (RCL; BCP);
PSALM 47:1-2, 5-6, 7-8 (RC)

This short psalm praises God as king over all the earth/nations, a refrain emphasized with a threefold repetition (47:2. 7, 8). His kingship is expressed by establishing Israel among the nations (47:3-4, invoking the exodus) and by controlling the nations (47:9). Hence all peoples are invited to join in worship (47:1) acknowledging God's reign as God "goes up" and is enthroned (47:5, 8). Presumably the words accompany a liturgical drama that imitates ancient Near Eastern rituals concerned with the king's enthronement at a coronation or state event.

PSALM 93 (RCL, alt.)

This psalm, like Psalm 47, perhaps employed in an entrance procession into the temple in the Festival of Tabernacles, celebrates God as king, clothed with majesty and strength (93:1a), the creator of the world that is "established" against all threats and chaos (93:1b), its everlasting ruler (93:2). Verses 3-4 employ very old understandings of the destructive threatening force of the watery abyss or sea (cf. Gen. 1:6-10; Pss. 74:12-17; 104:7-9) to depict threats to God's world, but God's rule is greater (93:4). In 93:5, the psalmist moves from creation to God's revealed will or laws for ordering human interaction. These decrees are, like God's world, "very sure" (93:5a). God's house "on high" (93:4, and represented by the temple) attests God's holiness or "set-apartness" as the majestic ruling king.

PSALM 110:1-5 (BCP, alt.)

This psalm, a likely coronation psalm spoken perhaps by a priest, might seem initially to celebrate not God as king but Israel's Davidic king. But the distinction cannot be forced. God authorizes the king in v. 1 to represent God's reign and order among the people. And God promises to act on behalf of the king and for the king's benefit (110:1b). This promise is elaborated in vv. 2 and 5 with assurances of expansive dominion and triumph over enemy kings and nations who serve other gods. That is, the vision of the king's power expresses the establishment of God's reign through the king over all of God's world. The difficult v. 3 includes at least the assurance that the king's people will be loyal and submissive. Verse 4 identifies the king also as a priest who represents the people before God and mediates God's will and purposes among the people. The king-priest is linked with the traditions of the ancient Melchizedek, a Canaanite priest-prince.

While the psalm may have originally affirmed the king as God's anointed ruler and agent of God's reign, it did not maintain that function throughout Israel's history, particularly in times when, under conquest, there were no kings. In such circumstances it functioned as a statement of hope anticipating the day when God's reign would be established over all enemies. The early Christian movement read the psalm eschatologically (Paul in 1 Cor. 15:25) and messianically in relation to Jesus (Matt. 22:41-45). Read as a statement about the ascended Jesus, it establishes that his rule cannot be spiritualized and restricted in impact. His rule will be asserted over all ruling powers and nations. For the early Christians, that meant a bold and subversive vision of Rome's demise and of all empires resistant to God's just purposes.

SECOND READING
EPHESIANS 1:15-23 (RCL, BCP);
EPHESIANS 1:17-23 (RC)

This complex text begins in 1:15-16 with thanksgiving for the church's relationships with God (faith) and with each other (love), and with reassurance of the writer's prayers (probably not Paul). Verse 17 elaborates the prayer's content. The writer prays that the church receives the revealing spirit, a Hebrew Bible expression denoting God's gift (Exod. 31:3; Deut. 34:9). Verses 18-19 particularize the revelation or knowledge. It concerns understanding the hope, inheritance, and God's power already at work in believers (note the extravagant language of v. 19). In context this power expresses God's love (1:4-5), grace (1:7; 2:7), and mercy (2:4). The writer points to the supreme demonstration of God's power in raising Christ from the dead and enthroning or exalting him (1:20), whereby he shares God's power over every ruling power (1:21). Verse 20 does not utilize the resurrection appearance or ascension narratives of the Gospels but invokes Ps. 110:1, a psalm that celebrates the enthronement of Israel's king. This very political language not only guarantees the resurrection of God's people (that has already been accomplished in 2:1-7, very different from Paul's anticipation of a future somatic resurrection in 1 Cor. 15:35-51), but also celebrates God's triumph through Christ over all ruling powers, visible and invisible, that seek control over people and God's world. Jesus' enthronement displays God's sovereign power over all resistant forces (contrast 1 Cor. 15:24) and asserts God's claim to God's world. This power is that which is at work among believers (1:19). Further, Jesus' exaltation renders him "head," or the source of and authority over the church (1:22-23). The language of "body" points to the church as a manifestation, an embodiment, of God's purposes and power. The church is connected to and reliant on the exalted Christ, manifesting him in the world and to the powers in a life of service (3:10; 4:12). Christ's rule as the exalted one is described as "filling" the church and the world (1:23), an image of the extension of God's presence and salvation through all creation.

> THE CHURCH IS CONNECTED TO AND RELIANT ON THE EXALTED CHRIST, MANIFESTING HIM IN THE WORLD AND TO THE POWERS IN A LIFE OF SERVICE.

Responding to the Text

Jesus' exaltation is interpreted in at least three ways here. It demonstrates God's power; it displays Christ's power over all claimants on human loyalty; it manifests his power over and through the church. The sovereignty model that pervades this and the other passages requires some reflection. First, sovereignty belongs to God, not to the church whose role is never of world dominion but of servanthood (4:12). The church that serves and advances itself ceases to be the church. But second, the use of imperial sovereignty language, borrowed from the political sphere, runs the danger of creating God in the image of kings and emperors and rendering "unto God the attributes which belonged exclusively to Caesar."[8] Even talk of God's loving rule does not solve the dilemma, since all rulers claim their rule benefits the ruled. The challenge is to find metaphors appropriate to God's just and life-giving purposes for all creation.

ACTS 1:1-11 (BCP)

See the First Reading for the Seventh Sunday of Easter.

THE GOSPEL
LUKE 24:44-53 (RCL);
LUKE 24:49-53 (BCP)

Interpreting the Text

The Emmaus road appearance of the risen Jesus dominates Luke 24 (24:13-35; see the Gospel for Easter Evening, above). Subsequent to it Jesus appears to the eleven and other followers (24:33, 36-43). They struggle to believe (24:38, 41), so Jesus offers a series of "proofs," first his scared hands and feet (24:39a), then his body (24:39b), then eating a piece of fish (24:41b-43).

Verses 44-47 are, effectively, his last words in the Gospel, and they underline key Lukan themes. Verse 44 emphasizes continuity between his pre-Easter and post-Easter teaching (9:22; 18:33), God's salvific purposes, and the witness of the scriptures. Verses 46-47 elaborate the scriptural witness: the Messiah must suffer (cf. 22:15), he will be raised, repentance and forgiveness are available in his name for all the nations (key themes for Acts). So far no actual scriptures have been cited and none exists that declares such things clearly (without "Jesus" glasses to provide the reading perspective). The point, of course, is that God's purposes are being accomplished.

Forgiveness, as indicated by Jesus' programmatic citation of the jubilee program of Isaiah 61 in Luke 4:18-19, means "setting at liberty" and refers not just to a personal renewal but to a socioeconomic transformation (see Leviticus 25, where the same term is frequently translated "jubilee"). The phrase "beginning from Jerusalem" anticipates the mission that Jesus will make explicit in Acts 1:8 and reverses the common eschatological expectation of the nations flocking to Jerusalem (Mic. 4:1-5). Verse 48 establishes the believers' key role (recall 24:33, more than disciples) as witnesses. Their new understanding (24:45), as well as the Holy Spirit, promised by God and sent by Jesus, will empower them for the task (24:49).

> FORGIVENESS MEANS "SETTING AT LIBERTY" AND REFERS NOT JUST TO A PERSONAL RENEWAL BUT TO A SOCIOECONOMIC TRANSFORMATION.

Jesus' final action is to "lead out" and bless the believers as he ascends into heaven. His departure has been signaled since 9:31, 51, as has his return in glory and power (9:26). That is, his departure into heaven closes this part of his ministry and anticipates his return. It also elevates his status as one approved by God (in contrast to those who rejected him, the Jerusalem and Roman elite, especially in the crucifixion) and as one who shares a crucial role in God's purposes. The disciples respond by obeying Jesus' words and returning to Jerusalem and the temple (cf. 24:49), and by worshiping God. Worship and witness belong together, nourishing each other.

Responding to the Text

The transitional nature of this Ascension Day between resurrection and Pentecost is evident as Jesus departs, but not before he commissions the church to mission and promises the empowering presence of the Spirit (24:49). That is, as with John's Gospel, his going away is a necessary and good thing in that it means, among other things, the sending of the Spirit who will enable the church to carry out its mission in Jesus' absence (John 16:7).

These ecclesial dimensions flow from the christological event of ascension. But this text does not dwell on Jesus' ascension. He departs, but most of the attention focuses on the implications for the church. In Luke-Acts there is no speculation about his relationship with God and no explanation of the significance of his elevation, only attention to his sending the Spirit so that the worshiping church can get on with its mission task. While this day draws us into worlds of mystery with its ascending Jesus, it keeps our feet grounded in the mission of the church, for which we will be held accountable at his return.

MARK 16:9-15, 19-20 (BCP, alt.)

This reading from Mark's longer ending, a latter addition to the Gospel, bears significant similarities to Luke's account. It begins with an appearance to Mary Magdalene who had earlier gone to the tomb (16:9-11) and refers very briefly, in a possible echo of the Emmaus road story, to an appearance to "two of them as they were walking in the country" who bear witness to unbelieving disciples (16:12-13). Jesus appears to rebuke their unbelief with teaching (16:14) and commissions them to worldwide mission (16:15-18) before ascending into heaven (16:19a). Verse 19b is a decisive expansion. It quotes Ps. 110:1, a royal coronation psalm, in which God invites Israel's new king to ascend to the throne. The use of this royal tradition emphasizes Jesus' exaltation not just (somewhat vaguely) to heaven, but to share in God's reign over creation as a king, and points to the eschatological consequences of the establishment of God's reign over all "enemies." The disciples obediently preach the message, supported by signs or miracles. There is no explicit mention of the Holy Spirit.

The Matthew scene is substantially different. It does not mention Jesus' ascension, though it could be inferred from the scene (where does Jesus go?). The scene is structured as a commissioning story with an introduction (28:16), confrontation (28:17), reaction (28:17), commission (28:18-19), reassurance, and conclusion (28:20). The risen Jesus has gathered the disciples in the marginal location of Galilee, not in Jerusalem, the center of political, social, and religious power, and deceit and hostility (28:11-15). From the margins, Jesus sends the disciples into this imperial world on a mission that challenges fundamental cultural commitments and Rome's mission to rule the world, and that calls people to loyalty to God. The scene's location on a mountain recalls both Sinai and Zion as places where God's will and rule are revealed and anticipated for the future (Isa. 25:1-10). Jesus shares in that rule in that God has given him "all authority in heaven and earth" as son of man (cf. Dan. 7:13-14). He commissions the disciples to make God's rule or empire known throughout the world (28:18-20), promising them his presence.[9]

SEVENTH SUNDAY OF EASTER

MAY 12, 2002

REVISED COMMON	EPISCOPAL (BCP)	ROMAN CATHOLIC
Acts 1:6-14	Acts 1:(1-7), 8-14 or Ezek. 39:21-29	Acts 1:12-14
Ps. 68:1-10, 32-35	Ps. 68:1-20 or Psalm 47	Ps. 27:1, 4, 7-8
1 Peter 4:12-14; 5:6-11	1 Peter 4:12-19 or Acts 1:(1-7), 8-14	1 Peter 4:13-16
John 17:1-11	John 17:1-11	John 17:1-11a

The Easter season closes, though the readings have emphasized that Easter life continues. Today's readings look forward to various futures: the coming of the Spirit in Acts 1, the believers' eschatological destiny in 1 Peter 4–5, and a life of bearing witness to Jesus and of unity in John 17. Again a key element in those futures concerns the difficult relation of church and world. Resurrection life sets up some boundaries, draws some lines, knows some distinctions, challenges death, and creates tensions and struggles because of its alternative focus. The readings urge us to reflect on the character of Christian existence and on our roles in God's world (an ownership emphasized in Psalms 68 and 47), challenging us to live accordingly.

FIRST READING

ACTS 1:6-14 (RCL);
ACTS 1:(1-7), 8-14 (BCP);
ACTS 1:12-14 (RC)

Interpreting the Text

Luke's account of Jesus' ascension marks a pivotal role in Luke-Acts. Jesus' post-Easter appearances end and the Spirit's coming at Pentecost is at hand (Acts 2). This reading divides into three sections. Verses 1-5 provide the book's introduction, linking it to Luke's Gospel (Luke 1:1-4) with references to a "first book," Theophilus ("lover of God") a model disciple (Luke 10:27), Jesus'

post-Easter appearances and ascension in Luke 24, and his promise of the Holy
Spirit (24:49). Especially significant is the Greek wording of v. 1: "all that Jesus
began to do and teach." The church's life, empowered by the Spirit, continues
Jesus' ministry.

Verses 6-11 concern the significance of the present. It is not the end (vv. 7-8)
but the time of Spirit-empowered, worldwide mission (1:8), in Jesus' absence and
until the ascended Jesus returns (1:9-11; cf. Luke 24:47-53). The third section,
1:12-14, has the disciples, the women, and Jesus' brothers obediently in Jerusalem
(1:4), prayerfully awaiting the Spirit's coming.

The passage narrates for the second time in Luke-Acts Jesus' ascension. The
emphasis falls on the on-going life of the church, especially the promise of the
empowering Spirit, and their mission task to the whole world.

Responding to the Text

We live in the "in-between" time following Jesus' ascension and before
his return. Both can motivate us to faithfulness, a life that requires the Spirit's
empowering and our obedience. The passage sounds a keynote for both Easter
and Pentecost, namely that the church does not exist for itself, but lives in God's
power for mission to the world. Such a radical perspective and agenda offer an
alternative to a self-centered focus and maintenance mode of ecclesial activity and
programming.

EZEKIEL 39:21-29 (BCP, alt.)

Interpreting the Text

Addressing the situation of Babylonian exile (587–539 B.C.E.), the
prophet Ezekiel offers a theological explanation for the catastrophe, and hope for
the future. He explains the exile in terms of God's purposes. Conventionally, a
people's defeat in battle, such as God's people suffered in the 587 B.C.E. fall of
Jerusalem, was understood to mean the defeat of their God or gods. But Ezekiel
resists such a view by locating this disaster in God's purposes. Exile was God's
punishment of the people for unfaithfulness to the covenant (39:21-24). But punishment is followed by deliverance, exile by restoration, judgment by mercy
(39:25). God will restore the people to their land and pour out God's spirit on
the returned exiles to help them live faithfully (39:25-29). The prophet is also
concerned for God's integrity and "glory" or good reputation among the nations
(39:21, 23, 27b-28). These actions of exile and restoration demonstrate to God's
people and the nations not God's weakness in defeat but God's purposes, power,
and faithfulness.

The Easter paradigm of death and new life is much older than Easter, because God is much older than Easter! This is God's way of working in the world. The Easter story utilizes a very old motif in the traditions to highlight a fundamental continuity across the scriptures. Likewise, God's promise to give the Spirit to the returned exiles (39:29) challenges Christian supersessionist claims that the Spirit is present only in Christian communities and only since Pentecost. This reading (and many others) undermines any such claim. God's spirit, operative since creation (Gen. 1:2), is regularly encountered in fresh ways at specific moments with varying effects throughout the biblical accounts.

RESPONSIVE READING

PSALM 68:1-10, 32-35 (RCL);
PSALM 68:1-20 (BCP);
PSALM 27:1, 4, 7-8 (RC)

This psalm seems to express the hopes of the marginalized and power-less poor (68:5-6) who, in lives of continuous threat, desperately look for God, the divine warrior, to leap into action against "the enemies" and "the wicked" who oppose God's ways (68:1-3). This demand for God's saving power is based on God's manifestation in the covenant as the one who helps the weak and punishes the "rebellious" (68:4-6). It is also based on the foundational events of the exodus, the Sinai revelation, and occupation of the land when "God provided for the needy" (68:7-10). God's faithful power on behalf of the weak has also been evident in battle (68:11-14). God's saving rule, even over death, is celebrated in the Jerusalem (Mt. Zion) temple worship (68:15-20). Therefore all nations are summoned to join in acknowledging God's rule and help for God's people by praising God.

The psalm reflects several influences. The language attesting God's cosmic reign and identity as divine warrior reflects early Canaanite religious claims. God's identity as "the one who rides upon the clouds" (68:4, 33) derives from Ugaritic descriptions of Ba'al, the storm and fertility god (68:8-9) who battles (68:17) and defeats the evil and deathly powers that would prevent such life (68:20), and who is enthroned as king. The language of liturgy is also influential. The cry of v. 1 accompanied the ark (Num. 10:35). Zion temple traditions (God's dwelling place) are frequently invoked (68:5, 16-18, 24, 29, 35). Very influential is the lived desperation of those whose only hope against the agents and instruments of death in the world is to cry for God to "arise!"

PSALM 47 (BCP, alt.)

See the Responsive Reading for the Ascension of Our Lord.

SECOND READING

1 PETER 4:12-14; 5:6-11 (RCL);
1 PETER 4:12-19 (BCP);
1 PETER 4:13-16 (RC)

Interpreting the Text

The focus of 3:8—4:11 on the suffering that 1 Peter's audience must endure as a minority Christian community in a hostile society continues (cf. 2:11-12). This suffering, identified in 4:12 as a "fiery ordeal," is not the irritations of daily human existence, nor does it result from doing wrong (4:15). It is specific to living as a Christian (3:14; 4:16), being "reviled for the name of Christ" (4:14). It does not consist of empire-wide state action but local social harassment comprising false accusations and misrepresentation (2:12) and verbal abuse (3:16; 4:14) because of living a distinctive, countercultural life (4:4). This "fiery ordeal," no surprise since opposition to God's will is inevitable, tests or proves Christian faithfulness (4:12; cf. 1:6-7; 2:20), indicates God's blessing and the Spirit's presence (4:14), and results from doing God's will (3:17; 4:19). In suffering, the letter's audience share in the suffering and rejection that Christ suffered while doing God's will (2:21-24).

Such faithfulness now means eschatological vindication and rejoicing in God's victory over all evil (4:13). To rejoice is not narcissism or mindless unreality; it is a perspective that is aware of the temporary nature of the suffering and that anticipates God's future, certain victory (4:12-13). This community experiences now a share in the future display of God's power and presence (glory, 4:13-14; blessing, 3:14). To suffer, then, not for wrongdoing (4:15) but for Christian faithfulness should not shameful (the verb indicates denying Christian faith) but a situation in which the suffering believer manifests God's power and presence ("glorifies").

Verse 17 places their suffering in another context. It is the beginning of God's judgment that will spread from God's household or community (cf. Isa. 10:11-12; Mal. 3:1-6) to nonbelievers, those who do not obey the gospel. Their fate will be worse (4:17b-18, citing Prov. 11:31). The point of the argument is to motivate Christian faithfulness by warning Christians to persevere and to encourage them by promising the demise of their opponents in the accomplishment of

God's purposes. Verse 19 provides the exhortation to "do right" and to trust God.

After a section on leadership and relationships within the Christian community (5:1-5), vv. 6-11 of chap. 5 return to the experience of suffering as Christians in the context of a hostile social environment. Using numerous imperatives, these verses largely repeat, and thereby emphasize, the teaching offered previously (e.g., 3:13-22; 4:12-19). The Christian readers are exhorted to rely on God, to look for God's eschatological vindication, to not be faithless, to not doubt God's care (5:6-7). They are also exhorted to vigilance (5:8a). Expressions of verbal opposition manifest the devil's work and reveal a larger context of spiritual warfare and opposition to God's purposes (5:8b). Resistance is required (5:9a, though its form is not specified), in solidarity with other suffering Christians (5:9b). Verses 10-11 look again to God's future in which God's grace will be victorious over all evil as God's power or dominion is established.

Responding to the Text

In any proclamation from this passage, the nature of the "suffering" involved in the passage must be made very clear. This is not general suffering. The passage offers not a general theodicy but specific pastoral address. It does not advocate "do nothing and it will be okay in heaven" as "the Christian response" to suffering. Rather the suffering involved is the social harassment ("persecution" is not a helpful term) experienced by a minority Christian community that lacks access to and protection from the elite holders of power or from legislation and cannot effect structural changes. That is, the experience of the text is quite foreign to many comfortable middle-class churches, with our commitments to the status quo, to being nice, to not making waves, to conformity, to cultural accommodation. Despite the claims of this scriptural letter that blessing is found in cultural tension and resistance (3:14; 4:14), we seem to be convinced that it is found in cultural imitation as we employ religious sanctions to pursue culturally conforming values of wealth and "fun," not disruptive justice, mercy, and faithfulness.

The very strangeness of this text could tempt us to dismiss it as having nothing to say to our situation. But therein lies a point worth pursuing. Its very foreignness offers us profound challenges. Perhaps in those places where we still see ourselves as culturally dominant, we will have to ask about whether we are the harassers in our treatment of other minority groups, including Christians of various minority persuasions and practices. Perhaps we are among those causing the suffering rather than enduring it.

THE SUFFERING INVOLVED IS THE SOCIAL HARASSMENT EXPERIENCED BY A MINORITY CHRISTIAN COMMUNITY THAT LACKS ACCESS TO AND PROTECTION FROM THE ELITE HOLDERS OF POWER OR FROM LEGISLATION AND CANNOT EFFECT STRUCTURAL CHANGES.

Or, alternatively, 5:9b indicates that opposition will break out wherever Christian discipleship is faithfully lived. That should give us pause for profound reflection on our ecclesial and personal practices and commitments. Interestingly, some of our kids, trying to live faithfully in various school and college situations, may find this passage life-giving. And some among our congregants who know that the gods Mammon, Status, and Fun cannot deliver what the advertising evangelists falsely proclaim may be strengthened in sustaining their alternative existence. Others might be mystified or angered, creating opportunities for pastoral conversation.

The Gospel
JOHN 17:1-11

Interpreting the Text

This reading continues the previous weeks' readings from the Farewell Discourse (John 13–17). Jesus' departure through his death, resurrection, and ascension is imminent (13:1-3; chaps. 18–21). But now, after four chapters of assuring, encouraging, and challenging his disciples, Jesus prays to God his "Father" (17:1, 5, 11, 21, 24, 25). A prayer at the close of the farewell or last testament of an important dying figure was common (Moses, Deut. 31:30-32:47; 33). Here we overhear and witness the intimate oneness of Father and Son, the oneness and divine life into which disciples enter (14:1-3; 17:1-3). Jesus' prayer to God, in which he refers to disciples in the third person, functions to provide understanding about God's purposes and his own departure, and to assure the gospel's readers of their participation in God's eschatological purposes in Jesus' "absence." Father, Son, and disciples dwell in eschatological unity.

The opening five verses concern Jesus' departure by death, resurrection, and ascension. Jesus recognizes that the "hour" of his death has come (12:23; 13:1). The imposition of the imperial elite's will through crucifixion is not its full explanation. Jesus prays for God to "glorify the Son." The term "glory" concerns the revelation of the power and presence of God (2:11) through Jesus' words and works/signs (12:45; 14:9-10) in his ministry (17:4-5) as the one sent from God (1:18; 3:14-17, 31-36). Now Jesus prays that God will manifest God's power and presence through Jesus' death. That will mean nothing other than his resurrection and ascension or return to God, the means by which the Son "glorifies you" (17:1) or manifests God's power and presence. Jesus will continue to manifest God's power and presence through giving people "eternal life" (17:2) or "life of the age" (5:21-30) with the gift of the Spirit (7:37-39). This eschatological life is marked by intimate knowing or union with the "true" or faithful God (17:3), and by life in a community that knows God's love, does God's will (14:15-24), and manifests it to one another (13:34-35).

Jesus then prays for the disciples (17:6-11). Verses 6-8 set the stage by elaborating Jesus' work in glorifying or revealing God (17:4, 6, God's name is God's character). This work has created a community of those who "received" his ministry, the community of disciples (1:12). This community is created "out of the world" by God's work ("whom you gave me") and by human response ("kept the word"). It has been "gifted" by God in an extraordinary way (17:7). Verse 8 describes the chain of revelation, from God to Jesus to disciples, and elaborates the disciples' response as their knowing and believing that Jesus originated from God. God has sent him. That Jesus is "of/from" God matters, because his origin with God legitimates and guarantees the truth of his revelation (1:1-18). It also determines his destiny; he returns to God (17:11) from whence he will return to take believers to God (14:1-3). Recognizing Jesus' origin enables disciples to become children of God (1:12-13) by being born from above (3:3-8), the basis for the community of disciples.

Jesus' prayer focuses on the disciples, not the world (17:9), the realm of humans whom God loves (3:16) but that rejects relationship with God (17:9; 1:10-11). Verse 9 indicates a particular focus in this context, not the withdrawal of God's favor from human beings or the denial of mission to them (17:15-18). Again God's work in bringing this community into being is emphasized with heightened focus on God and Jesus' ownership (17:9-10a). But the new dimension is the recognition of the disciples' task of "glorifying" Jesus, of recognizing and witnessing to God's power and presence in him. Jesus' departure to God (17:11) frames his prayer for the disciples. Discipleship is lived in the light of his "absence" and ascension.

Jesus prays that God will continue to "keep them" in a hostile environment ("the world," 17:14-15). The "keeping" is linked to God's name or to God's character. Jesus describes God in 17:3 as the "only true God." The notion of "truth" identifies God's powerful faithfulness by which God acts powerfully and faithfully on behalf of God's people. To "keep" them is ultimately to save them. In 17:11 God is addressed as "holy," an adjective denoting "setting apart for divine service." God is holy in that God is "set apart" for God's own purposes that include the saving of God's people. The disciples are set within God's saving purposes. Jesus also prays that God unite them, a demonstration of the unity (cf. 10:30) and love of the Father and the Son (elaborated in 17:20-24). Such unity is also very pragmatic as a means of sustaining the faithful, "against-the-grain" witness of the community of disciples in a hostile environment.

As with all these John readings, the preacher can helpfully unpack the distinctive and often bewildering Johannine vocabulary. Careful attention to the passage might help a congregation to move from being mystified by its words to encountering the mystery of the Word.

Three crucial but related affirmations about the church as an Easter people emerge in this passage as Jesus prays for the church. One is its origin with God and in God's purposes. God brings the community into being as a distinct entity. God possesses the church (17:11). We do not belong to ourselves. We are not our own masters. We have responded to and been empowered by God's love or grace to embody God's saving purposes.

> GOD BRINGS THE COMMUNITY INTO BEING AS A DISTINCT ENTITY. WE ARE NOT OUR OWN MASTERS. WE HAVE RESPONDED TO AND BEEN EMPOWERED BY GOD'S LOVE OR GRACE TO EMBODY GOD'S SAVING PURPOSES.

A second concerns the church's present. As much as this origin separates the church from the world and creates a tension between the two, it does not isolate the church from, or elevate it above, the world. The church's task of witnessing to the Son, even in the hostile sphere of the world, remains (17:10-11; 20:21). The church, knowing the gift of sharing intimately in God's life and love, makes these realities available to others.

A third affirmation concerns the church's future. Jesus, on the point of his departure, entrusts the church to God, to God's faithfulness and loving purposes. There the contemporary church with all its doubts about its identity, mission, and future and with all its possibilities abides. Originating with God, commissioned to mission in the present, kept by God in God's future—and prayed for by Jesus. How might such self-understanding focus and energize our priorities, programs, and personnel?

General

Hanson, K. C., and D. Oakman. *Palestine in the Time of Jesus: Social Structures and Social Conflicts.* Minneapolis: Fortress Press, 1998.

Pilgrim, W. E. *Uneasy Neighbors: Church and State in the New Testament.* Minneapolis: Fortress Press, 1999.

Psalms

Kraus, H.-J. *Psalms 1–59.* Minneapolis: Augsburg Fortress, 1988.

————. *Psalms 60–150.* Minneapolis: Augsburg Fortress, 1993.

J. L. Mays, *Psalms.* Interpretation. Louisville: Westminster John Knox, 1994.

Matthew

Carter, W. *Matthew and the Margins: A Socio-Historical and Religious Reading.* Maryknoll: Orbis, 2000.

————. *Matthew and the Empire: Initial Explorations.* Harrisburg, Pa.: Trinity Press International, 2001.

Davies, W. D., and D. Allison. *The Gospel according to Matthew.* 3 volumes. International Critical Commentary. Edinburgh: T. & T. Clark, 1988–97.

Luke

Green, J. B. *The Gospel of Luke.* NICNT. Grand Rapids: Eerdmans, 1997.

Johnson, L. T. *The Gospel of Luke.* Sacra Pagina 3. Collegeville: Liturgical Press, 1991.

John

Brown, R. *The Gospel according to John.* 2 volumes. Anchor Bible Commentary. Garden City: Doubleday, 1966, 1971.

Moloney, F. J. *The Gospel of John.* Sacra Pagina 4. Collegeville: Liturgical Press, 1998.

Acts

Johnson, L. T. *The Acts of the Apostles.* Sacra Pagina 5. Collegeville: Liturgical Press, 1992.

Ephesians

Barth, M. *Ephesians 1–3.* Anchor Bible Commentary. Garden City: Doubleday, 1974.

Perkins, P. *Ephesians.* Abingdon New Testament Commentary. Nashville: Abingdon, 1997.

1 Peter

Achtemeier, P. J. *1 Peter.* Hermeneia. Minneapolis: Fortress Press, 1996.

Craddock, F. B. *First and Second Peter and Jude.* Westminster Bible Companion.
    Louisville: Westminster John Knox Press, 1995.

Elliott, J. H. *1 Peter.* Anchor Bible. New York: Doubleday, 2000.

NOTES

1. F. Moloney, *The Gospel of John* (Sacra Pagina 4; Collegeville: Liturgical, 1998), 516.

2. W. Carter, *Matthew and the Margins: A Socio-Political and Religious Reading* (Maryknoll: Orbis, 2000), 543–47.

3. Ibid., 476–79.

4. Ibid., 305–8, 326–28.

5. E. Käsemann, *New Testament Questions of Today* (Philadelphia: Fortress Press, 1969), 135.

6. For a helpful discussion of John's distinctive vocabulary, see R. Brown, *The Gospel according to John*, 2 vols. (Anchor Bible; New York: Doubleday, 1966, 1971), Appendix 1.

7. Consult the commentaries for the extensive discussion of 3:19-20. I offer an interpretation that treats them as an integral part of this passage.

8. A. N. Whitehead, *Process and Reality: An Essay in Cosmology* (New York: Free Press, 1929, 1979), 342.

9. W. Carter, *Matthew and the Margins,* 1–2, 36–49, 549–54.

THE SEASON
OF PENTECOST

DIANE
JACOBSON

Welcome to the season of Pentecost, that great time of freedom and challenge for the preaching of the church. The freedom is the freedom of summer where schedules are loose, restrictions are few, vacations beckon, and the community is scattered until the excitement of Rally Sunday rolls around and we are off again. Challenges come with the freedom—attendance in church is less regular and folks are looking for a special spark or comfort. Pentecost is the season of the Spirit—so let the Spirit flow and call folks to new life and renewed hope in Christ.

The texts of Pentecost offer many opportunities for enlivened summer and fall preaching. You might consider a series of sermons. Three options readily come to mind: "Exploring Discipleship in Matthew's Gospel"; "Rediscovering the Rich Stories of Genesis" (in the summer) and/or "Exodus" (in the fall); or "Discerning the Gifts of the Spirit with Paul in Romans, Philippians, and/or 1 Thessalonians." Pentecost invites a certain openness and spirit of exploration in which one can consider how a theme speaks to us, what questions are raised, and how we might be open to the workings of the Spirit in our everyday lives.

One more challenge of the season to consider: Perhaps this Pentecost season can become a time of exploration and renewal for the preacher as well as for the parishioner. Visit some parishioners at work and mark how the Spirit is alive in their lives. Read up on some topic you know little about. Visit some obscure museum or listen to some different music. Re-read Augustine or Tillich or study a book of Scripture that you know less well than others. Offer your services to some community project. Take a class in woodworking or knitting. Let the freedom of Pentecost touch you so that through your new experiences your words are enlivened, God's church is renewed, and God's world is served. The Spirit is alive and calls us as well as our flocks to renewed hope in Christ.

THE DAY OF PENTECOST

MAY 19, 2002

REVISED COMMON	EPISCOPAL (BCP)	ROMAN CATHOLIC
Acts 2:1-21 or	Acts 2:1-11 or	Acts 2:1-11
Num. 11:24-30	Ezek. 11:17-20	
Ps. 104:24-34, 35b	Ps. 104:25-37 or	Ps. 104:1, 24,
	104:25-32 or	29-30, 31, 34
	Ps. 33:12-15, 18-22	
1 Cor. 12:3b-13 or	1 Cor. 12:4-13 or	1 Cor. 12:3b-7, 12-13
Acts 2:1-21	Acts 2:1-11	
John 20:19-23 or	John 20:19-23 or	John 20:19-23
John 7:37-39	John 14:8-17	

Come, Holy Spirit. We live in an age when many might identify with the centrality and urgency of this simple prayer. Folks all around us are hungering for the Spirit. Many folks who wouldn't dream of coming to church speak of themselves as "spiritual, but not religious." They are theoretically closed to church but ripe for the Spirit. And many others within the church are themselves looking for more spiritual fulfillment, even seeking out spiritual directors. So now the day of Pentecost arrives when we celebrate the arrival of the Spirit. Have we anything to say to those seekers outside and inside about the Spirit? Can we in the liturgical traditions really give space for the Spirit to enter and to enliven the church and the individuals within the church? This is our challenge.

To meet this challenge and to help breathe life into our prayer of V*enite Spiritus Sanctus,* we are given marvelous texts that teach us a great deal about the nature of this Spirit for whom we wait and yearn. These texts offer particular insights, invitations, and warnings for both the seekers and the church. To the church these texts say this: The community without the Spirit is dead. The church cannot speak the truth but for the Spirit of God. But with God's Spirit we are alive and united in Christ. To the seekers these texts also speak: You are not in this alone; the Spirit is with you. You are not alone—this is God's promise and invitation. But know as well that you cannot experience this gift in isolation. The Spirit is also with all those around you joined by Christ's name as one. The Spirit is God's communal gift.

ACTS 2:1-21 (RCL); ACTS 2:1-11 (BCP; RC)

The Day of Pentecost arrives, and the whole community is gathered. Pentecost is another name for the Jewish Feast of Weeks, the second of the great pilgrimage festivals (Exod. 23:14-17; 34:22-23; Deut. 16:9-12; 2 Chron. 8:13). Pentecost was originally a harvest festival in which the gathered gave thanks for the first fruits of the harvest. Today the gathered also give thanks, now for the first fruits of the Spirit. In the time of Jesus, this festival would have centered less on the gathering of the harvest and more on the celebration of the covenant and perhaps on the giving of the law at Sinai. During this great festival season, Jews would have gathered from throughout the diaspora to the central city of Jerusalem. Here in Acts, the initial concrete manifestation of the Spirit to the community—first as a sound, violent as a storm, then as fiery tongues—reminds us of and ties us to the many biblical theophany traditions of God appearing in fire and storm and, most particularly, in speech. Think of Sinai and the burning bush. Read Psalm 18 or Psalm 29 or Ezekiel 1. But you need not be attuned to the tradition to understand the power of fire and wind. You need only be in a windstorm or watch the attraction of a fire as the neighbors gather to see where the siren-blaring fire trucks will stop. Our attention is drawn by both tradition and experience to the coming of the Spirit, as surely as we are drawn by those sirens. Something mighty is happening here.

The gift of the Spirit is most often identified in this passage as the gift of tongues, seen as a reversal of Babel with its multiplication of tongues and its scattering of people throughout the earth. But the reversal is not what we would expect. In Acts, the multiplied tongues rather than being punishment for hubris are themselves part of the gift of the Spirit. Through the speaking of various tongues, the community is gathered rather than scattered. Moreover, while the wonder is certainly in the miraculous speaking of those tongues, the more significant miracle is in the understanding. The crowds are astonished at hearing, "each of us, in our own language." The gift of the Spirit is more in the hearing and understanding than in the speaking precisely because a shared understanding is the particular gift that forms the community as one. Here is a message for those among us today who believe that each person can be "spiritual" on their own, in their own way. The Spirit in Acts is manifest precisely within the common hearing that binds us together. The Spirit does not speak a different message for each spiritual seeker—you find your truth and I'll find mine. A quest for spiritual truth that would isolate us from our neighbors is flawed at the outset. The miraculous gift of Pentecost resides in our discovering our commonality.

A QUEST FOR SPIRITUAL TRUTH THAT WOULD ISOLATE US FROM OUR NEIGHBORS IS FLAWED AT THE OUTSET.

And the shared message that is heard tells of "God's deeds of power." The Spirit makes such deeds manifest. The Spirit points us outside of ourselves to God. The gathered people hear this message, and they respond with the marvelously catechetical question, "What does this mean?" Here, too, is a lesson for the spiritual seeker. As Luke so often illustrates, one learns through faithful questions. The doubters of the text have the ready response and the closed minds that trust only in their own limited perception. They perceive only drunkenness. But Luke would have us see that being faithful is not to be equated with certainty. Asking questions is often more a sign of faith and an openness to the workings of the Spirit than a ready answer.

The final gift of the Spirit in this passage is the use and enlivening of the tradition. In response to the faithful inquiries and the cynical doubt, Peter quotes from the prophet Joel (Joel 2:28-32 [English]). What marks Peter as a preacher touched by the Spirit is his capacity to speak the text of past tradition into the reality of the present. The tradition lives precisely when it is not merely a lesson in history. The last days of Joel are clearly seen as the present days of Peter in which distinctions—young and old, male and female, slave and free—are shattered, and the community is gathered in prophecies, visions, and dreams. Even nature is changed—see and hear the tongues of fire! And the speaking of the mighty acts becomes a uniting prayer such that all who call on the name of the Lord are saved. We preachers today are challenged to follow Peter's example, allowing the Spirit to show us where the tradition of this text from Acts is alive in our own churches and world. We cannot be content merely to describe what happened that "first" Pentecost. The Spirit of Pentecost is alive wherever boundaries are broken down and folks understand their common calling to ask faithful questions, to speak of God's deeds of power, to share dreams and visions, and to call on the name of the Lord.

NUMBERS 11:24-30 (RCL, alt.); EZEKIEL 11:17-20 (BCP, alt.)

For those who choose to celebrate the Day of Pentecost by reading one of the alternative Old Testament passages rather than the more traditional passage from Acts, the emerging pictures of the effects of the coming of God's Spirit have much to offer. The Numbers passage uses narrative to explore the freedom of God to bestow the Spirit wherever and on whomever God wills. The text calls into question the assumption that the Spirit will be manifest only through the expected orders of the community. While such is certainly possible (notice that the Spirit does, in fact, rest on the gathered seventy elders), such manifestations are not to be exclusively bound. Lo and behold, two men, Eldad and Medad, stay in the camp with the people rather than separating themselves and going to the tent, the proscribed holy place. There they prophesy and there they stand as a model and sign of God's free Spirit. Such a text might well be in order within any community tempted to claim exclusive rights to God's Spirit. Moses' cry, "Would that all the LORD's people were prophets!" stands as eternal challenge to insiders who claim that there is a proper order and method for spiritual discernment.

The text from Ezekiel, like the Acts text, speaks both to the gathering and common purpose of the people and to the signs of the Spirit in the eschatological future. Ezekiel also picks up on the tradition of Pentecost as a celebration of the covenant and the giving of the law. Indeed, as in the great passage from Jer. 31:31-33, the law is now written on the heart, making obedience as natural as breathing. Ezekiel finds it inconceivable to picture the coming of a new Spirit without a concomitant change in very real behavior. One cannot have a "spiritual" transformation that does not lead to following God's commandments. Such a passage speaks a very specific word to an age in which being "spiritual" often is more associated with how one feels rather than how one acts.

Responsive Reading

PSALM 104:24-34, 35b (RCL);
PSALM 104:25-37 or 104:25-32 (BCP);
PSALM 104:1, 24, 29-30, 31, 34 (RC);
PSALM 33:12-15, 18-22 (BCP, alt.)

The psalms assigned for this Pentecost Sunday supplement the picture of the Spirit portrayed in Acts. In Psalm 104 the Spirit's role in creation is emphasized, expanding the claim that nothing, not even creation, can live and breathe except for the presence of God's Spirit (note especially v. 30). Small wonder that that in the last days "the sun shall be turned to darkness . . . " or that God can cross the boundaries of different tongues. Psalm 33, like Psalm 104, begins with praise to the Lord as Creator. But the chosen portion of Psalm 33 supplements the final line of the Joel passage quoted by Peter by inviting us to respond to the Lord with trust and assuring us that those who do so will be delivered from death.

SECOND READING

1 CORINTHIANS 12:3b-13 (RCL);
1 CORINTHIANS 12:4-13 (BCP);
1 CORINTHIANS 12:3b-7, 12-13 (RC)

First Corinthians 12 is the perfect reflection in the epistles of the narrative text in Acts. So many of this text's lessons concerning the Spirit match and further illumine the manifestations of the Spirit is Acts. First, that which is only implicit in Acts Paul makes explicit: speaking in the Spirit of God has much to do with naming Jesus as Lord. The Spirit leads a person to recognize Jesus as Lord. In fact, such naming might be conceived as a test of the presence of the Spirit, much as Deuteronomy proposes tests for distinguishing true prophecy from false (Deuteronomy 13). I do find it worth noting, however, that, at least in this passage, Paul does not claim that *only* those who say Jesus is Lord are able to manifest the Spirit. Paul thus avoids the modern pitfall of the Numbers text that only Christians can claim the presence of the Spirit. What Paul does claim, much as Luke has done in Acts, is both

> VARIETIES OF GIFTS AND ACTIVITIES, MUCH LIKE THE VARIETY OF TONGUES, POINT NOT TO DIVISION AND HIERARCHY BUT RATHER TO UNITY AND EQUALITY.

the unifying and communal nature of the Spirit. Varieties of gifts and activities, much like the variety of tongues, point not to division and hierarchy but rather to unity and equality.

The most significant unity is the unity of God. Again Deuteronomy comes to mind—"The LORD our God, the LORD is one" (Deut. 6:4). So also Paul lays stress on one Lord, one God, one Spirit. Such a stress again helps us to guide the spiritual seeker in our modern world to understand that, though each person certainly has an individual right to believe whatever he or she pleases, that right is not matched by a great plethora of divine personages. In truth, any god will not do. More than this, individual spiritual gifts, each in their own way, point to the same God and the same Spirit. Here is an opportunity for proclamation whereby we name the gifts of the Spirit we see manifest around us and claim this as emanating from one God, one Lord, one Spirit. Real people surround us in our church and our world. Some have the spiritual gifts of wisdom, some of healing, some of faith. Our task and the task of our parishioners might well be to name such gifts precisely as spiritual gifts from the same Spirit who leads us to name Jesus as Lord.

More than this: When we name gifts as spiritual, a follow-up question is implied by Paul's description of the Spirit. In what way is the gift of each person serving the common good? For, says Paul, "the manifestation of the Spirit is for the common good." Again, spiritual gifts are not given for the sake of the individual but rather for the sake of the community. To be spiritual alone is not only impossible; it is manifestly sinful if not used in service to the community good. Precisely in this way, divine unity is matched by the unity of the community. Such unity is not to be confused with sameness. There is a variety of gifts and services. Community unity is shown rather in common purpose. And all this together points us once more to lack of distinction and hierarchy whereby all of us—Jews or Greeks, slaves or free, any distinction one might name—are made one body through baptism into Christ.

ACTS 2:1-21 (RCL, alt.);
ACTS 2:1-11 (BCP, alt.)

See the First Lesson for today.

THE GOSPEL
JOHN 20:19-23 (RCL, BCP, RC);
JOHN 7:37-39 (RCL, alt.);
JOHN 14:8-17 (BCP, alt.)

We come finally to the Gospel, which for this one day serves less as principal text and more as supplemental text to the account in Acts. All of our traditions give the option of John 20:19-23 as the Gospel of the day. If Acts is public Pentecost for strangers as well as believers, then John 20 is the first Pentecost for the inner circle of disciples. The text begins in fear, which is the disciples' justified reaction to the reality of the situation—a reaction to reality with which many today can identify. Jesus meets their fear with two responses: a double proclamation of peace and signs of the cross.

The first bestowing of peace speaks directly to the disciples' fear. Jesus had earlier left them his peace precisely when he had spoken of sending the Holy Spirit (John 14:25-27, right after the alternative Gospel lesson). The gift of peace is tied to the gift of the Spirit, a reassuring message to the disciples and to us. Having calmed their fears, Jesus then shows them the marks of the cross. Normally this gesture is seen as proving to the disciples that he is truly Jesus. And so it is. But this gesture is deeper than mere proof. These marks are not merely identification marks; they are marks of identity.

Truly this is Jesus. What is truly Jesus are these marks. Jesus is made known in these marks of the cross, linking him forever to the fear and suffering of the world. But also these signs of the cross, while they have marked and even defined Jesus, have not defeated him. Jesus is alive—fear, suffering, and death are defeated.

This reality leads to the second bestowal of peace, now not to comfort the fearful but to send them on their way. As surely as Christ is alive, as surely as he is sent from God, so also the disciples are no longer defined by death-dealing fear but rather by life-giving mission. They are no longer to be apart and hidden but on their way. And the instrument of their journey is the Spirit. For John the sending of the Spirit is indelibly tied both to the manifestation of the crucified and risen Lord and also to the mission of the church. The gift of the Spirit to the disciples is outward directed, more for others than for themselves, so that sins might be forgiven for Christ's sake. In this way, the Pentecost for the disciples leads directly to Pentecost for the world. And we are back to the relentless message of all of these texts: the gift of the Spirit is not a private affair. Always, always this gift is for others, for the wider community. But now we have an added word for spiritual seekers. We need not fear. We are granted both peace and forgiveness. A similar message is found in John 7: come to Jesus as a thirsting spiritual seeker and receive not only refreshment for yourself but also receive a heart overflowing with living water for others. (John 14 is the one text that takes Pentecost in a different direction, claiming that the one who receives the Spirit of truth cannot be received by the world.)

> AS SURELY AS CHRIST IS ALIVE, AS SURELY AS HE IS SENT FROM GOD, SO ALSO THE DISCIPLES ARE NO LONGER DEFINED BY DEATH-DEALING FEAR BUT RATHER BY LIFE-GIVING MISSION.

Most of the texts for this Sunday resound with invitation to spiritual seekers. Come, we have much to offer. Receive the gift of the Spirit, which will open up for you new questions and understandings and experiences of who you are in relationship to God, to Christ, and to others. Come; you have been gifted with the capacity to hear the story of God's power. Come; you have your own spiritual gifts to be named and joined with the gifts of others for the good of all. Come; know that the Lord is one, and we are one—no distinctions made here. Come; peace and forgiveness is God's gift to you. Come, join our prayer. *Venite Spiritus Sanctus.*

HOLY TRINITY SUNDAY (FIRST SUNDAY AFTER PENTECOST)

MAY 26, 2002

REVISED COMMON	EPISCOPAL (BCP)	ROMAN CATHOLIC
Gen. 1:1—2:4a	Gen. 1:1—2:3	Exod. 34:4b-6, 8-9
Psalm 8	Psalm 150 or	Dan. 3:52, 53, 54, 55, 56
	Canticle 2 or 13	
2 Cor. 13:11-13	2 Cor. 13:(5-10), 11-14	2 Cor. 13:11-13
Matt. 28:16-20	Matt. 28:16-20	John 3:16-18

Each year when I attend church on Holy Trinity Sunday, I carry with me a certain air of anticipation—maybe this year the Trinity will finally make sense. The years I am called upon to preach strike terror in my heart—how in the world do I explain the Trinity in a way that clarifies and engages? The whole notion of Trinity seems so radically entrenched in theological systems and historical councils and creeds. What is a preacher to do? The wonder of the texts for this Sunday is that they are not abstractly theological. Rather, they are radically contextual and thereby point us to the most significant truth about the Trinity: Knowing God as Trinity is not having information about God but responding to an invitation to a relationship with God. Knowing the Trinitarian God involves knowing and living into God's mission for the world and our own role in that mission. I am reminded of a story I like to tell whenever I teach the book of Job. A group of folks die and go to heaven. All the theologians, teachers, and pastors are shepherded into a lecture room to learn about God. The rest of the folks are ushered into the eternal throne room.

FIRST READING
GENESIS 1:1—2:4a (RCL);
GENESIS 1:1—2:3 (BCP)

The texts for Trinity Sunday begin with the first chapter of the Bible, clearly rooting the Trinity in God's reality as Creator of the world and all that exists. Some following the Revised Common Lectionary may want to note that the reading of Genesis will continue throughout the season and might provide a fine occasion for a series of sermons. Genesis 1 does more than relate the fact that God creates; this text begins the story of what manner of Creator our God is and to what purpose. Note God's declaration of the goodness of creation, that is, that creation is well ordered, beautiful, pleasing to the divine eye, and able to function as intended. If we believe that this very God created us, then we know as well that creation's goodness is part of the package. Moreover, God creates in such a way that all creation and its creatures are fully engaged. God's creative role does not leave us passive.

On Trinity Sunday, special mention might be made of v. 26, where God says, "*Let us* make humankind in our image, according to our likeness . . . ," the first inclination towards a Trinitarian God in the Christian imagination. Even knowing that the language of "us" has its origin in the ancient Near Eastern notion of a divine council supports this imaginative impulse in that it shows God to be self-relational at the outset. In our entire tradition, conversation with others is at the heart of the divine reality. This relational reality spills over into our reading of humans being made in the divine image. We, like God, are plural at the outset and partaking of just such divine sovereignty in our relationship with all creation. We must look to the remainder of God's story to understand the full nature that God's sovereignty takes. We will find that God ultimately rules from a cross and is crowned with thorns, a reality that must, particularly in our day of precarious ecological balance, define the dominion relationship we are commanded to have with the rest of creation.

Finally, the overall shape of this first story of creation is also worthy of note. God creates not only the stuff of the world but also establishes forever a creational order of time in which days and seasons have their place (days 1 and 4), and the seven-day pattern of six days of work and one day of rest (day 7) defines and claims all time (note the lovely chiastic structure, pointing to the central importance of time in creation). Imitating and upholding this creational pattern is part of how we function as images of God (see Exod. 20:8-11). Exploring the implications of Sabbath-keeping seems to be an important task for our overly busy world and, ironically, the lectionary allows us little time for such exploration.

EXODUS 34:4b-6, 8-9 (RC)

Exodus 34 offers its own perspective for Trinity Sunday with the marvelous narrative of God passing before Moses and proclaiming, "The LORD, the LORD, a God merciful and gracious, slow to anger, and abounding in steadfast love and faithfulness," the most quoted creedal formula about God in the Old Testament. This "revelation" about God is paradoxically given in the context of God showing only the divine backside and hiding the divine face (Exod. 33:17-23). Clearly, everything about God is not here revealed! But the all-important divine inclination towards mercy and forgiveness is revealed, again showing us that revelation is precisely about relationship—first God's relationship with us and subsequently our relationship of forgiveness and mercy with others.

RESPONSIVE READING

PSALM 8 (RCL);
PSALM 150 or CANTICLE 2 or 13 (BCP);
DANIEL 3:52, 53, 54, 55, 56 (RC)

Psalm 8, always an important companion piece to Genesis 1, takes the pronouncements of the Genesis text and, in light of the human self-understanding that ensues, offers them as praise. Psalm 150 invites all of creation to join in pure praise to God for all God's mighty deeds. The canticles, on the other hand, point us forward to the second person of the Trinity and the enfleshment of God's mercy.

SECOND READING

2 CORINTHIANS 13:11-13 (RCL; RC);
2 CORINTHIANS 13:(5-10), 11-14 (BCP)

One does not often look to the closing words of an epistle for a lesson. But the importance of the closing benediction of 2 Corinthians for Christian knowledge of the Trinity is clear. Here we have the earliest known Trinitarian formula in the church, written by Paul to the often-fractious Corinthians. And here as well, we hear one of those marvelous liturgical formulations that automatically unites our weekly and yearly experiences of Church with the words of Scripture. When we hear v. 13 (14) read we react as we might when the Aaronic blessing is read from Num. 6:22-27, "Oh, of course, that's where those words come from!" Their true familiarity derives from our own experience of these words as liturgical greeting. And as is so often true, the radically familiar can teach us a great deal if we consciously attend to their details. Note in particular the three nouns associated with each person of the Trinity and consider what this implies about God. Grace, love, and communion (in Greek, *charis*, *agape*, and *koinonia*). Our Trinitarian God offers these three gifts—first, through Paul to the Corinthians and subsequently to generations and multitudes of churchgoers. The Trinity offers us the same grace that is characteristic of divine offering in Exodus 34, a grace that denotes God's

> THE TRINITY OFFERS US THE SAME GRACE THAT IS CHARACTERISTIC OF DIVINE OFFERING IN EXODUS 34, A GRACE THAT DENOTES GOD'S ON-GOING FAVOR TO US.

on-going favor to us. The Trinity offers us God's abiding and engaging love, again matching the steadfast love of God proclaimed in Exodus. Moreover, this love is the very *agape* with which God loves the world in John 3:16, the Roman Catholic Gospel of the day. And climactically, the Trinity offers us communion, fellowship, *koinonia*. Again we are thrown into the underlying and crucial reality of the Trinity that we glimpsed first in Gen. 1:26. God, as Trinity, offers relationship and community. Consider the context of this original benediction. Paul urges the Corinthians to live in peace with one another, thereby reflecting the offered peace of God. He urges the building up of community precisely because that single action echoes the essence of God's character. Finally, finding communion with one another is the best reflection we have as images of our Trinitarian Lord. And surely we are no less fractious than those first-century Corinthians!

THE GOSPEL
JOHN 3:16-18 (RC)

As noted above, the Roman Catholic Gospel for this Sunday lays emphasis on the love that God gives by having the congregation hear once again this most beloved passage from John. The emphasis is not so much on the whole Trinity as on the intimate connection of love between the first two persons of the Trinity. Consistently, this love, this *agape*, is not for the sake of the Father or the Son, but for the sake of the world. God's relationship of love for the creation leads directly to God's sending Christ, his very Son, that the world might be saved. Here is a love that has a price; it costs the giver. We learn that the love of God is, at its core, self-giving, poured out for the sake of the other. God sent his Son "that the world might be saved through him." And we who are recipients of that love are called to respond in faith.

MATTHEW 28:16-20

The Gospel for the other traditions is Matthew's climactic proclamation of chap. 28. Attending to this "Great Commission" with true openness competes in its frightening consequence with preaching on Trinity Sunday. We are told, in Jesus' final words—surely aimed beyond the confines of history directly at us— to "Go therefore and make disciples of all nations." Ostensibly this commission would have been more daunting in those former years of Christendom when mission was always somewhere out there where folks we knew had not previously gone. But today, our mission task is to speak with that person next door, our friends, even our children. All nations have come home, and the task is ever more overwhelming. How dare we be so presumptuous, our modern selves say, as to impose our faith on others? The Good News for this day is that this text along with the other texts of the day opens up for us the possibility that the very character of God as Trinity prepares us to receive just such a commission. Baptizing in the name of the Trinity is truly an invitation to relationship with God and to community rather than a mere triumph of Christian theology.

Looking at the text one finds that some of the fear is as internal to the text as it is to one's own inner struggle. The setting is sparse, even austere. We are told only that the eleven disciples go to the Galilean mountain to which Jesus directed them. Not knowing the specific mountain causes us to conjure up all the mountains we know of, not only in Matthew but in all of scripture. We think of the mountain where Jesus gave his sermon, the mountain of instruction where "he taught them as one having authority" (Matt. 7:29). Or one thinks of the mountain of the Transfiguration where Jesus is joined by Moses and Elijah and identified by God as Son (Matt. 17:1-13). The transformation text leads us in turn to Moses' mountain, tradition's definitive location of revelation and instruction. Will this mountain be like those others, or will we be told, as was Elijah when he escaped to Moses' mountain for refuge (1 Kings 19:1-18), to go back into the world where the mission is to be found? At the Transfiguration, the disciples fell to the ground in fear. Now when they see Jesus, they worship, though some doubt.

This setting provides the context, but the full force of the text belongs to Jesus and his words. Jesus first claims the authority and the power earlier recognized in the Sermon on the Mount, but now his authority comes with the cosmic scope of all heaven and earth. This authority leads to Jesus' specific commission. He tells the eleven disciples to multiply their numbers, to increase the community. They are to "go" to and for the sake of the nations. Here is a final call to match God's initial call to Abraham, "Go from your country and your kindred . . . in you all the families of the earth shall be blessed" (Gen. 12:1-3). Now the disciples are to leave home and go to the nations. And the disciples are to do what to all the families of the earth? Baptize them "in the name of the Father, and of the Son, and of the Holy Spirit." This is the big moment for Trinity Sunday—the naming of the Trinity and the ultimate revelation of God's character. And the name is revealed precisely in service to God's ultimate mission of making disciples. Again we are reminded of Moses, this time at the burning bush (Exod. 3:1-15). Moses is called to set God's people free. And when Moses asks what he is to say to the people when they ask him God's name, then God answers not to give information but precisely to help Moses fulfill God's mission of saving God's people, Israel. In Matthew God's name is also revealed for action, now for God's saving mission to all God's people, for all God's nations. All people are to cross through the waters, now the waters of baptism.

As is the case for each new generation of Christians, we are now the disciples instructed to make more disciples. God is revealed as Trinity to us so that we might share this revelation with others. The purpose is not that they might be better informed as to the nature of God but that they be invited into discipleship. We offer an invitation to a relationship with the living God. We are to make disciples and to teach, says v. 20. At the heart of the mission is instruction not of a particular system or specific theological formulation, but instruction concerning all that Jesus has commanded: "Love your enemy and pray for those who persecute you" (5:44); "Do not worry about your life . . . (or) about tomorrow" (6:25, 34); "Ask and it will be given you" (7:7); "Enter through the narrow gate" (7:13); "Go and learn what this means, 'I desire mercy, not sacrifice'" (9:13); "Be wise as serpents and innocent as doves" (10:16); "Come to me, all you who are weary and are carrying heavy burdens, and I will give you rest" (11:28); "Whoever does the will of my Father in heaven is my brother and sister and mother" (12:50); "If any want to become my followers, let them deny themselves and take up their cross and follow me" (16:24). And oh, so much more. We are to teach for the sake of obedience the many things Jesus has commanded so that all nations and people, even those close to home, might know the grace, love, and fellowship of God—Father, Son, and Holy Spirit.

> AT THE HEART OF THE MISSION IS INSTRUCTION NOT OF A PARTICULAR SYSTEM OR SPECIFIC THEOLOGICAL FORMULATION, BUT INSTRUCTION CONCERNING ALL THAT JESUS HAS COMMANDED: "LOVE YOUR ENEMY AND PRAY FOR THOSE WHO PERSECUTE YOU."

And finally we are left not with commandment or even commission. We are left with promise, a promise of the constant and eternal presence of God. Such is always the way God takes leave from one who is called. So Moses is told at the burning bush "I will be with you; and this shall be a sign for you that it is I who has sent you" (Exod. 3:12). With the promise and sign of divine presence, we disciples of today are identified as called ones who are sent. God will be with us. For so we were promised at the very beginning of the Gospel of Matthew at the birth of Jesus when he is named Emmanuel, "God is with us" (Matt. 1:23).

Ultimately Holy Trinity Sunday need not be so scary if one approaches it as a disciple first and theologian second. To that end, I am strongly drawn to the hymn sung the day I was baptized together with my two sons, a hymn that has been the instrument of God's call to discipleship for well over a millennium:

> I bind unto myself today the strong name of the Trinity
> By invocation of the same, the Three in One and One in Three,
> Of whom all nature has creation, Eternal Father, Spirit, Word.
> Praise to the Lord of my salvation; Salvation is of Christ the Lord!
> —ST. PATRICK'S BREASTPLATE

SECOND SUNDAY AFTER PENTECOST

BODY AND BLOOD OF CHRIST
PROPER 4
JUNE 2, 2002

REVISED COMMON	EPISCOPAL (BCP)	ROMAN CATHOLIC
Deut. 11:18-21, 26-28 or Gen. 6:9-22; 7:24; 8:14-19	Deut. 11:18-21, 26-28	Deut. 8:2-3; 14b-16a
Ps. 31:1-5, 19-24 or Psalm 46	Psalm 31 or 31:1-5, 19-24	Ps. 147:12-13, 14-15, 19-20
Rom. 1:16-17; 3:22b-28, (29-31)	Rom. 3:21-25a, 28	1 Cor. 10:16-17
Matt. 7:21-29	Matt. 7:21-27	John 6:51-58

Two distinct themes are present for this Sunday. The Roman Catholic lectionary reflects the theme of the Body and Blood of Christ, while the texts read in the other traditions deal more particularly with the theme of righteousness. Given this distinction, I will deal first with one set of texts and then address the second set. We begin with Body and Blood and the cornucopia of texts calling us to attend to the gifts of the sacrament of communion.

FIRST LESSON
DEUTERONOMY 8:2-3; 14b-16a (RC)

The texts from Deuteronomy 8 tie communion to thirst and hunger in the wilderness. The text describes Israel's thirst, but the description of wandering in a dangerous wilderness taps into *our* fear, thirst, and hunger as well. God responds to this need with the great gift of manna. Deuteronomy explains this event in Israel's history and thus offers an explanation of our own experiences, in a very particular way. God allows us to hunger and thirst, even sends such trials, as a test to humble us, "and in the end to do [us] good." This explanation of suffering is certainly true at times and can be a great comfort, though scripture does not always view suffering in such a light. Job, for one, calls into question all universal and pat answers to suffering. Still, Deuteronomy drives toward this marvelous insight: "[We do] not live by bread alone but by every word that comes from the mouth of the Lord." Read on a Sunday dedicated to the body and blood of Christ, this insight sets the bread of communion in a particular context. That bread, like manna in the wilderness, is a pure gift of God. And the source of that bread's life-giving capacity is not the physical bread itself, but the very Word of God whereby the bread becomes the body of Christ.

RESPONSIVE READING
PSALM 147:12-13, 14-15, 19-20 (RC)

SECOND LESSON
1 CORINTHIANS 10:16-17 (RC)

The epistle moves to include the cup with the bread and to speak to another aspect of the gift of bread and wine—the unity of the church. Unity is at the heart of communion, just as communion, *koinonia,* is at the heart of God (just such fellowship was discussed at length regarding last week's texts). Here God's fellowship is manifest particularly in the broken body and poured blood of Christ. Community is linked directly from the cross to the table and from Christ's body to our body, the church. Church unity comes from a proclamation of precisely this unity, which begins at the cross. Certainly we all have different ways of understanding how this oneness is actually manifest in the life of the church. Maybe unity is only part of our apocalyptic future, or maybe unity comes when we celebrate the church catholic by working together in individual parishes or congregations. Ironically we engage in numerous fights about just where unity is or ought to be manifest, and such fights always tear at the fabric of our fellowship. Particularly in the midst of such struggles this text calls to us: Know, you Christian believer, that each time you come to the table you do not come alone. Christ is there as are a myriad of saints, living and dead. For me the ingrained vision of the true meaning of communion found at table comes from the 1984 movie, *Places in the Heart.* In a final scene, folks gather together in the country church—black and white, living and dead, lynched and lyncher—and they pass the communion one to the other.

> KNOW, YOU CHRISTIAN BELIEVER, THAT EACH TIME YOU COME TO THE TABLE YOU DO NOT COME ALONE. CHRIST IS THERE AS ARE A MYRIAD OF SAINTS, LIVING AND DEAD.

JOHN 6:51–58 (RC)

Going beyond both the Old Testament lesson and the epistle reading, this Gospel reading links the gift of Holy Communion to the gift of eternal life. As in 1 Corinthians, Jesus stands at the center. Jesus is the living bread and his blood the true drink. More than this, where Jesus stands, so also stands God. We know this both from the *ego eimi* that ties Jesus to Yahweh as the great *I AM* and also from v. 57. As the Father is alive, so Jesus lives and gives life. Jesus here speaks to us about the nature of true life found in the eating of the true bread. He compares this food to manna, certainly a gift from God, but only temporary. But the flesh and blood is something more, the embodied gift of eternal life. For many of the disciples this teaching is too difficult (v. 60) and many even leave him (v. 66). Jesus asks them to drink blood, an abomination under the law (Lev. 7:26-27). But God, in Christ, breaks the law both in disobedience and in breaking it asunder. Moreover, in breaking the law, God breaks the boundary between death and life, breaks the hold of death over life, and thereby offers eternal life. Eternal life is the ultimate gift of the body and blood of Christ.

As noted above, the other texts for this Sunday unite under a different theme. We begin with an age-old question: What do I need to do in order to meet with approval, blessing, and even salvation from God? Asked another way, how can I be righteous and what constitutes righteousness? This Sunday's texts help to illumine our ongoing struggle with these questions.

FIRST READING

DEUTERONOMY 11:18-21, 26-28 (RCL, BCP)

Deuteronomy 11 assumes that righteousness is well described and prescribed within the tradition in the commandments of Moses encapsulated in v. 13, "loving the LORD your God and serving him with all your heart and with all your soul." This tradition is a sacred trust externally bound as emblems on body and home precisely in order that they might forever be bound internally to heart and soul. The prescribed righteousness dwells not on the surface, but deep within. Moreover, the tradition is not just for the individual but for each new generation, to be taught and passed on at all times to the children. This tradition asks each generation to remember God's saving acts in bringing them out of slavery (salvation precedes the giving of the law) and tells each generation of the righteousness that must be done in gratitude and in order that it continue to go well with the community. The law is a gift from our gracious Lord, and the rules are clear. If you obey the commandments of the LORD your God, you will be blessed; if not, you are cursed.

GENESIS 6:9-22; 7:24; 8:14-19 (RCL, alt.)

This text, which continues the reading of Genesis, tells part of the story of Noah, notably designated as a righteous man and blameless. The story tells of life as it should be if it were clear who is wicked and who is righteous, and God ruled only according to just deserts. The righteous one gets saved (and gets to save creation's beasts with him) while the wicked drown. The rules are clear. Perhaps this is why the story of Noah is so appealing. We not only get animals two by two (a constant delight to children of all ages), but we also get a clear vision of justice. And then, of course, we hear God's promise that never again will the earth be so destroyed.

RESPONSIVE READING
PSALM 31:1-5, 19-24 or PSALM 46 (RCL); PSALM 31 or 31:1-5, 190-24 (BCP)

Two psalms are suggested for the day. Psalm 46 seems best suited as a partner for the Noah reading, with the references to shaking mountains and roaring waters in the first three verses. Psalm 31 takes up the issue of righteousness directly and unites with the epistle in stressing the righteousness of God.

SECOND READING
ROMANS 1:16-17; 3:22b-28, (29-31) (RCL); ROMANS 3:21-25a, 28 (BCP)

C. K. Barrett, in his insightful short reflections on Romans, calls 3:21-31 "perhaps the richest and most important paragraph in the whole letter."[1] Add to this the two verses from chap. 1, and Paul addresses our questions about righteousness head on. The Gospel, the Good News that Christ died for us, reveals the righteousness of God, which is the only righteousness that matters. What do I need to do in order to meet with approval from God? Nothing. Deuteronomy, in the most profound way possible, told us that we need to obey God's commandments. Ideally we are to be like Noah, blameless and righteous. But Paul in

Romans turns the whole system on its head. In v. 23 Paul recognizes a deep reality: "all have sinned and fallen short of the glory of God." Being Noah is not a real possibility. Trying to be Noah is always a set-up, always a trap. Going down that path leads to death. But in God's ultimate gift in Christ, God disarms the trap. God's own righteousness becomes the only righteousness needed to get right with God. While each of us can doubt our own righteousness, none of us can doubt the righteousness of God. This righteousness, God's very own righteousness, is God's gift to us so that our righteousness is no longer at issue. God's righteousness comes not at a price for us but at a price for God. We are bought, redeemed with life of Jesus though which our sin is wiped away. God's mercy is shown to be stronger, more essential to God's character than even God's justice, which is

GOD'S MERCY IS SHOWN TO BE STRONGER, MORE ESSENTIAL TO GOD'S CHARACTER THAN EVEN GOD'S JUSTICE, WHICH IS GOD'S JUDGMENT.

God's judgment. All is encapsulated in v. 28, "we hold that a person is justified by faith apart from works prescribed by the law." To grasp this is to grasp how righteousness now works. We are left only to believe that with God all things are possible, even the disarming of the trap accomplished through the sacrifice of Christ. This reality is apprehended by faith in Christ. The effect brings not only freedom from the burden of saving ourselves but also equality within the community. None among us is better than any other; none is more righteous—no more Noahs either to boast of or to be rewarded for righteousness. All are equally rewarded for Christ's sake. The result is not to be rid of the faithfulness of Deuteronomy. The law, says Paul, is still to be upheld (v. 31) but no longer as a test, as a trap. We are free.

THE GOSPEL
MATTHEW 7:21-29 (RCL);
MATTHEW 7:21-27 (BCP)

The amazing truth about questions of righteousness is that they do not go away. One can hear the message of Paul again and again, and we are still trapped. Everywhere, we look at life in categories of deserving. My family teases me every time we watch the movie *The Sound of Music*. We get to that deliciously romantic scene when the baron chases Julie Andrews out to the carousel and proposes. And then she sings that awful song (which song, I always at this point remind them, was not part of the original score), "Somewhere in my youth or childhood I must have done something right." That's it; that's the trap. She finds romance because somewhere, sometime she did something right. This assumption, so innocent in the movie, is lethal in the hospital room or when dealing with the AIDS epidemic. And this assumption is at work every time we ask the question: What do I need to do to have God reward me with the ultimate reward, salvation? In the Gospel for this day, we quite easily fall back into the trap. The text seems to tell us that we are, after all, saved by following the law. What is more, Jesus is laying it all out for us. "Not everyone who says to me, 'Lord, Lord,' will enter the kingdom of heaven, but only the one who does the will of my Father in heaven" (v. 21) One cannot get much plainer than this. It seems our righteousness does matter. But then again many will say: Look at all of the wonderful things we have done—prophesying and casting out demons, all in your name. And Jesus responds by calling them evil, rejecting them, and telling a parable about a wise man and a fool.

When I teach my class on biblical wisdom, I often ask my students to tell me how the Sermon on the Mount begins. They all know it begins with the Beatitudes. I then ask them how the sermon ends. Very few remember that it ends with this parable of the wise and foolish builders[2]—which is to say that, insofar as beatitudes and parables are both familiar forms of Jewish wisdom, the sermon begins and ends with language of and about wisdom. Paul ends his remarks in the epistle reading by saying that the law is still to be upheld. So also Jesus says in this sermon. The law is not dead; the law is wise. And the wise people know to build their houses on rock. One must choose the right foundation. And here is the challenge of the text: What is the right foundation on which to build a house of faith? What I want to say is this: I, like all of those around me, am always tempted to build my house on my own deeds of righteousness. Jesus' sermon keeps plugging away at me. Every time I think I get it, another new demand of the law comes at me, and I fall short. This or that I cannot do. Finally I stand before Jesus and say, but I have done all of these things in your name, and even this brings condemnation. If I build my house on the foundation of my own righteousness, it will always fall. So this parable, as all of Jesus' teaching, invites me in, invites me to be wise and build my hope on "nothing less than Jesus' blood and righteousness."[3] Build your house on any less of a foundation, and it will always fall. Wisdom here is throwing ourselves on the mercy of God, and trusting in God's righteousness rather than our own.

But here is the problem. In reading the parable in this way, I am not paying attention to the details of what Jesus is saying. Jesus specifically says, "Everyone who hears these words of mine and acts on them will be like a wise man,"(v. 24) and those who do not will be like a fool (v. 26). How we act matters! Our righteousness does matter. We who know Christ cannot act any old way. We cannot even hide behind acting in Jesus' name. Jesus presents a radical view of righteousness in his sermon that does not allow us to abandon the law. On the contrary, Jesus tells us to go beyond the law in love of God and neighbor and denial of self. The gate we are invited to enter is narrow. Jesus preaches that the ethics of the kingdom is a sign of who we are. And now, I am trapped. I believe what Paul says to be true. I also believe Jesus, in Matthew, presents us with a radical new vision of ethics we are called to live. What is more, Jesus says our life and even our entry into the kingdom depend on hearing and acting on what he says. Like it or not, we live with a biblical text that contains both Romans and Matthew. And finally, although I do not know that this is Matthew's intention, the sermon and this parable drive me to throw myself on the mercy of God. But even that mercy never finally diminishes the raw power of God's will that we follow Christ in all we do and say, even to the cross. If we are not struggling with this, we are not listening.

JESUS PRESENTS A RADICAL VIEW OF RIGHTEOUS-NESS IN HIS SERMON THAT DOES NOT ALLOW US TO ABANDON THE LAW. ON THE CONTRARY, JESUS TELLS US TO GO BEYOND THE LAW IN LOVE OF GOD AND NEIGHBOR AND DENIAL OF SELF.

This story, the climax of the sermon, prompts an astonished response from the crowd, because Jesus taught them as one having authority. The authority of these texts unsettles us and will not let us go. Our struggle with these texts calls to mind a scene from the more recent movie, *O Brother, Where Art Thou?* This modern-day *Odyssey* brings the "brothers" to a baptism scene by the river, where the baptized are singing an oft-repeated and haunting lyric about studying the "good old way" and then asking the "Good Lord" to "show us the way."

THIRD SUNDAY
AFTER PENTECOST

TENTH SUNDAY IN ORDINARY TIME / PROPER 5
JUNE 9, 2002

REVISED COMMON	EPISCOPAL (BCP)	ROMAN CATHOLIC
Hos. 5:15—6:6	Hos. 5:15—6:6	Hos. 6:3-6
or Gen. 12:1-9		
Ps. 50:7-15 or	Psalm 50 or 50:7-15	Ps. 50:1, 8, 12-13, 14-15
Ps. 33:1-12		
Rom. 4:13-25	Rom. 4:13-18	Rom. 4:18-25
Matt. 9:9-13, 18-26	Matt. 9:9-13	Matt. 9:9-13

For the next five Sundays, we are invited by lectionary texts from Matthew and elsewhere into a study of discipleship. What is it to be a disciple? This is scripture's way of asking what it is to be a spiritual person. Here is a great question to bring to one's fellow Christians through a series of sermons in the season of Pentecost. What are the challenges, comforts, changes, and commitments that come with being a disciple? Each Sunday brings its own distinct insights to these questions. This Sunday's texts are the appropriate starting gate, for they tell you where to begin. One starts on the road to discipleship by learning what this means, "I desire mercy and not sacrifice." The "I" who expresses this desire for mercy is God, who first expresses this desire in the book of Hosea.

FIRST READING
HOSEA 5:15—6:6 (RCL, BCP);
HOSEA 6:3-6 (RC)

The book of Hosea roots discipleship in the very character of God. In fact, Hosea is most striking in its remarkable glimpses into the interior life of God. This passage begins by sharing with us God's thoughts about how to ensure a dynamic and true relationship with believers. God has an idea. "If I withdraw," says God, "the people will see their sin and seek my renewed presence." And the people think that they do precisely this by reiterating their understanding of the divine promise that God will most certainly heal us and appear to us. Their response sounds so good, so like our own spiritual responses. "Let us press on to know the Lord; his appearing is as sure as the dawn!" But what the people want is surface faith. They want to be able to say these glorious words without repentance, without any true change. The people whom Hosea addresses are very much like Christians who want to call on Jesus when trouble comes and then merrily ignore God the remainder of the time. "We've got the promise of the resurrection," they say, "No worries!"

God's response is a cry from the divine heart. "What shall I do with you, O my very own people!" God repeats this cry again in the remarkable eleventh chapter where we learn that what makes God different from humans is that God's love, God's mercy, is always stronger than God's judgment (11:8-9). God cannot give up on the people of Israel, God's beloved children, despite their repeated rebellion. So also in chap. 6. God rec-

> THE PEOPLE WHOM HOSEA ADDRESSES ARE VERY MUCH LIKE CHRISTIANS WHO WANT TO CALL ON JESUS WHEN TROUBLE COMES AND THEN MERRILY IGNORE GOD THE REMAINDER OF THE TIME.

ognizes the fleeting nature of human faithfulness. Human love is like cloud or dew that quickly disappears. So God sends judgment in order to capture the attention that divine withdrawal did not accomplish. Perhaps then people will understand. God does not desire empty piety or surface spirituality. What God desires is steadfast love (*ḥesed*), that is, love that is loyal and true and has implications for action. Steadfast love favors the other and drives always to mercy. Only such love reflects true knowledge of God, knowledge that binds us to God so that we model our mercy on God's mercy. Discipleship begins with this deep connection and points us directly to the Gospel.

GENESIS 12:1-9 (RCL, alt.)

The alternative reading from Genesis 12 actually ties directly to the day's epistle, in that it centers on Abraham's faithful response and his role in the future of all nations. Abraham's call is so familiar to us that we often fail to recognize either the extravagant audacity of God's promise or the wonder of Abraham's response. That God would choose to bless all the families of the earth through one particular blessing and one particular family is a first glimpse of God's incarnational character. Our God never acts "in general," by-passing the particular. Rather the particular is the only way the promise of the infinite is made manifest. This characteristic of the God revealed in Scripture is often missed by folk who speak in terms of general spirituality. This same God will become very particularly incarnate for the salvation of all. For his part Abraham acts in this text, as in chapters 15 and 22, as a model of discipleship. His response to the call of God is immediate and unquestioning. He believes in the promise, a promise not only for himself but for all nations. God truly uses the discipleship of one for the blessing of many.

RESPONSIVE READING
PSALM 50:7-15 (RCL);
PSALM 50 or 50:7-15 (BCP);
PSALM 50:1, 8, 12-13, 14-15 (RC)

Psalm 50 begins with a summons not to one man but to all earth and heaven to come and bear witness to God's righteousness. In v. 7 and following God calls on Israel to hear testimony against her, reiterating Hosea's rejection of empty sacrifice. Pause and consider for a moment the remarkable capacity of Israel within even her liturgical tradition—here the psalms—to be self-reflective and even self-critical precisely of the liturgical tradition. Israel praises God for rejecting empty gestures, even her own. We in the church would do well to learn from such praise lest we think that going to church or even receiving the sacraments of baptism and communion are desired more by God than loving-kindness and mercy.

PSALM 33:1-12 (RCL, alt.)

The alternative psalm gives a vision of creation as it was intended to be. Obedience to the word of God is build into the very structure of creation. God speaks and the earth responds in fear and awe. So also should all nations respond, as should we, God's created beings.

SECOND READING
ROMANS 4:13-25 (RCL);
ROMANS 4:13-18 (BCP);
ROMANS 4:18-25 (RC)

This text both illumines the alternative Genesis text for this Sunday as well as continues and builds upon the reading from Romans begun the previous Sunday. Paul's discussion continues with the insight stressed in chap. 3—salvation comes not through law but through faith. For this reason Abraham is "father of us all." I am always thrown back to that old camp song about Father Abraham having many kids—"I am one of them, and so are you, so let's all praise the Lord!" Paul insists that we are Abraham's children not by virtue of blood (the law) but by virtue of faith. Paul paints a vivid picture of Abraham's faith. Against all reason, against even the laws of nature, Abraham believed in God's promise of descendants. "Therefore his faith was 'reckoned to him as righteousness' . . . not for his sake alone, but for ours also." Even here at this deep insight about Abraham's faith in God, we might be trapped, tempted to believe that faith is a new work, a work a good deal simpler than following the law. But faith is not a work. Faith is trust that God has done the work.

THE GOSPEL
MATTHEW 9:9-13, 18-26 (RCL); MATTHEW 9:9-13 (BCP, RC)

The Gospel begins with a direct call reminiscent of Abraham's call, now addressed to Matthew, sitting at a tax booth. While one certainly could learn a good deal by considering the status of folk like Matthew in the time of Jesus, the image of a tax collector at a booth also has immediately accessible impact. Here's a guy with a job that makes him the enemy. He is someone we fear, maybe even shun and despise, because he takes our money. And he is defined by his job. We have both a "Pharisaic" reaction of suspicion and an identification of sitting in our own tax booths. All the more striking is the immediacy of Matthew's getting up and following Jesus. Abraham's discipleship is amplified.

And then we move with Jesus to a meal—another immediately accessible image. We conjure up so many pictures of sitting down to eat with others: childhood memories of hoarding all the events of the day in order to share them with the family at dinner, awkward meals with those people you'd just as soon would drop off the ends of the earth; untold numbers of joyous meals where laughter was plentiful and friendships were deepened. Small wonder that the picture of Jesus at table has such appeal.

Several aspects of Jesus' table fellowship draw one's attention. While we might quote the modern quip "You are what you eat," with Jesus the more accurate saying would be "You are who you eat with." Jesus eats with tax collectors and sinners. His choice of companions has more to do with hospitality than with power. Or perhaps more accurately, Jesus' power

"YOU ARE WHO YOU EAT WITH." JESUS EATS WITH TAX COLLECTORS AND SINNERS.

comes not from eating with the powerful but from sitting with the unloved. No up or down power lunches here, rather Jesus reclines at table *with* (Greek, *synanekeito*), alongside of these outcasts. The full impact of his choice of companions is not lost on the Pharisees, whose question "Why?" may well imply more than suspicion of the wrong sort of people. The question suggests that they believe that by eating with such folks, Jesus becomes contaminated, polluted, unclean[4]—dangerous business for a leader of the community.

Jesus' dining habits also invite us to see him in the context of the biblical portrait of Wisdom. Matthew often presents Jesus as a teacher of wisdom or even as the embodiment of the figure of Wisdom presented in Proverbs 1-9; Ben Sira 1; 15; 24; and throughout the Wisdom of Solomon.[5] In Proverbs 9, Wisdom sends out a call and then sets her table for the simple, inviting them into the way of insight. Jesus' table fellowship offers the fruits of wisdom to sinners. I once had a student whose final project for her class in biblical wisdom was to create Wisdom/Jesus' table at the entrance to our seminary chapel. The full-sized round table was disordered and bedraggled, set with all manner of chipped, mismatched, and yet brilliantly colored dishes. Yet the chairs and place settings were strangely inviting, perhaps only for those with eyes to see. In Matthew 9, Jesus, our Wisdom, responds to the scoffing question first with a proverb, "Those who are well have no need of a physician, but those who are sick." He then quotes Hosea 6, showing that wisdom comes from the tradition. What he quotes is crucial, so crucial he repeats it in 12:7: "Go and learn what this means, 'I desire mercy, not sacrifice.'" Here is the insight that, once digested, marks a person as a disciple. This insight was what the experts who stood before him failed to understand. Positions or activities of privilege count for nothing. Sacrifice implies that we have something to give that changes the divine scales in our favor. We ultimately are still in control. Those gathered at the table knew themselves to be needers rather than givers. They were in need of a physician and having received mercy were able to give the same. They did not stand in judgment but sat at table open to wisdom and mercy. "Learn what this means," says Jesus, "'I desire mercy, not sacrifice.'" "For," he continues, "I have come not to call the righteous but sinners." And somehow the "I" who is God becomes the "I" who is Jesus. Jesus has come. Jesus, like God, calls, and Jesus, like God, desires mercy not sacrifice.

Being in need of a physician's healing sends us to the final portion of the Gospel reading. Here we meet both a leader of the synogogue and a woman who is bleeding continuously. These two are ostensibly at radically different ends of the social spectrum: he, a respected religious figure; she, isolated in her uncleanness (see Lev. 15:19-33). In some ways the synogogue leader, like Jesus, becomes legally unclean at her touch. And yet these two are more alike than the synogogue leader and the aforementioned Pharisees. The leader and the woman are united not only through textual intertwining, they are united in their knowledge that they stand in need of healing and that Jesus can meet that need. I have been amazed of late with what is happening in the churches today as we are rediscovering this common need among us. Services of healing are multiplying that, when well grounded in scripture and well considered by congregational leaders, bind a community together in remarkable ways. I have been struck by the total community involvement and the deep willingness of so many to let down the self-protective barriers that normally keep us walled off from both the pain and the blessing. Both mercy and healing are palpably present when the community gathers in need of divine forgiveness and presence. As we learn in Matthew 9, the power of Jesus' healing is not minor; even the dead are raised.

So what do we learn of discipleship from these texts? Disciples, like Matthew and Abraham, respond immediately to the Lord's invitation. And this invitation pulls us beyond ourselves toward the other. Disciples sit at table with all manner of folk. As disciples, we know that we are in need of healing and that Jesus meets that need. More than this, miracles of healing promote discipleship. And disciples know, deeply know, that the Lord has no need of nor any desire for our sacrifices. Our relationship as disciples does not begin with the Lord's need, but rather with our own. We stand in need of God's

> AS DISCIPLES WE KNOW THAT WHEN WE START WITH GOD'S MERCY, WE TOUCH OTHERS WITH THAT MERCY. MERCY, RATHER THAN UNCLEANNESS, BECOMES INFECTIOUS.

mercy, and the Lord our God is merciful beyond all imaginings. As disciples we know that when we start with God's mercy, we touch others with that mercy. Mercy, rather than uncleanness, becomes infectious. So we meet the Lord's desire for mercy, for loving kindness. As disciples we approach the world filled with God's compassion and love. I am reminded of a traditional table grace expanded by my friend, Gail Ramshaw. This expanded prayer has been a gift to our family meals. As we invite Jesus' presence at our table, we pray as well that our table fellowship opens us further to show mercy to the stranger.

Come Lord Jesus be our guest, and let these gifts to us be blessed.
Blessed be God who is our bread. May all the world be clothed and fed.[6]

FOURTH SUNDAY
AFTER PENTECOST

ELEVENTH SUNDAY IN ORDINARY TIME / PROPER 6
JUNE 16, 2002

REVISED COMMON	EPISCOPAL (BCP)	ROMAN CATHOLIC
Exod. 19:2-8a or	Exod. 19:2-8a	Exod. 19:2-6a
Gen. 18:1-15, (21:1-7)		
Psalm 100 or	Psalm 100	Ps. 100:1-2, 3, 5
Ps. 116:1-2, 12-19		
Rom. 5:1-8	Rom. 5:6-11	Rom. 5:6-11
Matt. 9:35—	Matt. 9:35—	Matt. 9:36—10:8
10:8, (9-23)	10:8 (9-15)	

The texts this Sunday invite us to continue our exploration of discipleship. Last week's Gospel emphasized what we should know if we are to be faithful disciples. This week the Gospel explores what disciples do. We begin to take on discipleship's implication for leadership. That is, once a person becomes a disciple, how does such a one relate to the community, to the world? And just in case any of us are tempted to think that discipleship is a picnic in the park, we might best prepare for the rainstorm. Discipleship, though it is life-giving, always comes at a cost.

FIRST LESSON

EXODUS 19:2-8a (RCL, BCP);
EXODUS 19:2-6a (RC)

Exodus 19 is one of the most significant chapters in the Old Testament. The people have been freed from slavery and at last arrive at the mountain where they will learn how to serve God rather than Pharaoh. That is, they soon will be given instructions in discipleship, beginning with the Ten Commandments. But before these instructions are given, chap. 19 puts the commandments in context through the introduction of some of the most memorable images in all of scripture.

The image of God as one who saves is elegantly presented in v. 4, "You have seen what I did to the Egyptians, and how I bore you on eagles' wings and brought you to myself." This image has most recently captured the hearts of many through Michael Joncas's moving anthem based on Psalm 91: "And I will raise you up on eagle's wings, bear you on the breath of dawn, make you to shine like the sun, and hold you in the palm of my hand." Joncas's song communicates God's promise and taps into a deep yearning for a personal relationship with God. Israel's relationship with God is rooted first in her experience as a community, seeing all that God has done in defeating the Egyptians, and then together being borne home by God as on the wings of an eagle. God is elsewhere described as a mother eagle who teaches her young to fly first by pushing them from the nest and then by "spreading its wings, catching them, [and] bearing them aloft on its pinions" (Deut. 32:11, "The Song of Moses"). This image thus illumines God's central claim of relationship: God has saved Israel, freed the people from slavery, and brought them safely to Sinai. Israel did nothing to merit this saving act nor did they save themselves in any way. They are dependent entirely on the supporting wings of this eagle. Another favorite hymn urges us: "Praise to the Lord, who o'er all things is wondrously reigning. And, as on wings of an eagle, uplifting, sustaining. Have you not seen all that is needful has been sent by his gracious ordaining?"[7]

Israel, for her part, is pictured and thus given identity in two different ways. God says, "You shall be my treasured possession out of all the peoples." Here is another image rich in biblical history (see Deut. 7:6; 14:2; 26:18; Pss. 33:12; 78:71; 135:4). The image is bursting with the promise of God but is linked as well to the need for obedience. Israel is also called to be "a priestly kingdom and a holy nation." Understanding this phrase is not an easy task. The two parts of the phrase might each refer to a different part of the community of Israel: the priests, whose job it becomes to rule, and the people, who are to maintain a high standard of holiness before God. On the other hand, the terms can be read as parallel, both referring to *all* the people of Israel. All of Israel is to be both priestly and holy through worship, service, and obedience to God's word. The people are themselves to be priestly in relationship to and for the sake of the whole world. They are to stand as mediators and as beacons for all the earth, pointing all people to the reality of the Lord's loving concern. In Rev. 1:6 and particularly in 1 Peter 2:4-10, we Christians are also asked to see ourselves as "a kingdom of priests and a holy nation." Martin Luther expands this image to speak of the church as "the priesthood of all believers." We, as disciples, are the priests of the world, serving the world, which is God's temple, and speaking the words of promise and forgiveness to God's ever-expanding congregation.

GENESIS 18:1-15, (21:1-7) (RCL, alt.)

For those following through the reading of Genesis, chap. 18 offers an opportunity to preach about Abraham in a manner often overlooked by Christians but very important for Muslims. The passage highlights Abraham as a model of hospitality rather than as the preferred Christian model of faith. Hospitality is a crucial virtue for people of all faiths and is an aspect of discipleship particularly relevant for our age. This passage stands behind the injunction in Heb. 13:2 not to neglect showing hospitality to strangers, "for thereby some have entertained angels unawares" (RSV)—yet another vivid image that captures the imagination. Sarah's role is equally worthy of comment. Abraham in this passage thinks Sarah is only important as a background figure, incidental to both the hospitality and the promise. But the strangers/angels know better. The marvelously humorous exchange about Sarah laughing is made richer in the Hebrew text. The word for "laugh" in Hebrew is *tzahaq*, a word that in chap. 21 becomes the name of Abraham's and Sarah's beloved son, Isaac (in Hebrew, *yitzhaq*). Laughter, even Sarah's laughter of skepticism (her "isaacing"), anticipates the fulfillment of the divine promise.

RESPONSIVE READING

PSALM 100 or 116:1-2, 12-19 (RCL);
PSALM 100 (BCP);
PSALM 100:1-2, 3, 5 (RC)

Psalm 100 is a classic hymn of joy, particularly known from the Old Hundredth and William Kethe's 1561 text, "All People That on Earth Do Dwell." The psalm perfectly matches the Exodus text with its emphasis on our being God's people. In the Exodus text, the proper response to that reality is awe and obedience. Here the invited response is praise of God's steadfast love and faithfulness. The alternative, Psalm 116, is equally familiar, particularly to those who commonly use vv. 12-18 as an offertory during services of communion.

SECOND READING

ROMANS 5:1-8 (RCL);
ROMANS 5:6-11 (BCP, RC)

In chap. 5, the strong witness of Romans continues. Because we are justified, says Paul, we have peace. But the peace we have does not look like the peace that we expect. This peace does not protect us from suffering but, oddly, enables us to boast in our suffering. Such a claim can sound masochistic. Boasting in suffering can be a dangerous idea, leading some to think that suffering is to be desired or is always good for a person. Coming to such a conclusion is to misunderstand Paul. Paul speaks here of the endurance and character that comes from suffering. And one endures suffering precisely because one has hope. Paul is not saying that suffering is good, but rather that if we live by the faith and the hope that is ours through Christ, then suffering cannot defeat us. We learn that part of the gift of faith is this remarkable capacity to bear suffering, not because we have to or ought to but because the love of God in Christ has made such endurance possible. The endurance is possible because we know our hope is not in vain. This is the work of the Holy Spirit in us and the basis of our boasting. The hope that is ours has everything to do with Christ dying for us in our weakness and sin. Paul then leads us through the logic of our hope. Some few of us might indeed die for a good person, for someone we love or admire. But who among us would die for someone we think does not deserve such a profound sacrifice? Yet God in Christ has such love for us that Christ dies for us in the midst of our undeserving. More than this, says Paul, Christ not only died but Christ also lives, so our hope is all the more. Finally we even boast in God through Christ, "through whom we have now received reconciliation."

THE GOSPEL

MATTHEW 9:35—10:8, (9-23) (RCL);
MATTHEW 9:35—10:8 (9-15) (BCP);
MATTHEW 9:36—10:8 (RC)

The Gospel begins with the work and compassion of Jesus. Jesus travels all around the countryside, teaching, proclaiming the gospel of the kingdom, and healing the sick. His attitude toward the people he serves is captured by v. 36. He does not see an unruly mob that he might send away because he is tired and needs rest. Rather, the crowds move him to compassion because they are tired and harassed. The crowd is his burden to carry. They are "helpless, like sheep without a shepherd." The people as sheep and the leader as shepherd is yet another rich biblical image, perhaps the most familiar biblical image we know, particularly because of the many passages about Jesus as a Good Shepherd and because of Psalm 23. William Holladay, in *The Psalms through Three Thousand Years*, traces the history, impact, and centrality of Psalm 23 in our modern American culture, highlighting such notable and far-reaching figures as Abraham Lincoln, Louisa May Alcott, Henry Ward Beecher, Eldridge Cleaver, and Garrison Keillor.[8] For many of us, the mere mention that we are like sheep suggests at least a half-dozen melodies from hymns and chorales, so that we can't stop humming.

But Jesus uses the image only to suggest that the crowd needs help and leadership. So Jesus turns to his disciples and, like Moses in the wilderness (Exod. 18:13-27), shares his authority. Sharing of authority might seem like a gift to those who receive some of it. Who doesn't like to get promotions? Jesus turns to the disciples, the chosen ones. As with Israel, the chosen nation, the Lord's "treasured possession," being chosen feels like privilege; discipleship implies a certain status. And look at the power the disciples receive. Jesus "gave them authority over unclean spirits, to cast them out, and to cure every disease and sickness." How easy it would be to get puffed up. The disciples quickly discover that the gift of this authority, this shared shepherd status, this shared leadership, is also a burden. The disciples are to take up the work of Christ with precisely the same compassion he feels when he sees the crowds; they are to take on the same burden. Jesus instructs them to travel to the lost sheep. He tells them that they, like him, are to proclaim the good news, to heal the sick, and more. And further he tells them that they will receive no pay. This is surely not a promotion most of us would willingly take on.

The job of the disciples also includes the exercise of discernment and judgment. They are to judge which town and which household is worthy and which is not. This necessity to judge adds considerably to the burden. Most of us much prefer leaving judgment in God's capable hands. Precisely in their need to exercise judgment they now become like sheep. But unlike the crowds, whose status as sheep means they need care and direction, the disciples are like sheep when they find themselves in the midst of wolves. Jesus gives them the remarkable advice to "be wise as serpents and innocent as doves." Animal imagery abounds.

THE DISCIPLES QUICKLY DISCOVER THAT THE GIFT OF THIS AUTHORITY, THIS SHARED SHEPHERD STATUS, THIS SHARED LEADERSHIP, IS ALSO A BURDEN.

They are told that as sheep among the wolves, they will be flogged and dragged before the authorities, though even then the Spirit will speak through them. They are told the cost will be great, with families torn apart, brother against brother, with parents and their children betraying one another. All this results in people's hatred of the disciples and their persecution. Here the burden of discipleship is vividly described. It is hard to be romantic about such a call to discipleship.

We in the church can identify with both sets of sheep in this passage. We are like the crowds, defined by our need for compassion and direction, looking for and needing a shepherd to lead us. We sing the 23rd Psalm together and we are drawn to the stained-glass windows of Jesus with the lost lamb gathered in his loving arms. But then we are also transformed. Once we are touched by Jesus, once we know his love, his forgiveness, and his compassion, we ourselves become disciples. We take on the shared leadership of the flock and thus are open to becoming sheep among wolves. When we, each of us, take on the leadership role that comes with discipleship, we take on responsibilities that come with very real consequences. It is difficult to know how far to take such a call. We receive no pay and considerable hatred. Who among us desires such a burden? We are, I believe, invited back to consider the lesson of the epistle. Because Christ died for us while we yet were sinners, we have hope. And because we have hope, we are able to boast in our sufferings.

The combination of this Gospel and epistle puts me in mind of a remarkable episode of the acclaimed TV show *West Wing*. The episode was entitled "Shibboleth," recalling the test of identity in Judges 12:6. The show begins with our hearing about some one hundred escaped refugees from mainland China who arrived in California in a boat, each sealed in their own container. We soon learn that some of the escapees have died on the journey; they now number eighty-three. We hear as well that they claim to be evangelical Christians escaping persecution. President Bartlett must decide whether their claim to discipleship, and thus their claim to asylum, is real or somehow faked. He must discover if they can say "Shibboleth." The highlight of the show is a remarkable encounter that takes place in the oval office between President Bartlett and one of the Chinese refugees, a chemistry professor by the name of Jen Wei. Jen Wei is an older man, possessed of nothing but a calm and quiet dignity. The president asks how he became a Christian. Jen Wei responds that he and his wife began attending a house church and then were baptized. When asked how he practices his faith, Jen Wei responds that they share Bibles, sing hymns, hear sermons, recite the Lord's Prayer, and do charitable acts. "Who," asks the president, "is the head of your church?" "The head of the parish," responds Jen Wei, "is an eighty-four-year-old man by the name of Won Ling. He has been beaten and imprisoned many times. The head of the church is Jesus Christ." President Bartlett asks him to name the disciples. He responds, "Peter, Andrew, John, Philip, Bartholomew, Thomas, Matthew, Thaddaeus, Simon, Judas, and James"—the same list we find in Matthew 10. And then Jen Wei continues with a remarkable speech. "Mr. President, Christianity is not demonstrated through a recitation of facts. You are seeking evidence of faith, a whole hearted acceptance of God's promise of a better world. For we hold that man is justified by faith alone. This is what St. Paul said, "'justified by faith alone.'" Faith is the true shibboleth. The witness is astounding.

Discipleship begins with faith and then leads to suffering for the sake of that faith. Discipleship may lead to kicking the dust off one's feet and moving on. It may lead to terrible persecution and trial, as in the case of the fictional Dr. Wei and his flock. The drive and call of discipleship is to share and witness to the faith. And the gift is the hope in Christ Jesus. Of this we may boast.

FIFTH SUNDAY
AFTER PENTECOST

Twelfth Sunday in Ordinary Time / Proper 7
June 23, 2002

Revised Common	Episcopal (BCP)	Roman Catholic
Jer. 20:7-13 or Gen. 21:8-21	Jer. 20:7-13	Jer. 20:10-13
Ps. 69:7-10, (11-15), 16-18 or Ps. 86:1-10, 16-17	Ps. 69:1-18 or 69:7-10, 16-18	Ps. 69:7-9, 13, 16, 32-34 (Heb. Bible 69:8-10, 14, 17, 33-35)
Rom. 6:1b-11	Rom. 5:15b-19	Rom. 5:12-15
Matt. 10:24-39	Matt. 10:(16-23), 24-33	Matt. 10:26-33

This week the Gospel and accompanying texts continue exploring the cost of discipleship. The expression "cost of discipleship" calls to mind the German theologian and ethicist Dietrich Bonhoeffer who, in 1937, in the midst of dominance of the Nazi regime in his country, wrote a book by that title.[9] Bonhoeffer's writings concerning discipleship are often insightful, but what makes Bonhoeffer memorable is that what he said was matched and surpassed by how powerfully how he lived and died. Having participated in a plot to assassinate Hitler, Bonhoeffer was imprisoned and then executed in 1945. His story stands as a twentieth-century beacon of discipleship, calling to mind many Christians past and present who have taken up the cross and followed Jesus.

FIRST READING
JEREMIAH 20:7-13 (RCL, BCP);
JEREMIAH 20:10-13 (RC)

On a Sunday given over to consideration of the cost of discipleship, one could have no more appropriate lesson from the Old Testament than one of the confessions (laments) of Jeremiah. Jeremiah, like Bonhoeffer, stands as a beacon. He not only delivers a clear and certain message from God to the people but also gives us remarkable glimpses into his interior struggle with both the message and the call. Seven times throughout his book we hear his lament, we hear what it costs Jeremiah to continue proclaiming the word of the Lord. We see him caught between his call to speak God's word of judgment and his own compassion for and frustration with the people he is called to judge. In chap. 20, we hear Jeremiah's excruciating complaint to the Lord that he has been enticed and overpowered by God. The effect on his standing in the community is dramatic. He has become a laughingstock; his friends watch for his stumbling and wait to take their revenge. He wants desperately not to deliver God's message, but the word of destruction burns so within him that he cannot keep it inside. God's judgment takes over like a warrior (an ironic twist on a primary image for the God who saves), and Jeremiah now himself looks for the destruction of those who persecute him. He then moves from lament to praise, knowing that the Lord of justice delivers the needy. We see very clearly the personal cost to Jeremiah of being a prophet of the Lord. What is less clear is how much this cost to Jeremiah perfectly reflects the cost to God as well. Terry Fretheim, in *The Suffering of God*, shows how often the lamenting words of the prophet closely correspond to the laments found on the very lips of God.[10] God also cries out lamentations that show divine anguish over the necessity of judgment and the power of the word burning like fire. Fretheim speaks of an identity between God and the prophet in which, through the word, "God is *absorbed into* the very life of the prophet."[11] Jeremiah, like the disciples of Jesus, participates in the life of the One who sends him. He embodies as well as delivers the word and thus shares the weight and the burden of divine grief that comes with both judgment and compassion.

WE SEE JEREMIAH CAUGHT BETWEEN HIS CALL TO SPEAK GOD'S WORD OF JUDGMENT AND HIS OWN COMPASSION FOR AND FRUSTRATION WITH THE PEOPLE HE IS CALLED TO JUDGE.

GENESIS 21:8-21 (RCL, alt.)

The Genesis reading once again exposes a part of the life of Abraham and his family not often considered. The text begins with a complicated, unflattering picture of Sarah, who demands the expulsion of her slave, Hagar, along with Hagar's son. Sarah is one of the few women in scripture to be portrayed, like Moses, David, Abraham, Jacob, and others, with enough depth and detail that we see her faults as well as her strengths. God then instructs Abraham to follow Sarah's instructions and delivers a promise to Abraham that this other son will also become a great nation. But what is most striking in this text is the story of Hagar. Her story is partner to two other texts in Genesis. The first, in Genesis 16, is clearly parallel to this text. There Hagar makes her first journey to the wilderness where she herself receives God's promise of a son and then actually names God. These texts taken together serve notice to us that God's story doesn't just follow

110

THE SEASON
OF PENTECOST
──────

DIANE
JACOBSON

one straight line (Abraham, Isaac, and Jacob), but God also attends to the slave, giving heed to her affliction and to the underside of the story. The second text that runs parallel to this one is less clear unless one attends to details. This story of Hagar and the near death of her child parallels the story in chap. 22 of the near sacrifice of Isaac. Beginning with v. 14, the words of the stories match each other: Abraham rises early, lays provisions on Hagar/Isaac, travels to a place. Abraham/Hagar is called to by an angel of God, and he/she looks and sees a ram/a well. The biblical text invites us to read these two stories in tandem so that we might ask any number of questions. For example, is Hagar's refusal to look on the death of her child any less faithful than Abraham's willingness to sacrifice his? Perhaps these are both acts of faith. Another question: Why is Isaac always named, with attributes heaped upon him? In 22:2 God names him to Abraham as "your son, your only son, Isaac, whom you love." Meanwhile this son of the slave girl goes nameless and presumably unloved in his story. We have to work to understand that this child also is a child of the promise. On this score, one detail of chap. 21 is worth noting. After Hagar lifts her voice and weeps, God hears the child. Many are confused by this seeming error in the text. But in Hebrew, the text reads, *vayishma' 'elohim*, which when shortened becomes *vay* (and) *ishma'el* (*ohim*). In God's hearing the child is named Ishmael.

RESPONSIVE READING

PSALM 69:7–10, (11–15), 16–18 (RCL);
PSALM 69:1–18 or 69:7–10, 16–18 (BCP);
PSALM 69:7–9, 13, 16, 32–34 (RC);
PSALM 86:1–10, 16–17 (RCL, alt.)

The lament of Jeremiah is rightly paired with a lament from the Psalter. In fact, more than a third of the psalms are laments, but we rarely say or sing them. Claus Westermann has noted the movement from lament to praise is shown in scripture to be part of the natural rhythm of the human relationship to God, yet, in the church, we have substituted confession for lament.[12] The implication is that all rather than some evil is a result of sin. Lament when well understood is a cry from the human heart born of faith. The lamenter so believes in the promises of God that he or she cries out to and at God when the promises are not fulfilled. Believers are not just permitted to lament; faith demands that we lament. Psalm 69 is a dramatic lament with verses that strikingly parallel the lament of Jeremiah.

Psalm 86 will be discussed on the Ninth Sunday after Pentecost.

ROMANS 6:1b-11 (RCL);
ROMANS 5:15b-19 (BCP);
ROMANS 5:12-15 (RC)

In Romans 5, Paul contrasts Adam and Christ as the ones who bring sin and thus death, on one hand, and life, on the other. This contrast, while clear, is not immediately accessible. In our scientific era so caught up in the identity of fact and truth, it is easy to identify the truth of the primeval stories in Genesis with their historicity. On one hand, we speak decisively of the life, death, and resurrection of Jesus. As Paul says in 1 Cor. 15:17, "If Christ has not been raised, [our] faith is futile." But when we speak of Adam, are we speaking in the same way? I think not. *'Adam* in Hebrew is the common world for a human being or even a collective for the whole human race. "Adam" continues to carry that meaning into the New Testament. What complicates this picture is the use of Adam as a proper name within the all-important narratives of Genesis 2-3. These texts teach us about ourselves through the stories of the one man, Adam. In precisely this way, Paul also teaches us about ourselves. Through comparing Adam and Jesus, Paul teaches us that "just as one man's trespass led to condemnation for all, so one man's act of righteousness leads to justification and life for all. For just as by the one man's disobedience the many were made sinners, so by the one man's obedience the many will be made righteous."

Paul's words in Rom. 6:1-11 (taken up by two of the traditions next week) are spectacular. Every line is a gem. He begins with such a straightforward question. If God's response to our sin is grace, why should we not continue to sin "in order that grace may abound?" Any number of us have run into folks who approach their lives as Christians with precisely this attitude. On the basis of this faulty reasoning, they scorn costly discipleship and rely on cheap grace. Paul will have none of it. He begins to speak of what many would refer to as sanctification, a term Paul will come to at the conclusion of this extended discussion. (See 6:19, 22, discussed with next Sunday's text). Paul speaks of our being joined to Christ both in his death and in his resurrection. In our death, as in his, we are dead to, that is, freed from sin. Just as "death no longer has dominion over him," so also death holds no dominion over us. Death and sin are inexorably linked. Similarly Christ's resurrection insures that we may "walk in newness of life." How then could we think of sinning? Newness of life is incompatible with such a notion.

THE GOSPEL

MATTHEW 10:24-39 (RCL);
MATTHEW 10:(16-23), 24-33 (BCP);
MATTHEW 10:26-33 (RC)

The Gospel continues from last Sunday with different lectionary traditions beginning and ending at different places. Chapter 10 is, in fact, a seamless discussion about the cost of discipleship. Much of what was said about last week's text is therefore relevant. Once again the relationship between Jesus and the disciples is emphasized. While the disciples do not stand above their teacher nor, as slaves, above their master, still they are like him, which is gift enough. Yet, as we have seen above and will see below, to be like Jesus can be costly. Verses 25-31 center around a triple instruction/assurance that Jesus gives the disciples: they move from a passive subjunctive, "have no fear" (v. 26), to an imperative, "do not fear" (v. 28), to a passive imperative, "do not be afraid" (v. 31). First, they are to have no fear of secrecy, for all will soon come to light. Second, they shall not fear loss of life, for while they can kill the body, they cannot kill the soul. I am reminded of the old spiritual, "Michael, Row the Boat Ashore," in which the "chilly and cold" Jordan River "kills the body, but not the soul." The center of the three injunctions thus anticipates the promise of the text in v. 39. And third, the disciples shall not be afraid of being discounted or undervalued. For just as God watches after the lowly sparrow, sold as cheap food in the marketplace, so much more will God value and uphold the disciples. We Christians often sing about God's injunction not to fear, but this text is a helpful reminder that being told not to fear is not an assurance that life will be smooth. It is only through God's grace that we need not fear.

> BEING TOLD NOT TO FEAR IS NOT AN ASSURANCE THAT LIFE WILL BE SMOOTH. IT IS ONLY THROUGH GOD'S GRACE THAT WE NEED NOT FEAR.

Our reasons to fear are many—everything from the malignancy of Satan (in this text, Beelzebul) to bodily death to the very judgment of God. Surely fear is the appropriate response. We are told to have no fear not because such things are not frightening but because such things do not have the final word.

Jesus next issues some clear, stern, and unambiguous warnings. His claim both of ultimate power and unique relationship with God is stunning. He states that those who acknowledge or deny him will, in turn, be acknowledged or denied by him before God, his Father, in heaven. Particularly striking is his announcement that he comes not "to bring peace, but a sword," and that he will continue to bring divisions to households (see above, v. 21). One can hardly afford to be romantic about Jesus when faced with such texts. Camp songs will not do. Most of us have never come close to experiencing such trauma. This was the text of my very first sermon, and there sat my mother-in-law in the congregation. I was acutely aware of my own family history, having been raised a Jew and become a Christian. I spent years fighting the call to be baptized precisely because of my fear of family rejection (a rejection that did not materialize). Nothing is more personally frightening, more personally costly, than family strife. I recall an evangelist from Tanzania speaking about the rejection he faced from his family when he acknowledged his faith in Christ. He was forced to choose between faith and family. Jesus is clear, "whoever loves father or mother . . . son or daughter more than me is not worthy of me." No one can escape the cost of discipleship here described. "Whoever does not take up the cross and follow me is not worthy of me." For the first time in Matthew, Jesus speaks of the cross, and it is not only his to bear. The demand is relentless and feels like loss. The fear, despite Christ's assurance, is palpable. But undergirding the demand is a final promise. Jesus says, "those who find their life will lose it, and those who lose their life for my sake will find it." That which looks like life is death, but what looks like death is life. Do not fear, because finally discipleship leads to life.

Having been presented so directly with the cost of discipleship, it seems appropriate to end with a quotation from Bonhoeffer:

> Cheap grace means grace as bargain basement goods, cut-rate forgiveness, cut-rate comfort, cut-rate sacrament; grace as the church's inexhaustible pantry, from which it is poured out without hesitation or limit. It is grace without a price, without costs. . . . Cheap grace means grace as doctrine, as principle, as system. It means forgiveness of sins as a general truth; it means God's love as merely a Christian idea of God. . . . Cheap grace is grace without discipleship, grace without the cross, grace without the living, incarnate Jesus Christ. . . . Costly grace is the gospel which must be sought again and again, the gift which has to be asked for, the door at which one has to knock again and again.
>
> It is costly, because it calls to discipleship; it is grace, because it calls us to follow Jesus Christ. It is costly, because it costs people their lives; it is grace, because it gives them their lives. It is costly, because it condemns sin; it is grace, because it justifies the sinner. Above all, grace is costly, because it was costly to God, because it costs God the life of God's son—"you were brought with a price"—and because nothing can be cheap to us which is costly to God.[13]

SIXTH SUNDAY
AFTER PENTECOST

THIRTEENTH SUNDAY IN ORDINARY TIME / PROPER 8
JUNE 30, 2002

REVISED COMMON	EPISCOPAL (BCP)	ROMAN CATHOLIC
Jer. 28:5-9 or	Isa. 2:10-17	2 Kings 4:8-11, 14-16a
Gen. 22:1-14		
Ps. 89:1-4, 15-18	Ps. 89:1-18 or	Ps. 89: 1-2, 15-16,
or Psalm 13	89:1-4, 15-18	17-18 (Heb. Bible
		89:2-3, 16-17, 18-19)
Rom. 6:12-23	Rom. 6:3-11	Rom. 6:3-4, 8-11
Matt. 10:40-42	Matt. 10:34-42	Matt. 10:37-42

We continue this Sunday with our Pentecost season's study of discipleship. Today the central drive is toward hospitality. I have been told of late that hospitality is a spiritual gift. What a wonderful thought! One so often associates spirituality with activities that have a rather inward-directed, monastic quality—prayer, meditation, silence. Certainly these activities can be positive, but one wonders about the role of the Spirit in community. The texts for Pentecost showed us from the start the importance of the connection between community and Spirit. Hospitality is a spiritual gift of and for community. In truth community without hospitality is always dying. Discipleship and hospitality are thus worthy themes to explore. As we shall see, this week's Gospel text speaks of very specific recipients of hospitality: Jesus, prophets, righteous ones, and "little ones." This variety accounts perhaps for the plethora of texts available for the First Reading for today, each with a different slant and each with its own connection to the Gospel.

FIRST READING
JEREMIAH 28:5-9 (RCL)

We return to Jeremiah, whose powerful lamentation was one of last week's lessons. In chap. 28, Jeremiah and another prophet, Hananiah, have a series of encounters that could be entitled "The Case of the Dueling Prophets." Hananiah prophesies that the Babylonian exiles and stolen temple vessels will be returned within two years. Today's lesson is Jeremiah's response. At issue is how one can distinguish true from false prophecy, a subject taken up in Deut. 18:9-22. Which of us, given a choice, would not choose good news over bad? We will want to believe the bearer of good tidings, and we will tend to dismiss or worse the harbinger of woe. So it was throughout biblical history. The people were wont to choose Hananiah and to dismiss or even to kill Jeremiah. Jeremiah responds to Hananiah's smug assurance with the same clear and obvious message as Deuteronomy—time will tell. He says, in effect "I certainly hope you are right," though of course, Jeremiah, true prophet of God, knows Hananiah to be speaking falsely. In their next encounter, Jeremiah predicts his rival's imminent demise, and time does tell—Hananiah dies that same year.

At one level the connection between this reading and the Gospel lection is clear. Matt. 10:41 reads, "Whoever welcomes a prophet in the name of a prophet will receive a prophet's reward." Well, be warned—receive the wrong prophet and you may die. But a second, subtler connection is more compelling. As is so often true in the biblical witness, when Jeremiah's responds to Hananiah he says more than perhaps he realizes. He says, in fact, "As for the prophet who prophesies peace, when the word of that prophet comes true, then it will be known that the LORD has truly sent the prophet" (Jer. 28:9). We Christians then are wont to ask, "Is Jesus this prophet truly sent?" In light of last week's Gospel (Matt. 10:34, "I have not come to bring peace, but a sword"), we might hesitate to make such an identity. Though as one looks forward to next week's Gospel, we know that in terms of bringing a deeper peace, the prophet has surely come.

2 KINGS 4:8-11, 14-16a (RC)

The suggested reading in the Roman Catholic lectionary also connects with Matthew 10:41 in a very direct fashion. Here is the paradigmatic story of one who offers hospitality to a prophet and receives a prophet's reward. The wealthy Shunammite woman habitually welcomes the prophet Elisha to her home. Her reward is plenteous. The prophet Elisha, the one so often spoken of as a forerunner of Jesus (see next Sunday's comments on Matthew), not only announces to her that she will give birth to her desired son (v. 16), he later even raises the child from the dead (vv. 32-35).

ISAIAH 2:10-17 (BCP)

The Episcopal lectionary goes in a different direction with a chilling text about the coming day of the Lord. That day will be a day of judgment in which the proud and lofty will be brought low and the haughty will be humbled. One is reminded of the same theme from the *Magnificat* (Luke 1:46-55), in which Mary proclaims that with the birth of her child, God "has scattered the proud in the imaginations of their hearts" (RSV) and "brought down the powerful from their thrones." Our God is consistent when considering the haughty. This text points directly to the earlier part of the Gospel reading (dealt with last week but part of this week's Episcopalian lectionary) that points to Jesus himself coming with a sword.

GENESIS 22:1-14 (RCL, alt.)

The final option for the first lesson continues with the reading of Genesis and brings us to the ever moving and terrifying text of the near sacrifice of Isaac. I commented last week on the significant connections with Genesis 21. For most Christians, however, this chapter looms large both because of the faith of Abraham, particular as examined by Søren Kierkegaard in *Fear and Trembling*, and also because of the all-important connections to the death of Christ, God's only and beloved Son. More recent treatments of this theme range from postmodern questions about divine child abuse to a fascinating and important examination by the Jewish scholar Jon Levenson.[14] The stark introduction of the narrative, the unrelenting movement toward the altar with such chilling details as the knife and the wood and the fire and the son, combined with the terse dialogue between Abraham and God and Abraham and Isaac, all unite to imprint this text forever on our hearts and minds. The questions stand before us: Why would God ask such a thing? Would Abraham really have slain his beloved son? Would I, could I, ever have such faith? Is this how faith works? This text is all about seeing (the Hebrew word for "provide" is from the verb "to see"). How are we tested, and where do we see God?

PSALM 89:1–4, 15–18 (RCL);
PSALM 89:1–18 or 89:1–4, 15–18 (BCP);
PSALM 89:1–2, 15–16, 17–18 (RC);
PSALM 13 (RCL, alt.)

Psalm 89 is an exultant royal psalm that becomes, in the end, a lament calling on God to remember the faithfulness God has sworn to David. The assigned section is about God's promise and steadfast love to David as well as about God's justice and righteousness that are the foundation of both God's throne and David's. Equally significant is God's ruling over heaven and earth with a mighty arm. The alternative psalm is 13, a classic lament that moves from complaint to petition to assurance of hope and confident thanksgiving.

SECOND READING

ROMANS 6:12–23 (RCL);
ROMANS 6:3–11 (BCP);
ROMANS 6:3–4, 8–11 (RC)

As discussed with last week's texts, Romans 6 contains Paul's marvelous discussion of why we as Christians, though no longer subjects of the law, are nevertheless to avoid sin. This avoidance is both a matter of our own activity—our obedience, and our new state as freed by grace—our sanctification. Our sanctification is strictly a result of God's activity; God has brought us from death to life. Our obedience then comes naturally to us; we present ourselves as "instruments of righteousness." The metaphor Paul takes up in vv. 16ff. is that of slavery. This is a common and dominant theme in scripture. God's initial act of redemption was the freeing of Israel from slavery. More correctly, they were freed from being slaves to Pharaoh so that they could become slaves to the LORD (Hebrew has one and the same word for "slave" and "servant.") Slavery is also a subject well understood by the Romans in Paul's day. A slave was one who gave himself or herself completely over to the master; slaves in truth gave up their lives to their masters. Thus, both the Old Testament background and the Roman reality stand behind Paul's use of this metaphor. What then does Paul say? All slaves are slaves to the one whom they obey. Once, says Paul, you were slaves of sin, of impurity, of iniquity. But now you are "slaves of righteousness." The righteousness, of course, is God's righteousness, so Paul, recalling Exodus, speaks in v. 22 of being "enslaved to God." If one pours out one's life as slave to God, the result is "sanctification," and "the end is eternal life."

THE GOSPEL

MATTHEW 10:40-42 (RCL);
MATTHEW 10:34-42 (BCP);
MATTHEW 10:37-42 (RC)

We have built up to the final verses of Matthew 9-10 over the last several Sundays under the rubric of discipleship. We began on the Third Sunday after Pentecost with the call to table fellowship and learning about God's desire for mercy. We then heard Jesus teaching the disciples about both the joys and burdens of following in his footsteps. We learned with the disciples that such following comes at a cost. Throughout these chapters, Jesus has spoken both to the particular disciples before him, the twelve, and to those disciples who will come after. Now at the end of chap. 10, Jesus sends the disciples out and, through his speech to them, he speaks more directly to those to whom the disciples go. Each new layer of followers is a new group called into discipleship. To all the new communities to whom these twelve go, Jesus says, "Welcome them, practice hospitality." Jesus says through the disciples directly to us, "Your job is to receive with joy and openness the one who is bringing you the saving word. You are to make your home their home, and your community their community. And part of the trick is that you can never really know who that one may be." We are reminded of the encounter of Abraham and Sarah with the two angel strangers.

Jesus enjoins this hospitality with a series of four proverbial statements. First, he says, "Whoever welcomes you welcomes me . . . and the one who sent me." We are thrown rather directly to Jesus' final parable in Matt. 25:31-46 about the master being hidden in the naked, hungry, imprisoned, and thirsty stranger. The righteous who care for and welcome the stranger have eternal life while those on the left who offer no such welcome depart into eternal fire—certainly a no-nonsense distinction! Second, "Whoever welcomes a prophet . . . will receive a prophet's reward." We have seen two examples in Jeremiah and Kings of just what such a reward can look like. Third, "Whoever welcomes a righteous person . . . will receive the reward of the righteous." Righteousness is an all-important idea in Matthew. The word "righteous" or "righteousness" occurs twenty-two times in this Gospel. Significantly, the first occurrence is the identification of Joseph as a righteous man precisely because he does not expose Mary to public disgrace because of her pregnancy and thus he welcomes Jesus as his own son. The reward of the righteous is also clear; as seen in chap. 25 and as we shall see in 13:43, "they will shine like the sun." Finally Jesus adds, "Whoever gives even a cup of cold water to one of these little ones in the name of a disciple—truly I tell you, none of these will lose their reward." "The little ones" here most certainly at some level refer to any followers of Jesus, but only insofar as the followers themselves become like little children. In Matt. 18:1-6 Jesus urges his disciples to become like the child before him saying, "Whoever welcomes one such child in my name welcomes me." The circle of discipleship and welcome is ever expanding. The ultimate reward for such hospitality is being enfolded into the ever-loving arms of Jesus.

One of the striking features of this last proverb is the lovely expression "even a cold cup of water" (see Prov. 11:25; 25:21, 25). Water, as we will explore a bit the week after next, is such an important notion in scripture. Water can deal death or give life. Clearly here water is life-giving. So also, of course, the "cup" carries with it the symbolism of inclusion and welcome. In Matt. 20:22 Jesus asks, "Are you able to drink the cup that I am about to drink?" We may not desire the inclusion that such a cup offers. But then again in 26:27-28, "He took a cup, and after giving thanks he gave it to them, saying, 'Drink from it, all of you; for this is my blood of the covenant, which is poured out for many for the forgiveness of sins.'" The cup of water or wine or tea or coffee is the ultimate sign of hospitality. Two stories serve to illustrate the effects of such hospitality. One took place in Tanzania, where my family and I visited several churches some years ago. This one Sunday we had walked several hours to a Massai church and had taken part in a wonderful three-hour service with sermons, baptisms, and confirmation. Our son Benjamin, then nine years old, was not so enamored. He had been patient, but when we were invited to the village for a bit of "chai," a cup of tea, he was distraught. He needed a touch of the familiar; hospitality that met him where he was. We arrived, sat among the guests, washed our hands, and out of the hut came a woman carrying a case of Tanzanian cola. Benjamin's eyes lit up; he was welcomed and revived, embraced by the familiar within the unfamiliar and able to rejoice in the dancing and friendship that followed. Just so is the gift of hospitality experienced by the receiver.

> "ARE YOU ABLE TO DRINK THE CUP THAT I AM ABOUT TO DRINK?" WE MAY NOT DESIRE THE INCLUSION THAT SUCH A CUP OFFERS.

But if the recipient of hospitality is blessed, even more is the giver. This is splendidly illustrated by the movie *Shadowlands*, a semi-fictionalized account of C. S. Lewis's meeting and eventually marrying the American divorcee Joy Gresham. The movie is very much about discipleship as hospitality. In the movie, Lewis moves from being a safely circumspect, closed-off "religious" man, molded by routine and his own certainty about religious truths. He was certain that ideas were every bit as good as experience and the life he knew with friends and events he could control and predict was life as it should be lived. Gradually he takes the risk of being hospitable to this somewhat eccentric American woman and her son. He moves from offering a cup of tea in a hotel, to a pot of tea and conversation in his home, to an invitation to Christmas dinner and week's lodging, and eventually to an agreement to offer citizenship through a surface marriage. With each new offering of hospitality, Lewis himself is transformed. Eventually he finds love that he had never known from his books and bounded life. What makes this story of hospitality considerably more than an overdrawn romance is that as Lewis discovers his love for Joy, they also discover her terminal cancer (true in life as well as in the movie). The cost of such joy is great. This joy that comes from his hospitality matches the discipleship Jesus so fully describes in Matthew, for it comes at a cost. Opening up and welcoming the other who brings the message of joy comes with a cost of change from the familiar, the tried and seemingly true. It comes with the cost of life. When we offer hospitality, when we truly welcome the one who has come, what we have known is given up. But in losing one's life for the sake of encountered truth, one, in truth, finds one's life. In the words of Joy Gresham, "That's the deal."

SEVENTH SUNDAY AFTER PENTECOST

Fourteenth Sunday in Ordinary Time / Proper 9
July 7, 2002

Revised Common	Episcopal (BCP)	Roman Catholic
Zech. 9:9-12 or Gen. 24:34-38, 42-49, 58-67	Zech. 9:9-12	Zech. 9:9-10
Ps. 145:8-14 or Ps. 45:10-17 or Song of Sol. 2:8-13	Psalm 145 or 145:8-14	Ps. 145:1-2, 8-9, 10-11, 13-14
Rom. 7:15-25a	Rom. 7:21—8:6	Rom. 8:9, 11-13
Matt. 11:16-19, 25-30	Matt. 11:25-30	Matt. 11:25-30

The last several weeks' examination of discipleship has certainly not been easy, with its emphasis on the many costs and burdens. This week we add one final text to the Matthean picture, and this text offers a gift. The call to follow Jesus, the call to discipleship, now becomes the gracious invitation of the Lord of love to bring to him our weariness and our heavy burdens. We are invited to give them to Jesus and to accept the Savior's gift of rest. Rest is certainly a gift we need. In talking about our need for rest, Wayne Muller, whose marvelous book *Sabbath* has often fed my soul, observes that in his own work, whether he visits the very rich, the very poor, or the very middle class, the universal refrain of modern lives is "I am so busy." He notes that we wear our overwork and our exhaustion almost as a trophy and adds that "the Chinese pictograph for 'busy' is composed of two characters: 'Heart' and 'killing.'"[15] These observations strike a powerful chord. The harmonic response is found in this week's text, "Come to me . . . and I will give you rest."

DIANE
JACOBSON

FIRST READING

ZECHARIAH 9:9-12 (RCL, BCP);
ZECHARIAH 9:9-10 (RC)

Today's Old Testament lesson captures the mood of the good news of today's Gospel. The prophet Zechariah is not much read or quoted. In the final chapters of his book, written between 500 and 400 B.C.E., Zechariah speaks, among other matters, of the hoped-for triumphant return of Israel's king. The prophet calls on daughter Jerusalem to rejoice because her king is coming. The most striking feature of the king's triumphant entry is, of course, the announcement that he will come "humble and riding on a donkey, on a colt, the foal of a donkey." This points Christians directly to Jesus' triumphant entry on Palm Sunday but also to the Gospel of the day where Jesus speaks of being "gentle and humble in heart." The coming king will bring peace: in Zechariah this peace is rest from war; in Matthew it is the personal rest and peace of discipleship. Though one's eye is naturally drawn to the king's entry, another expression in this lesson is equally noteworthy. Zechariah speaks of the people who receive this good news as "pris-

> ZECHARIAH SPEAKS OF THE PEOPLE WHO RECEIVE THIS GOOD NEWS AS "PRISONERS OF HOPE."

oners of hope," a phrase whose descriptive power was first brought to my attention by pastor and theologian Paul Santmire. As disciples of Christ we are, most certainly, "prisoners of hope." We are captured by God's promise so that, no matter what the circumstances, we cannot let despair rule our hearts and minds. The force of this Zechariah text is itself beautifully captured by the third verse of Charles Coffin's hymn, "The Advent of Our God":

Come, Zion's daughter, rise to meet your lowly king,
Nor let your lowly heart despise the peace he comes to bring.

We cannot help but come; we are "prisoners of hope."

GENESIS 24:34-38, 42-49, 58-67 (RCL, alt.)

Our continuing reading of Genesis brings us to yet another story often overlooked. This time we learn of the betrothal of Isaac and Rebecca. Betrothal scenes in scripture tend to follow a particular pattern. A man travels a distance and stops by a well. He then sees a woman, often in distress, and draws water for her. She runs home and tells her family. They ask her why she has not brought the man home for hospitality. The man is invited, and the woman is offered as a bride. If you know the pattern, then you have tremendous fun watching the details that make each betrothal scene take on its own character. For example, in his scene, Jacob, the trickster, is tricked and is given the wrong sister as a bride. Moses, raised an Egyptian but now identified with his people, is mistaken for an Egyptian. Jesus, when he encounters the woman of the well, makes the disciples very nervous. He and she then speak of her marriages, and she runs and tells the village to come and see. In this present text, Isaac ironically does not even show up for his own betrothal scene, but is represented by his father's servant! Rebekah rules the action: she draws the water from the well and offers drink. She is asked, unusually, if she will go with the man. This scene is a preliminary indication of the important role Rebekah, who becomes Isaac's love and comfort in v. 67, will play. Tradition speaks of Abraham, Isaac, and Jacob as the principal ancestors who receive the promise. The full text of Genesis speaks more specifically of Abraham, Rebekah, and Jacob.

RESPONSIVE READING

PSALM 145:8-14 or PSALM 45:10-17 or SONG OF SOLOMON 2:8-13 (RCL); PSALM 145 or 145:8-14 (BCP); PSALM 145:1-2, 8-9, 10-11, 13-14 (RC)

Psalm 145 is a glorious hymn of praise containing one of the many proclamations of the LORD's essential character as "gracious and merciful, slow to anger and abounding in steadfast love." The picture of a bounteous God builds throughout the psalm inviting all flesh to praise God's holy name. Psalm 45 and the Song of Solomon were undoubtedly chosen to match the Genesis text. Reading the Song of Solomon affords an opportunity to hear Scripture give voice to the joys of human love and devotion—"Arise my love, my fair one, and come away. . . ."

SECOND LESSON

ROMANS 7:15-25a (RCL); ROMANS 7:21—8:6 (BCP); ROMANS 8:9, 11-13 (RC)

We come now to the second half of Romans 7. (Romans 8 will be discussed over the next two Sundays.) Paul speaks to us about his honest quandary, "I do not understand my own actions. For I do not do what I want, but I do the very thing I hate." Surely his quandary is also very much our own. He describes what Luther will later call "the bondage of the will," following Paul's statement in

7:18, "I can will what is right, but I cannot do it." We have all had experiences of doing things we know are wrong, experiences of pushing the envelope despite all those good lessons our parents gave us. Something compels us—what Judaism calls "the evil impulse"—to break rules, overindulge, hurt our neighbor. Paul speaks of this and of something more. Here is the trap we find ourselves in that explains why the law, though "spiritual" (v. 14), "holy" (v. 12), as well as "just and good" (v. 12), is also the means of death and sin. We cannot stop ourselves from being self-seeking, looking for the angle to God, the way into divine favor. We thus always do the very thing we hate. Even once we know what God wants through the law, we turn God's good desire into our own self-serving even when doing good. We cannot escape what Paul calls being in the flesh. Paul returns then to talk of being captive and enslaved to sin, the slavery we described last week. This trap compels him to issue a cry that reaches across the centuries and grabs us by the throat, "Wretched man that I am! Who will rescue me from this body of death?" His answer rings out as well, "Thanks be to God through Jesus Christ our Lord!" The trap is sprung by God alone.

WE CANNOT ESCAPE WHAT PAUL CALLS BEING IN THE FLESH.

THE GOSPEL

MATTHEW 11:16-19, 25-30 (RCL); MATTHEW 11:25-30 (BCP, RC)

We move this Sunday to a different section of Matthew in which the conflict between Jesus and the authorities, the conflict that points us to Jesus' ultimate trial and death, begins in earnest. The conflict here is prompted by a comparison between the two leading figures of the Gospel, Jesus and John the Baptist. Jesus has told the people (vv. 1-15) that John, now in prison, is indeed the prophet Elijah, the herald of the one to come (thus explaining the comparisons of Jesus to Elisha, Elijah's successor, as discussed last week). Our particular Gospel text begins with another comparison: the crowds are like children sitting in the marketplace, the type of children who taunt and jeer at strangers. "Look," they say, "we play upbeat joyous music, but you don't dance." I hold a picture in my mind of former Negro slaves after the Civil War being forced to dance in the streets of some embittered southern city. Then again they say, "We wail as at a funeral, but you do not mourn." The crowds are like these children in their taunting of John and Jesus. They cannot be satisfied with their behavior. Robert Smith notes that the people's dissatisfaction with John and Jesus parallels the jeers of the children: John will not dance, and Jesus will not mourn.[15] John insists on leading the aesthetic life (neither eating nor drinking) and calling for repentance, so the people declare him possessed of a demon. Jesus, the Son of Man, feasts in inappropriate ways with inappropriate people (tax collectors and sinners), so the people declare him a drunk and glutton. The response to this jeering is stunning: "Wisdom [in Greek, *sophia*] is vindicated by her deeds."

In comments on the Gospel for the Third Sunday after Pentecost I addressed Matthew's tendency to compare Jesus and the Old Testament figure of Wisdom. In that text Matthew also evoked the comparison when speaking of Jesus eating with sinners. Interestingly the parallel passage in Luke 7:35 reads, "Yet is wisdom vindicated by all her children." Luke then moves immediately into a banqueting scene, where the true guest and host and child of wisdom is the outcast woman with the alabaster jar of ointment. In Matthew, chap. 11 is the center of the comparison between Jesus and Wisdom. This chapter first builds the rejection of John and Jesus on the Old Testament theme of the rejection of the prophets, significant throughout the Gospel. Yet something more than prophetic rejection is here. Rejection of Wisdom is also a common theme in the wisdom material. In Prov. 8:35-36, Wisdom says, "whoever finds me finds life and obtains favor from the LORD; but those who miss me injure themselves; all who hate me love death." Rejection of wisdom leads to death. In Matthew 11, directly after Jesus says "wisdom is vindicated by her deeds," he issues a series of woe oracles (vv. 20-24, not included in the lectionary readings). These speak to Jesus' "deeds of power" and the resulting judgment and death for those who reject these deeds. Our lectionary reading proceeds straightaway to the words of Jesus directed to his followers.

Jesus prays a stern prayer and issues a glorious invitation. He thanks God, his Father, for hiding truth from the wise and revealing truth through him to those whom the Son chooses. He invites the weary to come and take on his easy yoke. The details of both the prayer and invitation call for much reflection. Once again comparisons to Wisdom are very much present. In much of the wisdom tradition, only God, maker of heaven and earth, knows the way of wisdom, because wisdom is God's child with whom the world was created (Prov. 8:22-31). As is said in Job 28:13 and elsewhere, "mortals do not know the way," though often the seemingly wise, like Job's friends, think that they know. People in Paul's day were frequently seeking and thinking they had found wisdom (cf. 1 Cor. 1:22). We ourselves often look for some magic key to understanding how the world works or how we can lead better, happier, more fulfilling lives. Jesus here thanks God for hiding such things from those who think they are wise. Only true Wisdom knows what has been hidden. The key, says Jesus, is through me; "no one knows the Father except the Son and anyone to whom the Son chooses to reveal him." Finally, wisdom is not a collection of information but rather comes from having a relationship with God, through Christ. Jesus is the way of revelation, the path of wisdom, the opening up of the truth, truth that is hidden to those who know all of the rules. True wisdom is revealed only to those who come without prior wisdom, to "infants," to the "little ones" discussed last week. These come eagerly to Jesus and are able to hear the invitation. Jesus speaks of this relationship as a yoke to be taken. So also Wisdom in Sirach says, "Draw near to me, you who are uneducated, and lodge in the house of instruction. . . . Put your neck under her yoke, and let your souls receive instruction. See with your eyes that I have labored but little and found myself much rest" (vv. 23-27, NRSV, RSV). Or in Sir. 6:24-31 we are instructed to "put your feet into her fetters, and your neck into her collar. . . . Come to her with all your soul, for at last you will find the rest she gives, and she will be changed into joy for you." The rabbis of Jesus' day spoke of following the law as taking on the yoke.

The effect of these comparisons is dramatic. In Matthew, Jesus both builds on and challenges the tradition. He says to us, "Wisdom has come to you, now come to me and take on my yoke." The yoke is not the law, and wisdom does not consist of either following a list of instructions or achieving a certain level of knowledge or cleverness. All talk of wisdom is as nothing if we do not understand who Jesus is, how Jesus comes to us, and what Jesus offers. Jesus is the One whose coming John has announced. He is the Son of Man, the king triumphant, and God's true Wisdom. Jesus comes to us "gentle and humble in heart." After all the woes and the strong words, we are brought up short, brought back to the text from Zechariah that shows our Messiah to be the opposite of what is expected. Once we accept this relationship, stop fighting so hard with all that we know, the Christ we see before us comes gently. And he offers us rest. Not surface rest, but deep rest for our souls. Once we stop knowing all things and judging all things, we can simply stop. Jesus offers us the ultimate Sabbath rest. As is made clear in the stories that follow in chap. 12, "the Son of Man is lord of the Sabbath" (v. 8).

> IN MATTHEW, JESUS BOTH BUILDS ON AND CHALLENGES THE TRADITION. HE SAYS TO US, "WISDOM HAS COME TO YOU, NOW COME TO ME AND TAKE ON MY YOKE."

I began this week's textual reflections by quoting from Wayne Muller. His thoughts are again helpful. He notes that "sabbath requires surrender." During Sabbath we are invited to know that "the deep wisdom embedded in creation will take care of things for a while."[16] This is like the invitation that Jesus offers. We are to lay down our heavy burdens and let Jesus take them up. This particular invitation to discipleship is pure gift. We learn from true Wisdom that his yoke will not be a burden. All the trials of discipleship, though costly, are ultimately easy because they come from our relationship with God through Christ. We have a prayer in our tradition that gathers together the insights of Matthew 11, transforming Christ's invitation to us into our invitation to Christ. This prayer is the first of the antiphons from the fourth century, sung in the third week of Advent. We most often sing these antiphons through the hymn "O Come, O Come Emmanuel," though frequently this particular verse is not listed.[18] The prayer is as follows:

> O Wisdom, who proceeds from the mouth of the Most High,
> reaching out mightily from end to end,
> and sweetly arranging all things:
> come to teach us the way of peace.

Come, thou Wisdom of God, and bid us come that we might learn from you and find rest for our weary souls.

EIGHTH SUNDAY AFTER PENTECOST

FIFTEENTH SUNDAY IN ORDINARY TIME / PROPER 10
JULY 14, 2002

REVISED COMMON	EPISCOPAL (BCP)	ROMAN CATHOLIC
Isa. 55:10-13 or	Isa. 55:1-5, 10-13	Isa. 55:10-11
Gen. 25:19-34		
Ps. 65:(1-8), 9-13 or	Psalm 65 or 65:9-14	Ps. 65:10, 11, 12-13, 14
Ps. 119:105-112		
Rom. 8:1-11	Rom. 8:9-17	Rom. 8:18-23
Matt. 13:1-9, 18-23	Matt. 13:1-9, 18-23	Matt. 13:1-23 (13:1-9)

In France, July 14 is celebrated as Bastille Day, a day that marks the storming of the royal prison on July 14, 1789, ending centuries of oppression. Bastille Day is a day of liberation. In the church on this day we read texts that celebrate another sort of liberation, the liberation that comes from the word of the Lord. The Lord speaks, and we respond. We either fail to hear and thus we wither and die, or else we hear with our ears, see with our eyes, understand with our hearts and minds, and thereby prosper and grow. This hearing of the word is the work of God in us, captured in these texts by the metaphor of well-watered earth and sown seeds. We are drawn to the wonder of seeds. Seeds by themselves may look small and unimpressive, but given the right conditions—water, sun, proper soil, proper care—they grow, prosper, and provide nourishment. So it is with God's word. Given the right care and reception, the word goes forth and liberates and nourishes not just us but all the world.

FIRST READING

ISAIAH 55:10-13 (RCL);
ISAIAH 55:1-5, 10-13 (BCP);
ISAIAH 55:10-11 (RC)

The Episcopal lectionary begins today's reading from Isaiah 55 with vv. 1-5, showing the chapter to begin with our thirst, our hunger, and our need. Isaiah meets us where we are with the invitation, "Come." "Come to the waters";

come and buy; come and eat. We hear echoes of the invitation from last week's Gospel, "Come . . . , you that are weary . . . , and I will give you rest." We again hear echoes of wisdom's invitation (Prov. 9:5, Sir. 24:19-21) and the invitation of Jesus in John 7:37, "Let anyone who is thirsty come to me" (cf. John 4:13-14). Isaiah here invites us to come and to listen to the promise of an everlasting covenant. This promise is not casual or idle; indeed the source of the promise is God's sure and certain word. The text then moves from our need for metaphorical food and drink to the on-going power of God's promised and living word, described in splendid detail. Isaiah speaks of this word with a prime metaphor. Word comes from God like the waters of heaven. As I discussed briefly two weeks ago, water in scripture powerfully symbolizes both life and death. One need think only of the waters as controlled chaos in Genesis 1 and compare these waters to the stream in the midst of the garden in Genesis 2. Rain and snow from heaven can wreak havoc, expressing God's judgment (Ps. 78:47; Job 37:6ff.). Or, as here, the water from heaven comes to earth and effects growth; earth brings forth, seeds sprout, and ultimately the people are fed. God's Word, like this rain and snow, goes forth and accomplishes the very intentions of God. The effect can only be captured in poetry: "You shall go out in joy, and be led back in peace; the mountains and the hills before you shall burst into song, and all the trees of the field shall clap their hands. Instead of the thorn shall come up the cypress; instead of the brier shall come up the myrtle." The language carries us away and itself becomes the Word of God doing its work on us. We sing it; we celebrate; we are caught up in the promise and expectation just as surely today as were the exiles in the days of Isaiah. Isaiah speaks of the word as being both a memorial, pointing us to what God has already done in the past, and an everlasting sign that takes us from the present into the future. For all time God's word has this effect so that we too must join in this very song of Isaiah and make it our own.

> ISAIAH SPEAKS OF THE WORD AS BEING BOTH A MEMORIAL, POINTING US TO WHAT GOD HAS ALREADY DONE IN THE PAST, AND AS AN EVERLASTING SIGN THAT TAKES US FROM THE PRESENT INTO THE FUTURE.

GENESIS 25:19-34 (RCL, alt.)

The Genesis reading continues the story of Rebekah and Isaac. I spoke last week of the middle cycle of the stories of the ancestors centering more on Rebekah than Isaac. This pericope is certainly illustrative. Like so many of the matriarchs, Rebekah is at first barren and then she conceives. Such stories help us to recognize that ultimately, despite our modern "misconceptions," we are not in control of family planning. Our children are not really ours; they are a gift from God. What is most striking in this text is the Lord's response to Rebekah's pain in childbirth. Just as God did with Abraham and will do with Jacob, God bestows on Rebekah the promise of nations. For Rebekah, this promise of progeny is not so direct. The promise is delivered within an oracle announcing future struggle. Childbirth is an apt metaphor for how the promise will be delivered: "Two nations are in your womb, and two peoples born of you will be divided." The prediction of struggle certainly does not feel like promise. But, in truth, struggle is often the crucible of promise for us as well as for those ancient patriarchs and matriarchs. Promise is often hidden in the strife, precisely where so many of us actually live. Moreover, the promise is hidden as well in reversal. Rebekah is told that the younger shall not serve the elder, soon to be identified as the father's favorite. Rather the younger one—the fighter, the scraper, the trickster, the mother's chosen—becomes the reigning child of the promise. Here is not the world as we would have it, ordered and fair. Here is the world as God will have it; preference is for the un-entitled. This less than noble younger son, who buys his birthright for a mere serving of bread and lentil stew, shows us how God's promise works. Through the messiness of family strife, greed, hunger, and tricks, God will effect salvation. These very messy people make up the world that God so loves. Such grace is a constant source of wonder.

RESPONSIVE READING

PSALM 65:(1-8), 9-13
  or PSALM 119:105-112 (RCL);
PSALM 65: or 65:9-14 (BCP);
PSALM 65:10, 11, 12-13, 14 (RC)

Psalm 65 is a perfect psalm to reflect both the Isaiah and Gospel texts. We join the psalmist as well as the meadows and valleys themselves in joyously praising God for both watering the earth and providing bountiful harvests. Psalm 119, a love song to Torah, matches the other texts as well by centering on the word of the Lord as "a lamp to my feet and a light to my path."

SECOND READING

ROMANS 8:1-11 (RCL);
ROMANS 8:9-17 (BCP);
ROMANS 8:18-23 (RC)

We come now to Romans 8, which chapter will be taken up for the next two weeks with different readings in different lectionaries. Paul continues with his deep contrast between one life—a life that is truly death, under the law, in the flesh, without Christ—and the other life "for those who are in Christ Jesus," those without condemnation. The contrast in chap. 8 centers around being "in the flesh," and being "in the Spirit" (v. 9). Here begins what might be identified as Paul's Pentecostal sermon. Of the thirty-four times that Spirit (Greek, *pneuma*) is mentioned in Romans, twenty-one are in chap. 8. The Spirit gives freedom, freedom from "the law of sin"; freedom from death. And, most significantly for Paul, this freeing Spirit is always the Spirit of Christ. The freedom of the Spirit is the work of God in Christ Jesus who "has set you free" by sending his very own Son. This life in the Spirit makes possible "life and peace." The life of the Spirit is our resur-

> THE LIFE OF THE SPIRIT IS OUR RESURRECTED LIFE, THE LIFE THAT COMES FROM THE DEFEAT OF DEATH.

rected life, the life that comes from the defeat of death. God raised Christ from the dead. This very Spirit of the resurrected Christ dwells in us so we too, because the Spirit of Christ dwells in us, are alive. This is the ultimate gift of the Spirit— life, and life abundant. We are given a vision of life, more than this, we are given actual life not weighed down but truly free.

THE GOSPEL
MATTHEW 13:1-9, 18-23 (RCL, BCP); MATTHEW 13:1-23 (13:1-9) (RC)

This week and next we hear Jesus tell a series of seven parables, beginning with the parable of the seeds, which is actually a parable about the word. The message of the parable begins even before a word is spoken. Great crowds gather around Jesus, and so he climbs in a boat and speaks from the midst of the sea. We are back to the waters, as in Isaiah, but now in the form of a sea, and the sea always holds within it the threat of chaos and death. Both earlier and later in Matthew, Jesus tames the chaotic sea by stilling the storm and walking on the water (8:23-27; 14:22-33). His taming of the chaos is no less apparent here in his chosen place of speaking. He teaches from the midst of the sea, showing in this action also his ability to transform the sea into life-giving water. He tells the familiar parable in which four groups of seeds "fall" on four different sorts of ground. For a parable that Jesus will call "the parable of the sower," the one who sows certainly has little role. These seeds appear to fall rather randomly where they will. Three groups fall on ground that cannot promote or sustain growth. But one group falls on good soil and produces a variety of bountiful harvests. So many aspects of this parable are striking: how it is told, to whom it is told, how it is interpreted, and how it is heard.

The story is told, of course, as a parable. In v. 10, the disciples ask the question we so often want to ask. "Why do you speak to them [to us] in parables?" One might assume that Jesus speaks in parables to obscure the truth, to keep it hidden. Such an assumption views truth as clear and straightforward where parables are obscure and complicated. Mark may well look at parables in this way. But in Matthew Jesus responds differently. He tells the disciples that they have been given the privilege of understanding, and he then quotes extensively from the prophet Isaiah about those who hear the word but do not understand. But, as with the great prophet himself, Jesus' pronouncement can be itself heard as a warning rather than as a judgment. Some hear the word and understand; some hear the word and continue in ignorance, though Jesus bids them turn that he might heal them. To which group then will you, will we belong? As Arland Hultgren says, "Jesus speaks in parables *because* the people do not see, hear, or understand. The parables are media of revelation (cf. 13:34–35), not of concealment."[19] Thus Jesus ends the telling of the parable with the words, "Let anyone with ears listen!"

So Jesus speaks in parables to clarify the truth. This view of Matthew coincides with my own experience of reading parables. Certainly, the most direct answer to the question of why Jesus speaks in parables is not found inside the text but rather comes from our own experience and the experience of the church past and present of hearing these parables. We find that teaching through such stories invites us in. We bring our own logic, our own life experience, our own

WE BRING OUR OWN LOGIC, OUR OWN LIFE EXPERIENCE, OUR OWN HUMAN AND WORK RELATIONSHIPS TO THE HEARING OF THE PARABLES.

human and work relationships to the hearing of the parables. Stories such as these are true to life with all its complexity and subtlety. Their truth, like life's truth, is not so much propositional as narrative in quality. Thus we so often remember the stories from sermons. I am, in fact, reminded of a story of a former student. He tells of his first experience preaching from this very text. He was on internship in a rural community, and this was the occasion of his very first sermon. He studied long and hard, translating the text from Greek and reading many commentaries. He shared all he had learned with the parishioners, speaking of the multiple meanings of the crucial vocabulary and waxing eloquent about the nature of seeds and soil. He pounded on the pulpit and spoke of the cares of the world and the word bearing fruit. After the sermon, people exited the church with their obligatory handshake and "Nice sermon, Pastor"—until one weather-worn farmer paused and said, "Son, it's a lot simpler than that. Come on down to the fields sometime, and we will teach you something about planting." Stories invite us in. So perhaps the answer to why Jesus speaks in parables is this: parables continue Christ's invitation to discipleship, inviting us to come and to hear and to understand.

To whom then is the parable told? It is told both to those with ears to hear and to those who fail to understand. The audience is, in fact, described in the midst of the interpretation of the parable. For though the parable is ostensibly about the sower, it is very much about how we hear and receive the word of the kingdom spoken to us. The word remains constant, but we who hear the word find ourselves in different circumstances. So it is that the same word is both law and gospel. The word is heard as law to those of us who do not understand, who fail to respond with our hearts and therefore fail to act in accordance with the word. The word is law to those of us distracted by trouble or beset by cares or lured by wealth in such a way that we cannot allow God's word to speak to those troubles, cares, and temptations. As law, this parable itself is heard as warning, even as condemnation. But to those who are given the grace to hear the word with understanding, the gospel comes to us as both encouragement and blessing. We are blessed ourselves with the feeding of our own souls. And we are encouraged with the promise that this blessing will multiply beyond us in the growth of the reign of God.

How then do we hear this parable? I suspect we all hear to a degree both with the ears that do not understand and with ears that God has opened with grace. We cannot help but consider the times we ourselves have been blocked from hearing any word of good news. At times the block seems to come from outside of ourselves, from the "evil one" snatching away what has been sown in our hearts. At times the block seems willful, stemming from our own stubbornness or hurt or sin. But by God's grace, such reactions do not have the last word. We mostly hear this parable as a word of promise that God's word of Christ once planted in our hearts will with proper tending, grow, prosper, and spread.

A favorite poem by e.e. cummings comes to mind that brings together the texts of the day. It captures the joy of Isaiah's promise, with the trees clapping their hands. It captures Paul's Spirit of God dwelling in us and giving us life. This poem, whose first lines are "i thank You God for most this amazing / day" also captures our needful response of thanksgiving. It speaks of "the leaping greenly spirits of trees" and "(i who have died am alive again today . . .)." The poem ends with a lovely and moving coda, "(now the ears of my ears awake and / now the eyes of my eyes are opened)."[20]

NINTH SUNDAY AFTER PENTECOST

SIXTEENTH SUNDAY IN ORDINARY TIME / PROPER 11
JULY 21, 2002

REVISED COMMON	EPISCOPAL (BCP)	ROMAN CATHOLIC
Gen. 28:10-19a or Isa. 44:6-8 or Wisd. of Sol. 12:13, 16-19	Wisd. of Sol. 12:13, 16-19	Wisd. of Sol. 12:13, 16-19
Ps. 139:1-12, 23-24 or Ps. 86:11-17	Psalm 86 or 86:11-17	Ps. 86:5-6, 9-10, 15, 16
Rom. 8:12-25	Rom. 8:18-25	Rom. 8:26-27
Matt. 13:24-30, 36-43	Matt. 13:24-30, 36-43	Matt. 13:24-43 (13:24-30)

"For the Lord our God shall come and shall take his harvest home." We continue this week to dwell in the harvest, but, unlike last week's Gospel, the undercurrent of this week's parable of the harvest is the final judgment. That the harvest would represent both judgment and plenty should come as no surprise. Certainly the idea of harvest suggests the completion of a season of hard work, barns full to overflowing with the fruits of our labor. One thinks of Ps. 126:6, "Those who go out weeping, bearing the seed for sowing, shall come home with shouts of joy, carrying their sheaves." And the hymn quoted to open this day's reflections is a favored hymn for Thanksgiving. But harvest is also a common scriptural image of final judgment, often for judging the nations and redeeming the chosen (see Isa. 27:12; Hos. 6:11; Joel 3:13; Rev. 14:15). The two ways this image is seen reflects the two pulls of today's Gospel. The sure and certain judgment of God will come, a frightening prospect indeed. But we also put our trust in God's promised future, trusting in God's power, justice, and forgiveness.

FIRST READING

WISDOM OF SOLOMON 12:13, 16-19 (RCL alt., BCP, RC)

The First Reading common to the three lectionaries is from the Wisdom of Solomon, a book of the Apocrypha not often read in Protestant churches.

This book was written in Greek by a thoroughly Hellenized Jew somewhere between 200 B.C.E. to 50 C.E. in the city of Alexandria. The author, as if writing from Solomon himself, is calling on the Jews in Egypt and beyond to keep the faith and rest secure in the sure knowledge that their God is truly wise and worthy of worship. The particular text for this Sunday, a section from an excursus on divine justice and mercy, speaks to why the God of Israel outshines all other gods. Ostensibly the text addresses the gods of the ancient Egyptians and Canaanites, but most certainly the text is speaking of Roman gods and continues to speak loudly of the current gods of our own making. Why then worship the Lord, the God of Israel? Because no other God exists who cares equally for all people, not just the chosen. The Lord rules with both justice and mercy. Certainly the Lord rules with power that will brook no nonsense but also—and here is the central and astonishing claim—the Lord rules with kindness and forbearance. This fills all God's children, which is to say all people, with hope. The reason for such hope is clear; the Lord makes room for repentance of sins. Clearly any old god will not do. Why worship the Lord, the God of Israel? Certainly not because of God's raw power, but rather because forgiveness is at the heart of God. This central character of God is important to remember always and is important particularly as a context for the reading from Matthew.

ISAIAH 44:6-8 (RCL, alt.)

The text from Isaiah also asks us to compare God to other gods. Isaiah's claim is total. Other gods simply do not exist. The Lord God of Israel is both the first and the last. Historically such a claim is stunning. After all, the people were in captivity in Babylon. All evidence pointed not only to the existence of other gods but actually to their superiority. The exiles were surrounded by evidence of the power of other gods; Marduk, the god of Babylon, appeared to have been victorious over the God of Israel. But Isaiah would have none of it. All evidence to the contrary, faith teaches us more truly than apparent logic. Isaiah's lesson is worth considering today. What seems to have power is position, wealth, and might. But faith speaks to us of power in weakness, and Isaiah's claim still stands.

GENESIS 28:10-19a (RCL)

This Genesis text is more familiar than some we have seen this season. Jacob is traveling, both fleeing his brother's wrath and seeking a suitable wife. Traveling out of normal space and time frequently denotes danger. So it is with Jacob. He stops at an unknown mysterious place, at a precarious time as the sun had set. Danger lurks. One might speak of the narrative taking place at a liminal time in a liminal space. Here Jacob dreams of God, just as on the way back from his sojourn he will wrestle with God. Jacob lies down and dreams of a ladder or staircase connecting heaven and earth with angels going up and down. And there was the Lord in the midst of them, delivering the promise. The promise to Jacob is very specific—land and progeny. The promised land is tied to this place of the dream, a place that carries sacral weight. The promised progeny are not just for his own blessing, but, repeating the promise to Abraham, they will be a source of blessing for all the families of the earth. But more than this, the promise to Jacob is also personal. The Lord says, "Know that I am with you and will keep you . . . and will bring you back . . . , for I will not leave you until I have done what I have promised you." Thus the promise of God to Jacob is both cosmic in scope and personal in depth, setting the standard for all the promises of God. If we lose either dimension of the promise, we fail to understand its full dynamic. If we lose the personal, then the promise never speaks to our own particular hopes and fears. If we lose the cosmic, we run the risk of centering too particularly on ourselves and thereby losing sight of God's relationship to the community and the world. So often in our theology, we fall off one edge or the other. Jacob seems to understand the promise in all its breadth and depth. He understands that he personally has been in the presence of God. He also understand the sacredness of the space that reaches beyond him and into God's promised future. So Jacob marks the place with a stone and a name—Bethel, house of God.

> THE PROMISE OF GOD TO JACOB IS BOTH COSMIC IN SCOPE AND PERSONAL IN DEPTH, SETTING THE STANDARD FOR ALL THE PROMISES OF GOD.

RESPONSIVE READING

PSALM 139:1-12, 23-24 (RCL); PSALM 86:11-17 (RCL alt., BCP); PSALM 86:5-6, 9-10, 15, 16 (RC)

Psalm 86 is a lament coming from deep within a person in need. As was true of the author of the Wisdom of Solomon, this psalmist knows the character of God. Once again we hear a psalm that speaks of God as merciful, gracious, slow to anger, and abounding in love. (See Psalm 145, Seventh Sunday after Pentecost.) Psalm 139 is one of the great and memorable songs of the Psalter, with aspects of both hymn and lament. "O LORD, you have searched me and known me." You know everything about me. Your Spirit is always there. You formed me from the beginning and know me yet today. Strikingly, as with the Gospel, this divine knowing can be the source of either great comfort or great terror. And therein lie the anguish, consolation, and strength of the psalm.

ROMANS 8:12-25 (rcl);
ROMANS 8:18-25 (bcp);
ROMANS 8:26-27 (rc)

In today's epistle, Paul continues with his pentecostal sermon, speaking of life in the Spirit and the gifts that are ours—and the life that is ours. Paul picks up and moves beyond his earlier contrast between being a slave to flesh and a slave to Christ. He says we are more than slaves; we are in fact children of God, heirs of the kingdom. Here is yet another gift of the Spirit, adoption. The power of this gift is palpable. Consider the social system of Rome and the great contrast within both the household and the public square, between a slave and an heir. Where slaves give life; heirs receive life, all that belongs to the father. Christians as heirs are part of an intimate relationship. So, like Christ, heirs call God "Abba, Father." And as heirs, we inherit everything—the good with the bad, suffering with glory. With this insight Paul then invites us into a picture of the universe, of the effect of God in Christ not just on humanity but on all of creation. He speaks movingly of creation waiting "with eager longing." One is reminded of the many ways creation is viewed in the Old Testament—able to witness for or against humanity, able both to lament and to praise. Now Paul tells the story of creation: Creation is subject to humans (Genesis 1; Psalm 8). So when humans are slaves to sin, then creation, "not of its own will" but because of the bound will of humanity, is itself "subjected to futility, . . . in bondage to decay." But still creation has had hope; creation has longed for humanity's release from captivity so that creation itself might be free. In fact, says Paul, we are very much like creation in our longing, in our groaning, in our waiting in hope. We wait for adoption; we wait for redemption. We, like creation itself, hope. And, says Paul, "in hope we are saved." We are thrown back to the image of Zechariah; we are "prisoners of hope." Hope is the defining reality of Christians. We

> HOPE TAKES US BEYOND OUR FLESH, BEYOND OUR SIN, BEYOND OUR WEAKNESS, INDEED BEYOND OURSELVES INTO THE SPIRIT OF GOD.

don't hope for what we see or know but rather for what we are promised in Christ. Hope takes us beyond our flesh, beyond our sin, beyond our weakness, indeed beyond ourselves into the Spirit of God. And says Paul, "that very Spirit intercedes with sighs too deep for words."

These insights of Paul, which will continue throughout chap. 8, are strikingly captured by the verse about the Spirit in Charles Wesley's beautiful Trinitarian hymn, "Love Divine, All Loves Excelling":

Breathe, oh, breathe thy loving Spirit into every troubled breast;
Let us all in thee inherit; let us find thy promised rest.
Take away the love of sinning, Alpha and Omega be;
End of faith, as its beginning, set our hearts at liberty.

THE GOSPEL

MATTHEW 13:24-30, 36-43 (RCL, BCP); MATTHEW 13:24-43 (13:24-30) (RC)

In today's Gospel, Jesus puts forward another parable about the sowing of the seeds and yet another detailed, indeed, allegorical interpretation, after some intervening verses. This parable, which we are to compare to the kingdom of heaven, is both straightforward and troubling. A sower sows good seeds in his field. But the field is sabotaged by an enemy who plants weeds among the good seeds so that the weeds and wheat grow up together. The slaves put the question to the sower, "What shall we do to these weeds?" He tells them to leave them alone, that at harvest time the reapers will collect the weeds and burn them and will put the wheat in the barn.

How we hear the parable depends a good deal on whom in the story we identify with. Most of us would identify not with the sower or the reapers but with the slaves. What should we do to save the growing wheat? We assume we should do something, that somehow we have a responsibility and a job to perform. The parable is fairly transparent to our own situations. We often find ourselves in circumstances when good seed is being choked. In our congregations, at work or home, in our various communities, we come across thorns in our sides who cause trouble for the whole community through gossip, greed, ill will, and all manner of sinful or self-serving behavior. We desperately want to weed out the problems so that the community might thrive. Of course, there is always this rub: it is not so easy to tell the good wheat from the weeds, the troublemakers from the good citizens.[21] I remember the first time my husband, the gardener in our family, told me to go pull weeds. Despite his fine instruction, I destroyed a good many potentially beautiful and fruitful plants that day. The metaphor is apt. But, if we have ears to hear, the good news of the parable is very good indeed. Judgment is God's, not ours. We need not worry about distinguishing the wheat from the weeds; weeding is not our job. God will do the judging and send the weeders when the time is ripe. We need only continue to do the work of helping the wheat to grow and leave the weeds to God.

I am reminded of a character from Barbara Kingsolver's novel, *The Poisonwood Bible*.[22] Mama Bekwa Tataba was paid a small stipend to watch over and serve the Price family at the Kilanga Mission. She did most of the useful work for the family, from carrying water to building fires to splitting wood to killing snakes. Mama Tataba stands by as the Reverend Price, the holier-than-thou Southern Baptist preacher identified as Father throughout the novel, vainly attempts to plant a Georgia garden in the jungles of the Congo. At first she tries to tell him that the garden will not grow, to teach him about the soil and the poisonwood tree and the way to lay out the garden. But he, himself the weed that looks to be wheat, will have none of it. He stubbornly continues his attempt to grow Kentucky Wonder beans and such. She, like we who are reading the book, needs only to watch and to wait for the sure and certain judgment to come.

The intervening verses between the parable and its interpretation introduce two short parables that also offer encouragement when things appear problematic. The kingdom of God is like a mustard seed; it looks small—but just wait. The seed will grow into a mighty tree that will provide sanctuary. The kingdom of God is like yeast mixed in flour; it seems inconsequential—but just wait. The yeast will cause the flour to grow and thereby provide food. And we are told that Jesus taught all things to the crowds in parables in order to fulfill what was spoken through the prophet, in this case Ps. 78:2, "I will open my mouth in a parable." The psalm continues: "I will utter dark sayings from of old," which leads us rather directly to the interpretation by Jesus of the parable of the weeds where our own reading of the parable is turned on its head.

Indeed the Sower is Christ himself, the Son of Man, now a title of apocalyptic splendor, and the field is the world, the cosmos. But past these first two elements, we have a problem. The very ones we so identified with on hearing the parable in the first place are not even mentioned in the interpretation. Indeed, Jesus skips altogether the slave's questioning and the master's accompanying caution to wait. We find no hint of confusion between the good seed and the weeds. The good seed are the children of the kingdom, and the weeds are the children of the devil. The interpretation goes straight to the harvest with God's angels as the reapers. Their job is clear: find the weeds and burn them. Throw them in Daniel's burning fiery furnace. There will be weeping and gnashing of teeth. No comfort here nor counsel to wait—only harsh warning that strikes fear in our hearts.[23] We find it hard to see past the terror to the promise of the last verse that "the righteous will shine like the sun in the kingdom of their Father." Who are we to claim membership among the righteous across the deep chasm of that fiery furnace?

Matthew is hard here. "Let anyone with ears listen!" If we don't hear the warning, we most certainly are not listening. Perhaps this parable will always come to us with a double message: judgment will come, but be patient and know that the judgment is in God's hands. The parable is very much like *The Poisonwood Bible*— we are waiting for the axe to fall, for disaster to come. But also we cannot help but wait in trust that good will prevail, that the righteous will shine no matter

DIANE
JACOBSON

where we are standing in the end. We are finally "prisoners of hope." So the whole of the Thanksgiving song quoted in part at the start of this Sunday's comments seems appropriate:

Come, ye thankful people, come,
Raise the song of harvest home;
All is safely gathered in,
Ere the winter storms begin;
God, our Maker, doth provide
For our wants to be supplied;
Come to God's own temple, come,
Raise the song of harvest home.

All the world is God's own field,
Fruit unto his praise to yield;
Wheat and tares together sown,
Unto joy or sorrow grown;
First the blade and then ear,
Then the full corn shall appear:
Lord of harvest, grant that we
Wholesome grain and pure may be.

For the Lord our God shall come
And shall take his harvest home.
From his field shall in that day
All offenses purge away.
Give his angels charge at last
In the fire his tares to cast;
But the fruitful ears to store
In his garner evermore.

Even so, Lord, quickly come
To your final harvest home.
Gather thou thy people in,
Free from sorrow, free from sin,
There, forever purified,
In thy garner to abide.
Come, with all thine angels, come,
Raise the glorious harvest home.[24]

NOTES

141

THE SEASON
OF PENTECOST

DIANE
JACOBSON

1. C. K Barrett, *Reading through Romans* (Philadelphia: Fortress Press, 1977), 15.

2. This title comes from Arland Hultgren, *The Parables of Jesus* (Grand Rapids: Eerdmans, 2000), 130.

3. *Lutheran Book of Worship* (Minneapolis: Augsburg, and Philadelphia: Board of Publication, 1978), 294

4. Robert H. Smith, *Matthew* (Augsburg Commentary; Minneapolis: Augsburg, 1989), 139.

5. See Celia M. Deutsch, *Lady Wisdom, Jesus, and the Sages: Metaphor and Social Context in Matthew's Gospel* (Philadelphia: Trinity Press International, 1996); Diane Jacobson, "Jesus as Wisdom in the New Testament," in *The Quest for Jesus and the Christian Faith*, ed. Fred Gaiser (St. Paul: Luther Seminary, 1997), 72–93; Marshall D. Johnson, "Reflections on a Wisdom Approach to Matthew's Christology," *Catholic Biblical Quarterly* 36 (1974), 44–64; Ben Witherington III, *Jesus the Sage: the Pilgrimage of Wisdom* (Minneapolis: Fortress Press, 1994).

6. The additional stanza for this traditional grace was written by Gail Ramshaw for an ELCA hunger pamphlet.

7. "Praise to the Lord, the Almighty," text by Joachim Neander, translated by Catherine Winkworth; *Lutheran Book of Worship*, 543.

8. William Holladay, *The Psalms through Three Thousand Years: Prayerbook of a Cloud of Witnesses* (Minneapolis: Fortress Press, 1993). See particularly the first and last chapters.

9. Dietrich Bonhoeffer, *The Cost of Discipleship*, trans. Reginald Fuller (New York: Macmillan, 1959).

10. Terence E. Fretheim, *The Suffering of God* (Overtures to Biblical Theology 14; Philadelphia: Fortress Press, 1984).

11. Ibid., 153.

12. Claus Westermann, *Praise and Lament in the Psalms* (Atlanta: John Knox, 1981).

13. *The Cost of Discipleship*, pp. 43–45, as quoted by Wayne Whitson Floyd in *The Wisdom and Witness of Dietrich Bonhoeffer* (Minneapolis: Fortress Press, 2000), 44.

14. Jon D. Levenson, *The Death and Resurrection of the Beloved Son: The Transformation of Child Sacrifice in Judaism and Christianity* (New Haven: Yale University Press, 1995).

15. Wayne Muller, *Sabbath: Restoring the Sacred Rhythm of Rest* (New York: Bantam, 1999), 2–3. The title of the paperback edition is *Sabbath: Finding Rest, Renewal, and Delight in Our Busy Lives*.

16. Smith, *Matthew*, 156.

17. Muller, *Sabbath*, 82, 83.

18.   O come, thou Wisdom from on high,
         Who orderest all things mightily;
         To us the path of knowledge show,
         And teach us in her ways to go.

19. Hultgren, *Parables*, 462.

20. e.e. cummings, "i thank You God for most this amazing," as quoted in *The Mentor Book of Major American Poets,* ed. O. Williams and E. Honig (New York: Mentor, 1962), 448

21. Hultgren, *Parables,* 294, 299. Hultgren's reading of both the parable and interpretation, pp. 292–303, is helpful throughout.

22. Barbara Kingsolver, *The Poisonwood Bible* (New York: HarperCollins, 1998).

23. Hultgren, *Parables*, 301.

24. *Service Book and Hymnal* (Minneapolis: Augsburg, 1958), 363, alt.

TENTH SUNDAY
AFTER PENTECOST

SEVENTEENTH SUNDAY IN ORDINARY TIME
PROPER 12
JULY 28, 2002

REVISED COMMON	EPISCOPAL (BCP)	ROMAN CATHOLIC
1 Kings 3:5-12 or Gen. 29:15-28	1 Kings 3:5-12	1 Kings 3:5, 7-12
Ps. 119:129-136 or Ps. 105:1-11, 45b or Psalm 128	Ps. 119:121-136 or 119:129-136	Ps. 119:57, 72, 76-77, 127-128, 129-130
Rom. 8:26-39	Rom. 8:26-34	Rom. 8:28-30
Matt. 13:31-33, 44-52	Matt. 13:31-33, 44-49a	Matt. 13:44-52 (13:44-46)

Today's readings provide an insight into the benefits of being in right relationship with God. Solomon, who loved the Lord and walked in God's ways and the statutes of his father, David, receives from God not only what he asks for but also many additional blessings as well (1 Kings 3:5-12). Jacob, the beloved son of Isaac and recipient of covenant promise, is blessed with two wonderful wives (Gen. 29:15-28). Even when one is uncertain about how to pray for what one needs, the Spirit is given as an intercessor (Rom. 8:26-27). Such love on the part of God attests to the unfolding reign of God in the here and now, so often spoken about in the Gospel of Matthew (Matt. 13:31-33, 44-52). Those who love God and walk in God's ways can expect all things to work together for good (Psalm 119; Rom. 8:28).

FIRST READING
1 KINGS 3:5 12 (RCL, BCP);
1 KINGS 3:5, 7-12 (RC)

Interpreting the Text

Dreams are common in the biblical tradition, and perhaps the most famous dream recorded in the Old Testament is Solomon's. It takes place at night at Gibeon, one of the most important high places, where Solomon often offered sacrifices. Gibeon was about seven miles northwest of Jerusalem. In the dream

God initiates a conversation with Solomon, inviting him to ask for what should be given to him (v. 5). The heart of the dream consists of Solomon's response (vv. 6-10).

In his response, Solomon first acknowledges God's goodness and the faithfulness and righteousness of his father David, which were part of the covenant fidelity and steadfast love shared between God and David (v. 6). Solomon next acknowledges his own divinely ordained place on the throne and a sense of his feeling of inadequacy (vv. 7-8). Such a feeling triggers his forthright request: Solomon asks God to give him wisdom—not for himself personally but for the sake of those under his governance (v. 9). God in turn acknowledges Solomon's humility and grants him his request while bolstering Solomon's self-confidence.

Responding to the Text

In ancient Israel one of the most beloved of all kings was David, a man who himself loved the Lord. His son, Solomon, followed in his father's footsteps and became known as the wisest of all Israel's kings. He was an astute political leader, excelling in foreign negotiations and economic expertise. During his reign Israel became a world-class nation. Solomon's major religious contribution to his own people was the building of the Temple, a site central to Jewish life still today. What was the source of such great wisdom? The story of Solomon's dream shows us that God was at the heart of and indeed the source of Solomon's great gift.

The content of Solomon's dream was different from that of most dreams that occur when napping during the day or sleeping at night. Solomon's dream is an experience of and an encounter with God in which both parties are actively engaged in conversation. Many of the great mystics of a later time help to shed light on this ever-ancient, ever-contemporary experience of God. For example, the fourteenth-century mystic Julian of Norwich often had such experiences of God, which she records as "showings." Such experiences are characteristic of what has become known as the mystical tradition.

Solomon's dream reveals to us the intimate relationship that the king had with God. Solomon's honesty with God is heartwarming; he is not afraid to become vulnerable, and he trusts enough in God to ask for what he needs. His primary concern is for the people of his kingdom. And God responds accordingly.

SOLOMON SERVES AS A MODEL AND A REMINDER THAT TRUE WISDOM, DISCERNMENT, AND UNDERSTANDING ARE GIFTS ATTAINED ONLY IN PART BY HUMAN EFFORTS.

Solomon's dream also reveals to us something about Israel's God. First, Israel's God participates in the events of daily life. Second, Israel's God is exceedingly generous and responsive. Third, Israel's God has a close relationship with the leadership of the day, and vice versa.

Today people of all nations struggle to identify leaders who have wisdom, insight, charisma, and political, social, economic, and national and international astuteness. Solomon serves as a model and a reminder that true wisdom, discernment, and understanding are gifts attained only in part by human efforts. Perhaps the key to wise and just leadership in the future rests in the development of one's spirituality and openness to the Divine, who waits to inspire and empower.

GENESIS 29:15-28 (RCL, alt.)

Interpreting the Text

Justice, trickery, and deception are the major themes of the Laban-Jacob narrative, which describes the fortune of Leah and Rachel, who became Jacob's wives. The story opens with Laban, Jacob's kinsman, offering to pay Jacob for his services even though Jacob is a relative (v. 15). A comment by the narrator reveals that Laban had two daughters, Leah the elder and Rachel the younger, whom Jacob loved (v. 18). It is agreed between the two men that after Jacob's service of seven years was completed, Laban would grant him Rachel's hand in marriage (vv. 19-20).

Upon the completion of the seven years, Jacob requests that Laban fulfill his part of the promise—which he does, but without recourse to Jacob's wish for Rachel. Instead, Laban tricks Jacob at night and offers him Leah, his firstborn, whom Jacob unknowingly takes as his wife only to discover in the morning that indeed he was deceived (vv. 21-25). Deception leads to confrontation on Jacob's part, which in turn leads to justice for all three: Leah, Rachel, and Jacob. Leah, Laban's firstborn, is given in marriage to Jacob before Rachel, but Rachel, whom Jacob loves, is also betrothed to Jacob after seven years of his additional service to Laban (vv. 25-28). Thus a father's shrewdness in the guise of trickery and deception leads to a just reward for his daughters and his kinsman.

Responding to the Text

Relationships within families, especially when certain standards are to be maintained, are never easy. The story of Jacob, Laban, Rachel, and Leah is one that involves social standards, negotiations, trickery, and marriage. Jacob and Laban make all the decisions; Rachel and Leah remain silent throughout the text.

Jacob, the son of Isaac and the future father of the twelve tribes of Israel, falls in love with Rachel, the younger of Laban's two daughters, and desires to take her as a wife. The problem is that Leah, the older daughter, is unmarried and according to custom should be the first to be given in marriage by her father. This dilemma causes Laban to resort to trickery and deception.

Heard in a contemporary setting and a social location that critiques women's experiences, this story bears all the marks of patriarchy and hierarchy. The males of the community make decisions without consulting the women; family traditions and social customs pit two women against each other with one being more favored by a courtier than the other, and trickery and deception become the only way to solve a dilemma of the heart. One wonders what Rachel and Leah's feelings would have been toward Jacob, toward their father, and toward each other if the writer of the text had included their perspectives and voices in the story.

On the surface, the text presents a picture of all issues eventually being resolved: both women will be cared for by a responsible and righteous husband, Laban's trickery and deception end up having positive results, and Jacob does receive the woman he really loves. On a deeper level, however, Laban's deceit highlights the problem that external and oftentimes rigid social standards can create especially when love and obligation come into play. The choice of the writer not to include the voices and feelings of the two women concerned reflects the culture of the day and would not be appropriate if the story were to be retold today.

RESPONSIVE READING

PSALM 119:129–136 (RCL, BCP); PSALM 119:129–136 (BCP, alt.); PSALM 119:57, 72, 76–77, 121–128, 129–130 (RC)

With awe and sincerity, the psalmist proclaims the greatness of God's law and word (vv. 57, 72, 76–77, 129–131), begs God for help and guidance (vv. 121–135), and expresses deep sadness over the failure to keep God's law (v. 136).

No words other than single-minded, single-hearted, righteous, and expectant can best describe this psalmist, whose life is so obviously committed to God and God's ways. In a reflective and intimate tone, the poet talks to God, and from that conversation one learns that God's law is delightful and liberating, God's steadfast love offers comfort, God's mercy sustains life, God's word enlightens, and God's power brings redemption from oppression. The person of the psalmist comes to life through the text of the psalm and reveals that in ancient Israel some people had a dynamic relationship with God, one that was deeply personal, candid, and honest.

PSALM 105:1-11, 45b (RCL, alt.)

A cultic hymn of the covenant community, Psalm 105 is a song of praise that calls the community to celebrate God and God's wonderful deeds.

The psalmist proclaims that Israel's God is a God of action whose many deeds call forth praise and thanksgiving from those among the community who marvel at such deeds, revel in them, and enjoy them. Israel's God remembers promises of old, keeps the promises, and remains faithful to covenant. The challenges that the psalmist sets before the congregation are for the people to seek God continually, to remember all the works that God has done, and to tell others about such wonderful deeds in song.

PSALM 128 (RCL, alt.)

Psalm 128 is comprised of three distinct literary units: a beatitude (v. 1), a series of blessings (vv. 2-4), and a benediction (vv. 5-6), all of which describe the good fortune that comes with loving God and walking in God's ways.

In this psalm one can see that the fruit of loving God and walking in God's ways is an abundance of blessings: prosperity, fertility, children, and a long life. This is quite a different view of family than the picture presented in the Jacob-Laban story. There is, however, a common thread that runs through these two texts. Like the Jacob-Laban story, this psalm text focuses on the good fortune either gained by or promised to the male heads of households. Israelite family structure was predominately patriarchal as we have already seen, and this paradigm is still operative today in some cultures but shifting or almost nonexistent in others.

SECOND READING
ROMANS 8:26-39 (RCL);
ROMANS 8:26-34 (BCP);
ROMANS 8:28-30 (RC)

Interpreting the Text

Three themes emerge in this segment of Paul's address to the Romans: (1) the role of the Spirit in one's life (vv. 26-27); (2) the destiny of those who love God (vv. 28-30); and (3) God's unsurpassable and faithful love made manifest through Christ Jesus (vv. 31-39).

Paul makes clear to his audience that the Spirit's role is to be one of assistance, particularly in helping one to pray. In this regard, the Spirit acts as an intercessor with sighs too deep for human words or comprehension. Paul's focus on the sighs of the Spirit becomes a foundation for understanding the content of genuine prayer. The notion of the Spirit as one who intercedes is unique to Paul's writings. Earlier Old Testament texts speak of human intercessors acting on others' behalf (see, e.g., Gen. 18:23-33; Exod. 8:8; 12, 28-30; Lev. 16:21-22; Num. 6:23-27; 2 Sam. 12:16; 1 Kings 18:22-40; Isa. 53:12). Moreover, the Spirit, as Paul indicates, has a special relationship with God who knows the mind of the Spirit. This sense of knowing implies an intimacy beyond human capabilities but one that does not exclude human life. The understanding of God as one who searches the heart is rooted in the theology of the Old Testament (see, e.g., 1 Sam. 16:7; 1 Kings 8:39; 1 Chron. 28:9; Pss. 7:11; 17:3; 139:1).

THE NOTION OF THE SPIRIT AS ONE WHO INTERCEDES IS UNIQUE TO PAUL'S WRITINGS.

With regard to divine providence and one's destiny, Paul is clear. With a tone of affirmation and certitude, Paul states that it is already known that all things work together for the good of those who love God, who are called according to God's purpose. Paul's reference to "all things" most likely includes sufferings, glory, the groaning of creation, and hope (see Rom. 8:17-27). One's love for God does not go unrewarded. God's ultimate plan for humanity is salvation and glorification (vv. 29-30).

Finally, Paul instructs his audience on the depths of God's love realized through Christ Jesus. With a series of rhetorical questions, a list of seven dangers, and an appeal to Ps. 44:23, Paul proclaims that God's love made manifest through Christ is a love for all eternity. This love is an unchangeable and unshakable gift given to humankind forever.

Responding to the Text

As seen in the psalms that are prayers and poems to God or about God, in ancient times God's people usually talked to God about everything,. Not all people were then or are now adept at conversation with God. Paul reminds everyone that the sighs of the Spirit are at the heart of all genuine prayer. This manner of praying requires that one simply be in the presence of God. Allowing the Spirit to intercede with sighs presumes that the one praying is in a posture of quiet and attuned to one's own depths wherein dwells the Spirit.

Paul's comment about all things working together for those who love God echoes the theme of Psalm 128. Paul associates the love of God with being called, predestined, justified, and glorified. In essence the love of God is linked to one's becoming transformed into Christ, an event that happens gradually and one that attests to the risen and glorified Christ. Are not these words of Paul at the heart of the Christian vocation for the entire Christian community everywhere?

MATTHEW 13:31–33, 44–52 (RCL);
MATTHEW 13:31–33, 44–49a (BCP);
MATTHEW 13:44–52 (13:44–46) (RC)

Interpreting the Text

The series of parables contained in this passage captures one of the central themes of Matthew's Gospel: instruction on the kingdom of heaven. Here Matthew depicts Jesus as a teacher who uses metaphorical language with concrete images to explain a simple yet complex concept.

The first parable compares the kingdom of heaven to a mustard seed that grows to be the greatest of shrubs, a tree in which the birds make their home (vv. 31–32). Classifying the mustard seed as the smallest of all the seeds appears to be an exaggeration but its growth into a shrub/tree crystallizes the intent of the parable: the small beginnings of the kingdom of heaven will flourish and become unexpectedly great.

The second parable compares the kingdom of heaven to yeast mixed in three measures of flour (v. 33). Yeast is a fermenting agent that, when added to a batch of dough, causes the dough to rise and expand into what is commonly known as a loaf of bread. The three measures of flour are the equivalent of fifty pounds of flour. Hence a little yeast goes a long way, and the effects of the kingdom of heaven are both transformed and beyond expectation.

The third parable compares the kingdom of heaven to a treasure hidden in a field, which, when discovered, causes the discoverer to sell everything in order to purchase that field (v. 44). Because the threat of invasion was part of the fabric of life in the world of the first century, the hiding of one's treasures was a common way of protecting them. To be noted is the joy of discovering the treasure and not the sorrow of what has to be let go in order to gain the treasure.

The fourth parable compares the kingdom of heaven to a merchant who discovered a pearl of great value and who then sold all that he had to purchase it (v. 45). The parables of the hidden treasure and the pearl of great price both express the extraordinary value of the kingdom of heaven that brings joy and is worth the letting go of everything in order to obtain it.

The fifth parable, about the net, is a bit more complicated. It draws on a life experience common to first-century people: fisherman casting a net, hauling in the catch, and separating the good fish from the bad ones. Embedded in this parable is a message about final judgment whose description suggests apocalyptic influence.

Matthew's final words feature Jesus addressing his disciples, inquiring whether they have understood the parables. He then makes one final comparison that helps them to understand that both "the new" and "the old" are valued, another Matthean theme.

Responding to the Text

Matthew's five parables depict Jesus as one who is gifted with imagination and able to take difficult concepts, like the kingdom of heaven, and make them clear through ordinary comparisons reflective of people's lived experiences. Jesus' examples provide contemporary readers with an insight into Jesus' and Matthew's social locations. The first-century world was both an agrarian and urban society whose ordinary people—bakers, merchants, fishermen—became not only the backbone of Jesus' mission and ministry but also the resources for his teachings as recorded by Matthew. Of note is the significant role that the natural world plays in both the Jewish and Christian religious traditions.

OF NOTE IS THE SIGNIFICANT ROLE THAT THE NATURAL WORLD PLAYS IN BOTH THE JEWISH AND CHRISTIAN RELIGIOUS TRADITIONS.

Central to the theology of Matthew's Gospel is the kingdom of heaven. All five parables deal with this concept, and common to each is the element of surprise. The smallest of all seeds grows into the greatest of all shrubs; a small amount of yeast turns a batch of dough into numerous loaves of bread; a person unexpectedly finds a treasure hidden in a field; a merchant finds a pearl of great value; fisherman, not knowing what they will find in their net, haul in a catch with fish of every kind.

Each of these parables reminds the people of Jesus' and Matthew's day about the impact that the reign of God will have on all creation, inclusive of non-human life forms as symbolized by the mustard seed and the shrub. The parable of the net poses the greatest theological difficulties. The description of final judgment at the end of the narrative probably originated with Matthew and bears the imprints of an ancient theological construct: the deuteronomistic theology of retribution (see Deuteronomy 28). This construct is incongruous to the all-compassionate love of God, especially for sinners, made manifest through the life and death of Jesus. Readers today are cautioned against such dualisms when considering God's universal plan of salvation for all creation.

In the spirit of Matthew's Gospel, come, search for the reign of God, and discover it already blossoming in our midst.

ELEVENTH SUNDAY AFTER PENTECOST

EIGHTEENTH SUNDAY IN ORDINARY TIME
PROPER 13
AUGUST 4, 2002

REVISED COMMON	EPISCOPAL (BCP)	ROMAN CATHOLIC
Isa. 55:1-5 or	Neh. 9:16-20	Isa. 55:1-3
Gen. 32:22-31		
Ps. 145:8-9, 14-21	Ps. 78:1-29 or	Ps. 145:8-9, 15-16, 17-18
or Ps. 17:1-7	78:14-20, 23-25	
Rom. 9:1-5	Rom. 8:35-39	Rom. 8:35, 37-39
Matt. 14:13-21	Matt. 14:13-21	Matt. 14:13-21

God's promise to make an everlasting covenant based on steadfast love (Isaiah 55) is fulfilled again and again throughout the biblical tradition and within people's lives. God's faithful presence and gracious love often take people by surprise, as in the case of Jacob who unknowingly wrestles with God at Peniel (Gen. 32:22-31). God's covenant fidelity and commitment to steadfast love remain constant in the face of human weakness, transgression, stubbornness, and rejection (Neh. 9:16-20; Rom. 9:1-5). Although covenant often pertains to the Israelite people in particular, it includes all of creation as well (see Gen. 9:8-17) and is made known through acts of care and kindness (Psalm 145; Matt. 14:13-21). Today's readings celebrate the Lord who is good to all, and who has compassion over all that has been created (Ps. 145:9).

FIRST READING
ISAIAH 55:1-5 (RCL); ISAIAH 55:1-3 (RC)

Interpreting the Text

With gusto the prophet Isaiah delivers a bold message full of divine sarcasm, promise, and cajolery. Part of a larger work (Isaiah 40-55), this passage is addressed to a general audience and features God as the main figure, speaking through the poet Deutero-Isaiah. A tightly woven passage of rhetorical artistry, the passage opens on a sarcastic note that has traditionally been understood as a joyful invitation extended to the poor to come and join in a grand feast. In the first verse, God, through the poet, invites everyone to come and eat and drink without any worry of having to pay. Wine and milk can be bought without money, without price. On first hearing, such an invitation does sound wonderful, but embedded in it is a tongue-in-cheek note of disdain that becomes obvious through the rhetorical question in v. 2a.

In vv. 2b-3a God implores the people addressed to listen carefully to God, to eat what is good, to delight in rich food, to incline their ears to God, to come to God, and to listen that they may live. The list of divine imperatives serves to shift the people's attention away from physical satiation to a deeper level of satisfaction that flows from a receptivity to God's word, the word that promises an everlasting covenant to be made between God and themselves (vv. 2b-3). This everlasting covenant is not a new one but refers to the fulfillment of promises made earlier (see, e.g., 2 Sam. 7:8-16; 23:5; 1 Kings 8:23-25; Ps. 89:2-38). Verse 4 speaks of a vision of a new leader to follow in the line of David. For the exiled Israelite community that has experienced the fall of both its northern and southern kingdoms, this is good news. Indeed the Israelites will be restored as a nation and glorified as a people (v. 5).

Responding to the Text

One of the many gifts of a prophet is the ability to manipulate words to surprise listeners in order to sting their moral consciences and wake them from their stupor of irresponsibility or to soothe their hearts and spirits wearied from injustice and exile. Isaiah's so-called invitation to abundant life is a rhetorical masterpiece laden with sarcasm and to-the-point questions, all of which are aimed at not only pointing up the foolishness of some Israelites but also highlighting the great promises to which they are called.

ONE CAN IMAGINE HOW THE PROPHET ISAIAH WOULD DELIVER THIS MESSAGE TODAY TO A PEOPLE STEEPED IN CONSUMPTION AND RELYING ON PLASTIC MONEY.

One can imagine how God, speaking through the prophet Isaiah, would deliver this message today to a people steeped in consumption and relying on plastic money. One might hear something like this: "Yo! Come, eat, drink, and be merry! Have a grand ole' time! Don't worry about not having any money; just come and buy, buy, buy. Eat, drink, and get fat!" The mood of indulgence changes to sobriety by means of a rhetorical question that underscores the pointlessness of investing in temporal things. To be preferred is the good and rich food that God has to offer—food that will provide real and lasting sustenance. This food is God's word and God's everlasting covenant, complemented by the promise of strength, leadership, and the respect of other nations. Isaiah's proclamation challenges people today to evaluate their choices and investments.

GENESIS 32:22-31 (RCL, alt.)

Interpreting the Text

Jacob wrestling with God is one of the most famous stories in the Old Testament. The event takes place at night, when Jacob is by himself. The details of the story describe Jacob wrestling with a man until daybreak. The climax of the story occurs in v. 28 when, after the wrestling match had come to an end, Jacob asks his opponent for a blessing (v. 26), which in turn prompts his opponent to inquire about Jacob's name (v. 27).

After Jacob reveals his name to his opponent, the opponent makes two astounding statements to Jacob: first, he would no longer be called Jacob but Israel and, second, that his name would be Israel because he had striven with both God and humans and had prevailed (v. 28). Jacob eventually receives his opponent's blessing, which both he and the readers now understand to be a divine blessing. Jacob names the site where the event happened Peniel, for he had seen God face to face and lived (cf. Exod. 33:11, 20). A narrative comment at the end of the story links the tale to Jewish ritual (v. 32).

The story as a whole makes use of a variety of ancient sources, many of which can be traced back to early folklore. The story's significant points include how Jacob's name became Israel, the relationship that existed between God and Jacob that foreshadowed Israel's ongoing struggle as a community called to live in covenant with God, and an explanation of the dietary rule that prohibits Israelites from eating the sciatic nerve.

Responding to the Text

What a surprise Jacob receives when he learns that the person with whom he has been wrestling is God! This Genesis story reflects the struggles endured by the Israelite community as it tried to remain faithful to God and the struggles encountered by the human community today as it tries to deal with what it means to be in "right relationship." For believers this right relationship pertains to God and to all creation as we face together the struggles involved in making right and just choices for the common good of all life on the planet.

NEHEMIAH 9:16-20 (BCP)

Interpreting the Text

The context of this passage is Ezra's prayer, which begins in v. 6 and ends in v. 37. The prayer focuses on the relationship between God and Israel. Verses 16-20 comment specifically on Israel's infidelity and God's graciousness toward Israel despite the community's shortcomings. In this section of the prayer, Ezra recounts the disobedience, stubbornness, and idolatrous ways of his ancestors (vv. 16-17). Ezra sets this most unpleasant picture in contrast to one that exemplifies the majesty of God, who shows great mercy to the people even when they had committed great blasphemies (vv. 18-19). Perhaps the most poignant verse in this portion of the prayer is v. 20 where Ezra, speaking directly to God, comments that God had given the Israelites God's good spirit to instruct them and did not withhold from them either manna or water when they were hungry and thirsty.

Ezra's prayer provides a social and religious overview of Israel in a historical setting and celebrates God's faithfulness to Israel in the midst of the people's social and religious struggles to remain true to Torah and covenant promises.

Responding to the Text

After pondering the content of Ezra's prayer, one cannot help but marvel at the long-suffering of Israel's God, who continues to remain faithful, gracious, merciful, and compassionate to a people presumptuous in their deeds and arrogant in their attitudes. And yet the Israelites are a microcosm of humanity, with all its goodness and depravity. If God were not a God of long-suffering, steadfast love, what hope would humankind have?

RESPONSIVE READING
PSALM 145:8-9, 14-21 (RCL);
PSALM 145:8-9, 15-16, 17-18 (RC)

God's compassion and all-encompassing love for all creation are celebrated by the psalmist. Psalm 145 has three parts: (1) Verses 8-9 affirm God as gracious, merciful, slow to anger, and abounding in steadfast love to all. (2) In vv. 10-12 the poet addresses God personally, speaking on behalf of all God's works that thank and bless God and tell of the glory of God's kingdom and God's power. (3) In vv. 13b-20 God's fidelity and benevolent graciousness are made known along with God's justice viewed in the light of kindness.

Of all the many qualities and virtues attributed to God, perhaps the greatest is compassion, which is preferred not only to humanity but to all creation. God's compassion is linked to God's justice: Israel's God hears and responds to all in need.

For contemporary believers, this psalm poses a tremendous challenge from an ecological perspective. All forms of life—and indeed the earth itself—suffer today because of human injustice and irresponsibility. Many voices are crying out, some audible such as those of women and young children, some not understood, such as those of the salmon trapped by dams, and some inaudible, such as that of the land as it lies stripped of nutrients, parched in some places and polluted in others. The voices that call upon God represent the magnificence of a grand biodiversity. If God cares for all creation and responds to all who cry out, then what does this psalm suggest to the human community called to be tillers and caretakers in God's image?

PSALM 17:1-7 (RCL, alt.)

The poet sincerely and humbly entreats God to hear his (her) case, attend to his (her) cry, and give ear to his (her) prayer so that he (she) might be vindicated by God from what would seem to be his (her) enemies as inferred by the last line of the psalm (v. 7). From the psalmist's perspective, he (she) is worthy of God's response to the petitions made because the psalmist's life has been one of truth, goodness, and fidelity to God and God's ways. The psalmist stands ready to be examined by God who will find a life worthy of divine assistance in this time of apparent need (vv. 3-6). Underlying this psalmist's petition to God is a profound confidence that God will indeed act on behalf of the righteous.

The one who stands just and upright before God can expect to be helped by God. This psalm encourages people to ask for what they need in a manner that is sincere and straightforward and then to wait patiently for God to respond.

PSALM 78:1-29 or 78:14-20, 23-25 (BCP)

Fervently and directly the psalmist calls listeners to attention: to give ear to the teaching that is about to be proclaimed, namely, a recapitulation of Israel's history and God's activity in that history (vv. 5-29). This recapitulation describes the past infidelities of the Israelite ancestors and a God whose deeds are liberating and salvific, on the one hand, and harsh, on the other hand. Such divine harsh deeds are attributed to God's expression of justice, one that is understood by the psalmist in the context of the theology of retribution (see Deuteronomy 28).

The recapitulation of God's powerful deeds in the lives of the ancient Israelites becomes a source of inspiration to nurture and enliven the faith of all people. Today one might call this psalm a ballad.

SECOND READING

ROMANS 9:1-5 (RCL)

Interpreting the Text

Filled with deep emotion and expressing his thoughts from his depths, Paul addresses his listeners in a spirit of honesty, profound conviction, and great sadness (v. 1). After a personal reflection, he proudly enumerates seven privileges granted by God to the Israelites, who are to Paul his brothers and sisters. These privileges include divine adoption, glory, covenants, the giving of the law, worship, promises, and the patriarchs from whom the Messiah descended, whose sovereignty extends to all creation, and who is the one blessed by God forever. With such statements, Paul affirms the prominent place and role that the Jewish people have among Christians.

Responding to the Text

The person of Paul as an apostle to the Gentiles, as a Christian, and as a Jew comes to life in this passage where he bares the true feelings of his heart. He is in agony over the Jews' failure to accept the gospel and even more because they are his kindred, his own people. In this regard, Paul's experience is no different from Jesus' experience among some of his people—rejection. Paul's gospel is rejected, just as Jesus and his teachings were rejected. Paul accents the dilemma that such rejection poses by referring to the Jewish people as "Israelites," an honorific title bestowed upon them by God. The enumeration of the seven God-given prerogatives, to which Paul adds an eighth, sheds further light on why Paul experiences such deep anguish.

> THE PERSON OF PAUL AS AN APOSTLE TO THE GEN-TILES, AS A CHRISTIAN, AND AS A JEW COMES TO LIFE IN THIS PASSAGE WHERE HE BARES THE TRUE FEELINGS OF HIS HEART.

Paul's statement to the Roman Christians is both cathartic and instructive and reveals the deep love that he has for his own. He is willing even to suffer the loss of his own relationship with Christ if it would mean transformation and salvation for his own people. Such passion is heroic; such love and commitment are an inspiration for people today engaged in the preaching and mission of the gospel.

MATTHEW 14:13-21

Interpreting the Text

This popular Matthean narrative of Jesus feeding five thousand has par-allels in the other three Gospels (Mark 6:35-44; Luke 9:12-17; and John 6:1-15). It is the only miracle story to appear in all four Gospels, which indicates its promi-nence and importance in the memory and life of the early church. This story also helps to develop one of Matthew's overarching themes: the importance of both the "old" and the "new." The backdrop to the narrative is Jesus hearing about the beheading and death of John the Baptist, which becomes the impetus for Jesus taking off in a boat to a deserted place to be by himself in response to such hor-rendous news (14:12-13).

Jesus' desire for seclusion is only a temporary experience, however, because the crowds discover where he has gone, and when he comes ashore he is greeted by a great multitude whom he in turn greets with compassion: he heals their sick (v. 14). In the midst of this crowd and long past the hour for dinner, Jesus decides to care for their needs further. He feeds them, much to the chagrin of his disciples, who had wanted the people sent away (vv. 15-21).

> THE BLESSING AND BREAKING OF THE FIVE LOAVES AND TWO FISH FORESHADOW THE LAST SUPPER AND THE CHURCH'S FORMAL EUCHARIST/COMMUNION CELEBRATIONS.

The blessing and breaking of the five loaves and two fish foreshadow the Last Supper and the church's formal Eucharist/Com-munion celebrations.

The fact that there were five loaves and two fish has no special symbolic sig-nificance. The mention of five thousand men who ate, a number that did not include women and children, adds to the grandeur of the setting and the event. The story as a whole reflects two ancient traditions: (1) the feeding of the Israelites by God in the desert (Exodus 16) and (2) the feeding of one hundred men with twenty loaves of barley and ears of grain, as ordered by the prophet Elisha (2 Kings 4:42-44). Thus Matthew's narrative reflects older traditions drawn on for the telling of this new event, traditions that situate Jesus theologically in relationship to God and as one who stands in the prophetic tradition.

Responding to the Text

Jesus' feeding of the five thousand who have gathered around him is another example of compassion, a virtue ascribed to God in Psalm 145. In this story of the loaves and fish, Jesus' compassion comes across as an act of human response to a group of people who have among them sick ones in need of care.

Jesus heals their sick. The virtue of compassion continues when Jesus offers to feed them. The miracle of the story is not the multiplication of the loaves but the fact that people shared what they had without leaving anyone in need.

Read in the context of the Old Testament story of God providing manna in the desert for the wandering Israelites, and heard against the backdrop of Psalm 145, one is able to see that Jesus not only embodies the spirit of God but also does what God does. Furthermore, Jesus' acts of healing—his liberating others from whatever oppresses them—becomes a sign of the reign of God already unfolding in one's midst. Finally, Matthew's version of this story suggests deep theological implications: Jesus is the Son of God and the living embodiment of God.

Would that the rich meaning of such a simple story be discovered again and again so that people could come to understand that God's self-revelation takes place among ordinary human beings in the most unlikely places, times, and situations of everyday life.

TWELFTH SUNDAY
AFTER PENTECOST

NINETEENTH SUNDAY IN ORDINARY TIME
PROPER 14
AUGUST 11, 2002

REVISED COMMON	EPISCOPAL (BCP)	ROMAN CATHOLIC
1 Kings 19:9-18 or	Jon. 2:1-9	1 Kings 19:9a, 11-13a
Gen. 37:1-4, 12-28		
Ps. 85:8-13 or	Psalm 29	Ps. 85: 8, 9, 10-11, 12-13
Ps. 105:1-6, 16-22,		(Heb. Bible 85:9,
45b		10, 11-12, 13-14)
Rom. 10:5-15	Rom. 9:1-5	Rom. 9:1-5
Matt. 14:22-33	Matt. 14:22-33	Matt. 14:22-33

With confidence the psalmist proclaims, "Surely his salvation is at hand for those who fear him, that his glory may dwell in our land" (Ps. 85:9). Today's readings focus on the theme of salvation. God spares Elijah's life because of his fidelity (1 Kings 19:14-18), Joseph escapes death because of Reuben's intercession on his behalf (Gen. 37:22), Israel's poets recite God's saving deeds (Psalm 105), Jesus saves Peter from drowning (Matt. 14:28-31), and Paul proclaims that God's salvation is for all (Rom. 10:5-13). The Joseph story in particular reminds us of our responsibility toward one another and of our potential to be instruments of salvation even in the bleakest of circumstances.

FIRST READING
1 KINGS 19:9-18 (RCL);
1 KINGS 19:9a, 11-13a (RC)

Interpreting the Text

Elijah's encounter with God on Mount Horeb is familiar to many readers. God comes to Elijah in a most unexpected way—in the silence and not in the wind or an earthquake or a fire. The great and awesome God comes in silence. How remarkable!

The story opens with Elijah responding to God, who asks him what he is doing in a cave (v. 9). Elijah promptly explains that he has been very zealous for the Lord, that the Israelites have forsaken their covenant with God and have killed God's prophets, except for himself, whose life is now endangered (v. 10). God then tells Elijah to go and stand on Mount Horeb. There Elijah encounters God a second time who then asks him what he is doing on Horeb. Elijah responds to God with the exact same answer as he did when God asked him what he was doing in the cave (vv. 11-14; cf. vv. 9-10). Following Elijah's response, God gives Elijah a series of directives that offer the prophet hope (vv. 15-18) and, more specifically, that deal with the problem of covenant infidelity. Israel will be "purified," and what will remain will be a faithful remnant of seven thousand people (v. 18).

The story highlights the centrality of a prophet's mission despite the fact that his life may be seriously threatened. The prophet's task is to remain faithful to God and God's ways, and to work to preserve, safeguard, and renew the covenant made with God's beloved ones.

Responding to the Text

The story of Elijah provides a first-hand glimpse into the perils and struggles of a prophet who chooses to remain faithful to God, faithful to his community, and faithful to the task and mission that have been entrusted to him. The story opens with Elijah "on the run," taking refuge in a cave, and fearing for his life. Israel's prophets are being killed by some of the Israelites themselves. What has caused such violence among God's people? Elijah's conversation with God brings the situation to light. Some of the Israelites have become entangled in apostasy and idolatry, forsaking their covenant with God. Elijah, being zealous for God and trying to be faithful to his vocation, probably confronted the Israelites' infidelity, much like the other prophets, only to experience either rejection or death—or both. And where is God in the midst of all these events? The story tells us that God is at the still point—at the center of such swirling events, bringing a silent yet active presence to Elijah to redirect his mission. Now Elijah will anoint kings, assured by a divine promise that the lives of those Israelites who have remained faithful to God will be spared.

> THE STORY TELLS US THAT GOD IS AT THE STILL POINT—AT THE CENTER OF SWIRLING EVENTS, BRINGING A SILENT YET ACTIVE PRESENCE TO ELIJAH TO REDIRECT HIS MISSION.

The text offers several theological points for further reflection. First, the role of a prophet is not to be successful; it is to be faithful to the prophetic mission at hand in the face of adversity. Second, a prophet needs to remain committed to God and God's ways while taking appropriate caution for his or her life. Third, as the prophet remains committed to God, so God will remain committed to the prophet. Fourth, God is self-revelatory to the prophet. Finally, the mission of the prophet is not self-chosen; it is revealed by God.

The Old Testament focuses on certain individuals and their prophetic activity. The New Testament, however, focuses on the gift of prophecy present within the

Christian community (see, e.g., Acts 2:14-21; Rom. 12:6). Many situations today, such as the ecological plight of the planet and the unjust suffering that both humans and non-humans are forced to endure are just two areas of concern in need of a prophetic response. Dare Christians today embrace their God-given vocation for the sake of hastening God's plan of salvation for all life?

GENESIS 37:1-4, 12-28 (RCL, alt.)

Perhaps one of the best-loved stories in the Old Testament is the one about Joseph, his coat of many colors, and his jealous brothers. Comprised of three distinct sections, the first part of the narrative provides readers with background information on Jacob, his family, his partiality toward Joseph, and the negative report that Joseph delivers to his father about his brothers (vv. 1-4). This incident fueled their resentment against Joseph, whom they stripped of his coat and then threw into a pit. His life was spared only because two of his brothers, Reuben and Judah, interceded for him and talked the others out of the death plot that they were scheming for Joseph (vv. 19-24). This section of the story reflects two different traditions, the Yahwist and the Elohist.

The third part of the narrative features the brother Judah, who also opposes Joseph's death on the grounds that Joseph is their brother, their own flesh. Together, Judah and the other brothers plot to sell Joseph to the Ishmaelites for twenty pieces of silver. The plot is carried out, and Joseph is carried off to Egypt (vv. 25-28).

This story reveals the depth of jealousy that is possible within a family when another member favors one member over the other members. The narrator also sets the stage for Joseph's future dealings with his family members whom he saves from starving to death.

Responding to the Text

Sibling rivalry is common in many families, but when a parent shows favor toward one child, especially when he or she is perceived by the other siblings as a "snitch" against them, as in the case of Joseph giving Jacob a "bad report about his brothers," sibling rivalry can become exacerbated. Joseph is the one most loved by his father, Jacob; Joseph is the one most despised by his brothers. He is his father's "fair-haired" one who becomes the scapegoat for the brothers' unexpressed anger toward their father, the recipient of their fierce jealously, and the brunt of their foul intentions and play: except for Reuben and Judah, they all want him dead. Both of these brothers buck up against the others, and Joseph does not face the violent death intended for him by his other brothers.

This is a remarkable story of sibling rivalry at its worst and at its best. If Reuben and Judah had not had the courage to speak out against their brothers'

162

THE SEASON
OF PENTECOST
─────────
CAROL J.
DEMPSEY

plot, Joseph would have been killed. The story of Joseph illustrates that there are ways to incite and avert domestic violence. Reuben's and Judah's voices challenge people today to find their own voices against violence, especially against domestic violence, which continues to remain the most silent of all crimes.

JONAH 2:1-9 (BCP)

Interpreting the Text

Nestled in the midst of the infamous prose narrative that describes Jonah's ordeal with God and a great fish is Jonah's prayer to God from the belly of the fish. It is a psalm of lament that bears witness to Jonah's confidence in God and reveals his innermost thoughts and feelings about his perilous experience in the fish's belly. In this prayer, Jonah acknowledges to God what God has done to him (v. 3), which has caused him to fear that he has been driven from God's sight (v. 4). Jonah reminds God about what has happened to him while revealing how God indeed did help him in the midst of his turmoil (vv. 5-7). His reference to the worship of vain idols indicates that some members of Jonah's original audience may have been struggling with idolatry (v. 8). Jonah ends his prayer on a note of thanksgiving with a promise of sacrifice and a proclamation that, indeed, deliverance belongs to God (v. 9). Through an experience with the natural world elements and a sea creature, God teaches Jonah a powerful lesson about God and God's ways.

Responding to the Text

Imagine yourself in the belly of a great fish. Imagine yourself having the presence of mind to pray to God while in its belly. This portion of the Jonah story is fantastic and fictitious, but there is an element of realism in it: God's elemental will for creation is life. Jonah and the great fish manage to survive their encounter, and Jonah's prayer reveals one person's trust in God's power to bring about salvation and restoration. Jonah had remained faithful to God, and thus God remains faithful to Jonah. The story calls people to faithfulness and encourages people to ask for help when in need, confident that God will respond. Heard from an ecological perspective, the story shows how the natural world—the sea and the fish—plays a dynamic role in the lives of God's people and the divine plan of salvation.

PSALM 85:8-13 (RCL);
PSALM 85:8, 9, 10-11, 12-13, NRSV; (RC)

With anticipation and enthusiasm, the psalmist awaits God's word as he paints a descriptive picture of a beautiful future that he envisions will indeed come to pass: steadfast love and faithfulness will meet, righteousness and peace will kiss each other, faithfulness will spring up from the ground, and righteousness will look down from heaven (vv. 10-11). These images reflect a world characterized by harmonious and complementary relationships.

What a beautiful and hopeful vision the psalmist proclaims. After a long exile comes the promise of salvation. The Israelites will experience a time of peace—the fruit of justice and righteousness—and their land will flourish. God's glory has come to dwell in their midst. The psalm reminds us that this divine vision of peace and prosperity for all life has yet to reach its fullness. There is the work of justice and righteousness to be done in our world so that peace can be an enduring experience for all creation. The vision goes before us; the promise waits to unfold.

PSALM 105:1-6, 16-22, 45b (RCL, alt.)

This song of thanksgiving celebrates God's greatness (vv. 1-6) and wonderful deeds done in history (vv. 16-22). The middle portion of the psalm recounts a part of the Joseph story (vv. 16-22). The remembrance of God's deeds in general and Joseph's struggles as a captive in particular have the purpose of moving the poet's audience to fidelity for God's statutes and laws (v. 45b). Torah and faithfulness are at the heart of Israelite life.

The psalmist's enthusiastic address of the Israelite community encourages believing communities today to become self-reflective, to discover God in the midst of daily life, to remember and talk about the wonderful works of God throughout history and in the present moment, and to be mindful of God's plan of salvation that continues to unfold from one generation to the next.

PSALM 29 (BCP)

In this theophanic hymn of praise the poet addresses the heavenly beings, beckoning them to acknowledge God's glory and strength and to worship the LORD in holy splendor. The heart of the psalm focuses on the voice of God—as earth-shaking thunder—in all its grandeur and power. This voice of God breaks cedars (lightning) and makes Lebanon skip like a calf (hail). It flashes flames of fire, shakes the wilderness, and strips the forest bare. What a contrast to the voice of God that Elijah hears in 1 Kings 19:9-18! In the last two verses God is seated on the divine throne in the Temple, and the worshipers shout, "Glory!" (Hebrew: *kabod*, God's presence).

In this psalm two images of God converge: the storm God and God as king. For people who have never experienced the incredible power of nature's force and who have not lived in a monarchical setting, such images of God and God's power may be difficult to relate to. They are, however, part of an ancient people's experience and tradition and need to be understood in that context. The challenge for believing communities today is to create new metaphors from present-day life experience that can capture the wonder and grandeur of God whose ultimate work is to empower and to bless.

SECOND READING
ROMANS 10:5-15 (RCL)

Interpreting the Text

In a provocative discourse that appeals to a Greco-Roman style of argumentation fleshed out by an appeal to Scripture used to interpret Scripture, Paul tackles the difficult question of faith and its relationship to salvation. In his opening statement, Paul sets up a contrast between righteousness that comes from the law and righteousness that comes from faith. For Paul, salvation involves much more than the keeping of the Torah. Salvation is connected to the Christ-event—belief in his person and belief that God raised him from the dead. Paul's understanding of salvation is inclusive and expansive. Salvation is a gift not only for the Jews but also for the Gentiles. Furthermore, in Paul's understanding of salvation some basic boundaries collapse. No longer is there to be a distinction between Jew and Greek; the same Lord is Lord of all and exceptionally generous to all. Paul makes the bold assertion that everyone who calls on the name of the Lord will be saved (vv. 5-13).

> IN PAUL'S UNDERSTANDING OF SALVATION SOME BASIC BOUNDARIES COLLAPSE.

Continuing his line of thought and argument, Paul picks up on the theme of call and poses a series of rhetorical questions aimed at removing the blame from Israel with respect to Israel's narrow view of salvation (vv. 14-15). In essence, the word of faith must be proclaimed if people are to arrive at a full understanding of salvation.

What a refreshing message Paul brings to the Roman Christians! Salvation is no longer dependent upon a person's ability to keep law after law after law, as prescribed by Moses. Paul focuses on faith as the primary means to salvation: faith in the person and resurrection of Jesus and belief that God who raised Jesus from the dead. Salvation is not related to one's ethnic background. God's salvation is all-encompassing. For certain people in Paul's day who adhered to the law religiously, Paul's message was most likely quite scandalous. For others excluded by the Jewish community because of ethnic background or failure to keep the law to its letter, Paul's proclamation was indeed good news.

How Paul uses Scripture needs further comment. In several instances in this portion of his letter, Paul appeals to Scripture to bolster the point he is trying to make and to lend authority to his teaching. He either adapts certain passages to fit his context or he takes certain passages out of their original context, thus ascribing a new meaning to the original passage. In the early church, this was a common way of using Scripture. Today this use of Scripture is called proof-texting and reflects an older, noncritical use of the text. One could view Paul's use of Scripture as perhaps one of the earliest methods of biblical interpretation that emphasized application and re-readings that often failed to understand or take into account the texts' original settings and historical and social influences that shaped the texts.

This passage portrays Paul as a master of rhetoric, a person of enlightened understanding of the gospel, and someone courageous enough to put forth new theological ideas no matter how disconcerting or liberating they may be.

THE GOSPEL
MATTHEW 14:22-33

Interpreting the Text

The scene for this Gospel account is the sea, a place that provides a livelihood for fishermen and offers them a great challenge from time to time when storms come up and toss their boats to and fro. Jesus' disciples are caught in a storm at sea. One can imagine a certain anxiety associated with being in a fishing boat in bad weather. No storm, however, could ever cause them the feeling of terror they experienced when suddenly they saw Jesus walking on the water and coming toward them. For Peter, such terror is magnified when he bravely does what Jesus asks of him: to get out of the boat and begin walking toward him. Suddenly, the strong wind captures his attention, he becomes scared, experiences himself starting to sink, and immediately calls out for Jesus to save him, which Jesus does—but not without a comment about Peter being of little faith.

This story is about faith that becomes ever stronger through one's lived experience, which may at times include periods of doubt. The story reaches its climax at the end when the disciples recognize and name Jesus as the Son of God (v. 33).

In addition to being a story about faith, Matthew's narrative also sheds light on the person of Jesus and provides readers with a glimpse into his divinity made explicit by the disciples' final comment. Prior to his taking a walk on the sea, Jesus is pictured as a man of prayer who, after feeding more than five thousand people—some of whom he also healed—goes up to a mountain by himself to pray. Throughout the Old Testament, mountains are often associated with one's experience of and encounter with God (see, e.g., Exod. 19:2). In Jesus' life, mountains are significant. He is transfigured on Mt. Tabor; he goes to the Mount of Olives after the Passover feast. Jesus' presence on the mountains links him to the experiences of his ancestors. Moses receives the Decalogue on Mt. Sinai. When Jesus stills the storm, he does what God does (see Ps. 107:29), and his walk on the water is also associated with God's activity (see Exod. 14:13–31; Ps. 77:20; Job 9:8; Isa. 43:16; Hab. 3:15).

> THIS STORY IS ABOUT FAITH THAT BECOMES EVER STRONGER THROUGH ONE'S LIVED EXPERIENCE, WHICH MAY INCLUDE PERIODS OF DOUBT.

Thus, embedded in Matthew's Gospel is a statement about Jesus' divinity long before the disciples proclaim it. Whether or not the event at sea happens as Matthew relates it is uncertain. What is certain, though, is the fact that faith is a God-given gift, sustained by God, and deepened through one's experience of the extraordinary in the midst of the ordinary events of life.

Responding to the Text

Matthew earlier depicted Jesus swamped by a crowd of more than five thousand people, some of whom he cured of their sicknesses and all of whom he broke bread with at the end of the day. Anyone who has been engaged in work with or spent time with a large crowd knows how tiring and draining the experience can be. It is no wonder then that Matthew's next story about Jesus opens with him going up to a mountain alone to pray. A man of tremendous activity, Jesus was also a man of solitude whose solitary communion with his God was not only the source of his energy, wisdom, insight, and understanding but also his greatest source of rest. His solitude, however, does not last for long. Duty calls him down from the mountain. A storm has come up, and his disciples are about to sink in their boat.

The heart of the story is Peter's doubt and his exclamation, "Lord, save me!" For Peter to believe, he has to have some sort of experience, which he does. With

Jesus and at Jesus' invitation he gets out of his boat and walks on the sea. About to sink, he cries out to Jesus, and Jesus saves him from drowning. When Peter's faith fails him, Jesus takes over.

Paul, in his letter to the Romans, stressed the role that faith plays in salvation. Matthew's story sheds light on Paul's message, and vice versa. In sum, Matt. 14:22–33 offers listeners and readers today several theological points for further reflection: (1) Jesus was a man of deep prayer and spirituality whose life was centered in and on God; (2) experience often informs and strengthens faith; (3) God's work of salvation is ongoing in the course of everyday life.

Embrace Jesus' rhythm of life; be bold like Peter to ask for a sign of the reality of God's presence, dare to jump out of the boat, and be courageous enough to ask Jesus for help when help is needed.

THIRTEENTH SUNDAY AFTER PENTECOST

TWENTIETH SUNDAY IN ORDINARY TIME
PROPER 15
AUGUST 18, 2002

REVISED COMMON	EPISCOPAL (BCP)	ROMAN CATHOLIC
Isa. 56:1, 6-8 or Gen. 45:1-15	Isa. 56:(2-5), 6-7	Isa. 56:1, 6-7
Psalm 67 or Psalm 133	Psalm 67	Ps. 67:1-2, 4, 5 (Heb. Bible 67:2-3, 5, 6, 8)
Rom. 11:2-2a, 29-32	Rom. 11:13-15, 29-32	Rom. 11:13-15, 29-32
Matt. 15:(10-20), 21-28	Matt. 15:21-28	Matt. 15:21-28

Two hallmarks of Jewish and Christian life are justice and righteousness. The ancient people experienced both of these in their interactions with their God, who called them to practice these virtues in daily life (Isa. 56:1). The psalmist proclaims that God judges people with equity. Paul highlights divine mercy offered to the disobedient (Rom. 11:30). Joseph offers his brothers hospitality instead of revenge (Gen. 45:1-15). Jesus heals a Canaanite woman's daughter even though she is not a member of the house of Israel (Matt. 15:21-28). Today's readings show us a way of life reflective of being in right relationship with God and with God's people regardless of people's past faults, differences in ethnic backgrounds, or whatever else may cause a sense of separation. The ethical and religious challenges the readings pose are ever ancient and ever new.

FIRST READING
ISAIAH 56:1-8 (RCL);
ISAIAH 56:(2-5), 6-7 (BCP);
ISAIAH 56:1, 6-7 (RC)

Interpreting the Text

This proclamation of Third Isaiah describes who will be welcomed in God's new Temple and offers a word of hope to Jews and non-Jews alike. In the first verse God, speaking through the prophet, offers a word of encouragement to a people exiled: salvation and deliverance will surely come, but in the meantime the people are to maintain justice and continue doing what is right. The second verse is a beatitude that looks back to v. 1 and adds a comment about keeping the Sabbath holy.

Verse 3 introduces two new groups into the picture—the foreigner and the eunuch. The prophet gives a directive to foster an attitude of inclusivity with regard to these two groups of people. Verses 4–5 concern the eunuchs specifically. Eunuchs were often used in many courts but were excluded from the Temple. God now lifts this ban. Verses 6-7 concern foreigners. In Judaism, a foreigner who became joined to Yahweh was a proselyte. This group was also controversial, being members of the community without being Israelite by birth. Hence many within the prophet's community were reticent to grant full covenant rights to foreigners. Through Isaiah, however, God makes it clear that both the foreigners and their sacrifices will be accepted and welcomed in the Temple.

The last verse of Isaiah's message continues the theme of God's inclusive graciousness. God will gather more "outcasts" than those already welcomed. The text speaks of a wideness of God's love rooted in right relationship, love, and fidelity and not ethnic or religious background.

Responding to the Text

"Maintain justice and do what is right," proclaims Isaiah to an Israelite community that is no stranger to the difficulties involved in trying to act ethically and walk humbly with God. The prophet's message, however, is not just aimed at how the Israelites act toward one another or toward their God. It now pertains to their attitudes toward other people, especially toward those who were not welcomed among their members. Salvation is no longer contingent upon whether one is a Jew by birth. Salvation is based on justice and righteousness—on showing hospitality to the eunuch and the foreigner who keep God's Sabbaths, choose the things pleasing to God, and hold fast to God's covenant. Those whom the Israelites have excluded from their midst and from their Temple are the ones who will be welcomed in God's new Temple. "Maintain justice and do what is right"— the Israelites are called to let down their boundaries and welcome the unwanted.

What a powerful message this is for people to hear today! We live in a world of great diversity—indeed great biodiversity. We also live in a world where people tend to cast out, cast aside, step over, and write off others who appear to be "different" from themselves in any given way regardless of another's genuine goodness. To those who suffer such injustice, Isaiah's words offer comfort. To those who unjustly exclude others, Isaiah's message offers a pointed directive: "Maintain justice and do what is right." Whom do we welcome into our lives, our homes, our communities, our places of worship?

GENESIS 45:1–15 (RCL, alt.)

Interpreting the Text

Revelation, recognition, reconciliation, and restoration are the major themes of this segment of the Joseph story, which takes place in Egypt. There Joseph reveals his identity to his unsuspecting brothers, who had come into the country from Canaan to buy grain lest the family die of starvation during a severe famine that had struck their land.

Responding to his brother Judah's appeal (see Gen. 44:18–34) and overcome by emotion, Joseph finds himself no longer being able to hide his identity from his brothers. Alone with them, Joseph takes them by surprise and admits to them that he is their brother whom they had sold to the Ishmaelites (vv. 1–3). Joseph then reveals to his brothers what he perceives to have been God's divine plan, namely, that he should end up in Egypt so that he could eventually help his family when they came seeking food in a foreign land. Joseph is able to offer them not only food but also refuge in a nearby land called Goshen (vv. 4–11). The story closes with Joseph sending his brothers back to their father to tell him the good news about his being alive and the good fortune that awaits the entire family in Egypt.

The most poignant part of the story occurs in the last two verses, where Joseph and Benjamin weep upon each other's neck and Joseph then kisses all of his brothers, an act that initiates conversation among them once again. Benjamin was the son of Joseph's own mother and thus one of the closest to Joseph. This story of Joseph's encounter with his brother attests to God's grace working through the events of daily life.

Responding to the Text

After experiencing the violence done to him by his brothers, one would expect that Joseph would seek revenge upon meeting them again. After all, his cultural and religious world prescribed "an eye for an eye and a tooth for a tooth." Contrary to expectations and to the justice norms of his day, Joseph, when he meets his brothers after the long separation, chooses to respond to them with kindness. He surprises them by disclosing his identity and takes them by surprise with his response to them. When he speaks to them, he tells them not to be distressed or angry with themselves for having allowed him to be sold into Egypt. Joseph puts a positive spin on the past events, and in the end he and his brothers are reconciled.

Joseph's kind response was probably something his brothers did not expect. It may have even come as a surprise since he was in a position of power and could have "gotten even" with them. Joseph chooses instead to act with compassion that opens the door to reconciliation.

The story of Joseph's encounter with his brothers and their reconciliation illustrates how important family life and right relationships were in the ancient world. Today much conversation revolves around family values. Many families suffer from broken relationships yet to be reconciled after years of hostility. This story from the Joseph cycle raises a composite question for further reflection: What must family members do to reconcile their differences? And in the case of an impasse, might not one member be able to "cancel all debts" and resolve all hostility with the disarming justice of compassion?

THE STORY OF JOSEPH'S ENCOUNTER WITH HIS BROTHERS AND THEIR RECONCILIATION ILLUSTRATES HOW IMPORTANT FAMILY LIFE AND RIGHT RELATIONSHIPS WERE IN THE ANCIENT WORLD.

RESPONSIVE READING

PSALM 67 (RCL, BCP);
PSALM 67:1-2, 4, 5, NRSV (RC)

The cultic and liturgical setting of this psalm was most likely a harvest-thanksgiving festival with links to the ancient Aaronic blessing (Num. 6:24ff.) and the Sinai theophany. The psalm celebrates the abundance of a rich harvest, a blessing from God indicative of divine loving kindness and grace. All the nations are called to rejoice and give praise to God, the giver of good gifts, whose judgments are righteous and whose guidance is cause for great joy.

Believing communities who hear this psalm proclaimed today in an American setting against the backdrop of the text's own ancestral vision may find themselves facing a challenge to look at the relationship between faith, leadership, justice, and governance today just as the people of ancient Israel had to address such concepts in its own day so that God's ways could be known upon earth and God's saving power among all nations. Ancient words continue to offer hope.

PSALM 133 (RCL, alt.)

This psalm, whose opening lines have parallels in ancient Egyptian literature, is a Wisdom saying that affirms family life. The reference to kindred living together in unity (v. 1) reflects the ancient Jewish law concerning the levirate marriage (Deut. 25:5). With two similes, the psalmist concretizes the goodness and delight of harmonious relationships within a family.

The first simile compares kindred unity to precious oil on the head of Aaron (Moses' brother) and running down his beard onto the collar of his robes (v. 2).

Scented oil dripping down one's head and onto one's beard was regarded by the Israelite, Egyptian, and Greek cultures as something exquisite and refined. The second simile uses natural imagery to compare pleasant familial relationships to the dew of Hermon that falls on the mountains of Zion (v. 3).

The thought and images of this psalm capture the beauty and charm of family unity that the psalmist holds up as an ideal way of life. What an appropriate response to be sung after the story of Joseph's reconciliation with his brothers!

SECOND READING
ROMANS 11:2-2a, 29-32 (RCL);
ROMANS 11:13-15, 29-32 (BCP);
ROMANS 11:13-15, 29-32 (RC)

Interpreting the Text

Paul's stirring message heralds God's plan of salvation for Jews and Gentiles alike. Paul opens his address by stating emphatically that indeed God has not rejected the Israelites. He then presents himself as an Israelite, a descendant of the great patriarch Abraham and a member of the tribe of Benjamin, a son of Jacob (v. 1). Paul next appeals to the Old Testament as scripture and draws on the example of Elijah (v. 2). Elijah, a prophet of the ninth century B.C.E., took the lead against the introduction of Baalism into the kingdom of Israel (see 1 Kings 18:1-46; 19:1-8). The reference to God's foreknowledge of the Israelites indicates that there is a divine predilection toward Israel and the people's salvation.

Paul addresses the second part of his message specifically to the Gentiles and reveals to them his shrewd plan, boasting that his salvific mission to the Gentiles will make his own Israelite family jealous and thus save some of them as well (vv. 13-15).

Paul addresses his final remarks to the Roman Christians. Here he uses the Gentiles' disobedience to teach the Christians a lesson. Gentile disobedience stemmed from a basic disbelief in God that resulted in divine disfavor. Now Paul views disobedience as an occasion for divine mercy. Thus the disobedience of Christians and Gentiles is an opportunity for God to be merciful to all. For Paul, God's plan of salvation includes all people.

Responding to the Text

Paul's message, which he begins on a very personal note, appeals to the story of Elijah's encounter with God that we heard in the first reading for last Sunday (1 Kings 19:9-18). Paul reminds the Jews and Gentiles of his day that God's salvation is not limited to one specific group of people nor is it contingent on perfect fidelity to God and God's ways. Paul points out that both groups have been unfaithful to God and that their "disobedience" has been an opportunity for God to be merciful.

Paul's closing theological statement about God imprisoning all in disobedience so that God may be merciful to all warrants further comment. First, Paul's statement is a generalization. It assumes that all people are disobedient—which may or may not be the case. Second, by making a statement like this, it seems as though Paul presumes to know the mind and will of God, a presumption that remains unfounded. Paul's concluding words are perhaps best understood as his own interpretive theological understanding of God that he adds to the end of his discourse to strengthen the point of his argument and draw it to a close on a didactic, authoritative note.

> GOD'S SALVATION IS NOT LIMITED TO ONE SPECIFIC GROUP OF PEOPLE NOR IS IT CONTINGENT ON PERFECT FIDELITY TO GOD AND GOD'S WAYS.

THE GOSPEL

MATTHEW 15:(10–20), 21–28 (RCL); MATTHEW 15:21–28 (BCP, RC)

Interpreting the Text

In order to stress for his community the importance of morality, Matthew depicts Jesus teaching a lesson to the crowd. Also present are Jesus' disciples and the Pharisees. Jesus tells them that only that which comes out of the mouth can defile a person. Such a statement goes against the notion of Jewish ritual purity, and it incites the Pharisees. Matthew has now established a polemic: Jesus' teaching versus the Pharisees' teaching. To stress his point further, Matthew has Jesus use a parable as part of his instruction. The parable seems not to be readily understood by Jesus' listeners, which leads Peter to ask for an explanation. Jesus responds bluntly with two rhetorical questions aimed at underscoring his listeners' inability to "get" what the issues are. Jesus then lays the issues out clearly. Matthew's story has a threefold function: (1) It makes clear for his community and for the people of Jesus' day that moral rectitude and the condition of one's heart are far more important than the laws of ritual purity, which involve certain foods and the washing of one's hands before eating. (2) It lends authority to Jesus' teaching, which goes against the grain of the Pharisees' teachings. And (3) it frees Matthew's and Jesus' audiences from the ritual and ceremonial bonds set down in the Old Testament and offers them a deeper challenge and insight as they move among the Gentiles who are part of the divine plan of salvation as well.

The themes of freedom and the Gentile mission continue in Matthew's next narrative (15:21-28), which features Jesus healing a Canaanite woman's daughter because of the woman's faith. The woman's persistence helps Jesus clarify and broaden his sense of mission. Through the example of the Canaanite woman, Matthew helps his community understand that God's grace and saving acts are for Jews and non-Jews alike.

Responding to the Text

The first part of the Gospel for today is at the same time liberating and challenging for both its original and its contemporary audiences. It focuses on what is essential to holiness—not holding fast to sacred traditions and ritual practices that can become an end in themselves but rather working to maintain a certain "purity of heart" (see Matt. 5:8) that can inform one's ethical choices and way of life. Purity of heart here refers to the sense of being attentive to God and God's law, a law that the prophet Jeremiah proclaims to be written on the heart (Jer. 31:33). This law on the heart becomes more clearly understood in Matt. 22:36-40, where it is associated with love.

> PURITY OF HEART HERE REFERS TO THE SENSE OF BEING ATTENTIVE TO GOD AND GOD'S LAW, A LAW THAT THE PROPHET JEREMIAH PROCLAIMS TO BE WRITTEN ON THE HEART.

The second part of Matthew's message develops the theme of justice and righteousness, which are introduced in the previous readings of the day. Isaiah's proclamation focused on maintaining justice and doing what is right, with an emphasis on salvation being for all and not just for the Jews. The story of the Canaanite woman's encounter with Jesus illustrates Isaiah's point. This woman, a Canaanite, asks Jesus, a Jew, for mercy. She wants him to free her daughter from the torment of a demon. Jesus' ethnically oriented response shows Jesus' personal understanding of his mission and its limits: "I was sent only to the lost sheep of the house of Israel" (v. 24); "it is not fair to take the children's food and throw it to the dogs" (v. 26). The woman's candid response about the dogs eating the crumbs that fall from their master's table receives an equally candid response from Jesus. The daughter is healed because of her mother's great faith. Jesus' mission expands, and people then and now see the wideness of God's mercy and the essence of the divine plan of salvation. This part of Matthew's Gospel also drives home the message made by Paul in last Sunday's second reading: "Everyone who calls on the name of the Lord shall be saved" (Rom. 10:13).

The reign of God is in our midst and will come to greater fruition if only we have the Canaanite woman's persistence and Jesus' openness to look into another's heart and his willingness to go beyond unnecessary boundaries for the sake of another's well-being.

FOURTEENTH SUNDAY AFTER PENTECOST

TWENTY-FIRST SUNDAY IN ORDINARY TIME
PROPER 16
AUGUST 25, 2002

REVISED COMMON	EPISCOPAL (BCP)	ROMAN CATHOLIC
Isa. 51:1-6 or	Isa. 51:1-6	Isa. 22:19-23
Exod. 1:8—2:10		
Psalm 138 or Psalm 124	Psalm 138	Ps. 138:1-2, 2-3, 6, 8
Rom. 12:1-8	Rom. 11:33-36	Rom. 11:33-36
Matt. 16:13-20	Matt. 16:13-20	Matt. 16:13-20

Artistic in expression and rich in theological thought, today's readings bring together three themes: salvation, promise, and divine assistance. The righteous are encouraged to remember God's saving deeds done for their ancestors and to anticipate that God will do such deeds again (Isa. 51:1-6). The ingenuity of Moses' mother and other women save the life of her baby son (Exod. 2:1-10). A psalmist recounts God's saving help during the exodus and places full confidence in God's name (Psalm 124). God promises to raise up a new leader for Judah (Isa. 22:19-23). Crowning all these events are Paul's confession of the majesty and wonder of God (Rom. 11:33-36) and Peter's confession of Jesus as the Son of God (Matt. 16:16). Wonder and awe fill God's people of old, and we are invited today to join in their delight.

FIRST READING
ISAIAH 51:1-6 (RCL, BCP)

Interpreting the Text

Proclaimed to a people in exile, Deutero-Isaiah's message offers the Israelites comfort and hope. The prophet, speaking God's words, calls upon the righteous—those who seek the Lord—to listen and to have confidence in God and to remember God's fidelity and goodness to Israel's ancestors, specifically Abraham and Sarah (vv. 1-2). Deutero-Isaiah assures the exiled and faithful remnant that God indeed will restore and renew Zion—the holy city Jerusalem—and its surrounding territory (v. 3). This is the first of God's promises.

The second promise is universal salvation. God, through the prophet, again calls the people to "listen." Their deliverance from exile is about to come swiftly. God will assert divine sovereignty but the people need to be patient and "wait." The reference to God's arms is a metaphor for divine power (vv. 4-5).

The third promise reinforces the second one. This time God tells the people to look up to the heavens above and the earth below—to observe the cosmos and to know that while creation is temporal, divine deliverance will be unending (vv. 5-6). God's ultimate plan is one of salvation that, although realized, continues to be eschatological.

Responding to the Text

When the Assyrians invaded and took over the Northern Kingdom, Israel, in 721 B.C.E., and the Babylonians captured the Southern Kingdom, Judah, leaving the Temple and the capital city Jerusalem in ruins, the Israelites became "landless" and thought that God had completely abandoned them. This was not the case, however, as Deutero-Isaiah makes known to us and to his people living in exile. Although all things in the heavens and on earth may come to naught, God's salvation and deliverance from pain, suffering, and oppression will never end. With patience and confidence one must wait and trust in God's redeeming activity at work in all situations.

Deutero-Isaiah's words of hope and comfort remind those who struggle today that God indeed will act on their behalf. Embedded in this text is a message to the natural world as well. When Israel was redeemed from exile, the people were also restored to their land, which itself was restored to life after the ravages of the battles it endured. God's words that promise restoration to Jerusalem's waste places and deserts need to be heard by all environmentalists today working for the care, preservation, and restoration of the earth. Indeed God is at work in their activity and their work is a sign of God's saving grace in our midst.

> GOD'S WORDS THAT PROMISE RESTORATION TO JERUSALEM'S WASTE PLACES AND DESERTS NEED TO BE HEARD BY ALL ENVIRONMENTALISTS TODAY WORKING FOR THE CARE, PRESERVATION, AND RESTORATION OF THE EARTH.

EXODUS 1:8—2:10 (RCL, alt.)

Interpreting the Text

The composite story of the Israelites' oppression, the cleverness of the Hebrew midwives, the blessing given to a Levite couple, the risk that the woman took on behalf of her baby son, the compassion of Pharaoh's daughter, the shrewdness of the infant child's older sister—all reveal how God's wonderful plan of salvation is set in motion by means of human beings, especially women, regardless of political edicts or people's ethnic backgrounds.

Fearing that the Israelites would become more numerous and thus more powerful than the Egyptians in whose land the Israelites were residing, the Egyptian Pharaoh tries to suppress their vigor by draining their strength through forced and harsh labor. Concurrent with this plan is his other plan: to have all Israelite baby boys die at the hands of the Hebrew midwives whom he commanded to obey him. Both plans fail. The more the Israelites were oppressed, the more they multiplied and spread and, in defiance of the Pharaoh's edict, the Hebrew midwives concocted a story that they relayed to Pharaoh about the Hebrew women giving birth before they arrived on the scene (1:8-22).

The well-known story of Moses' birth and early childhood begins with his mother sending him down the Nile in a basket because she feared for his life. His life is spared by the Egyptians because the Pharaoh's daughter hears his cries, has compassion on him, and takes him as her own even though she knows he is a Hebrew baby. To save the baby, she goes against her father's wishes but seems not to care. The life of the child at that moment is more important than an edict. Pharaoh's daughter's maid, Miriam, helps tend the child and with ingenuity seeks Moses' mother to come to nurse him. Thus Moses is reunited with two of his family members in the setting of Pharaoh's household (2:1-10).

As a whole, the story provides the backdrop for God's plan of salvation for the Israelite people as it begins to unravel, with both Hebrew and Egyptian women having a significant role to play.

Responding to the Text

Leaders of countries often set a tone for the people they govern, and they have power to make policies and decisions that can affect people's lives positively or negatively. When Joseph dies and a new king comes into power in Egypt, the time of security and plenty is ended for the Israelites residing there. Hard labor is now their lot, with death to their baby boys becoming the law of the land. In the midst of such pain and suffering, God's plan of salvation continues to unfold creatively and defiantly. Through the women of the day, Moses, God's chosen servant destined to lead the Israelites out of oppression, is born to a Levite man and woman. Because of Pharaoh's edict, his short life is threatened with death. Because of his mother's creativity, his sister's foresight and ingenuity, and Pharaoh's daughter's compassion, baby Moses' life is spared. If Pharaoh's daughter had not had pity on the child whom she found crying in a basket in the Nile among the reeds, and if such pity had not moved her to ignore her father's command to have all Hebrew baby boys thrown into the Nile, perhaps Israel's salvation history story would have turned out much differently.

The main point of the narrative, a common theme in other literature of its time, is that God is a God of justice who will act on behalf of those suffering from unjust oppression. God accomplishes the work of liberation and salvation through ordinary people whom God inspires and strengthens to accomplish the task at hand. For women who hear this narrative, it is good news because it illustrates the prominent role that women have had in the divine plan of salvation, a plan that crosses over the lines of ethnicity and religious background. This exodus story calls women today to join together and move forward with God's vision for life, realizing that they have been empowered by God's spirit and walk in a rich tradition.

> GOD ACCOMPLISHES THE WORK OF LIBERATION AND SALVATION THROUGH ORDINARY PEOPLE WHOM GOD INSPIRES AND STRENGTHENS TO ACCOMPLISH THE TASK AT HAND.

ISAIAH 22:19-23 (RC)

Interpreting the Text

The central character of Isaiah's proclamation is Shebna, a steward in the royal household of Judah who has used his position of power for self-enhancement at the expense of justice on behalf of the common good. Shebna receives from God, through Isaiah, a word of judgment that will eventually displace him from his duties (v. 19). Isaiah announces to Shebna that God intends to replace him with Eliakim, son of Hilkiah, upon whose hands and shoulders authority shall rest. This authority will be in keeping with the Davidic ancestral promises and heritage (vv. 20-23). Shebna, a historical figure, represents the old, failed Judah; Eliakim, an eschatological figure, embodies the new Judah that will rise out of the ash heaps and ruins of the old.

Responding to the Text

Throughout the course of their history, the people of Israel often had to endure living under difficult circumstances because of its leaders' failure to take to heart what was right and just for the good of all. One such official in Judah was Shebna, the focus of this reading. The prophet Isaiah delivers him the message that God will depose him and put in his place Eliakim. For the Judahites, this promise of a change in leadership brings hope. It is obvious from the text how the prophets of old interpreted all events as directly caused by the hand of God. In the ancient world, God was considered Lord of creation and Lord of history. God was "in control" of both.

Today perhaps a better way of understanding God as Lord of creation and Lord of history is to see God working through and in the midst of creation and history. A re-reading of this narrative would enable us to see God working through

the prophet Isaiah to bring the people of his day a new vision of leadership that
will act through the ordinary events of history to make justice a living reality.

RESPONSIVE READING

PSALM 138 (RCL, BC);
PSALM 138:1-2, 2-3, 6, 8 (RC)

In this song of thanksgiving the psalmist, singing praise to God in the
sanctuary precincts while gazing on the Temple, extols God's steadfast love,
fidelity, and graciousness toward those in need. The poet stresses that God has a
particular care for the lowly. For the haughty, however, there is a sense of divine
distance (v. 6). To accent God's salvific goodness, the poet inserts personal experience, stating that God was quick to respond in time of need (v. 3).

What encouragement this psalm offers to those in need of God's help, particularly in situations where one is rendered powerless! The psalm also serves as a
reminder that with the psalmist, we are called to give thanks to God for help
received whether in unusual circumstances or in the course of everyday life.

PSALM 124 (RCL, alt.)

Speaking on behalf of the community, the psalmist thanks and praises
God for saving deeds done at the time of Israel's exodus from Egypt. With
metaphorical language from the natural world, the psalmist compares Israel's
escape to that of a bird who has managed to evade the snare of fowlers, a snare—
a bondage—that was eventually broken (vv. 6-7).

This psalm invites us to reflect on our own history and recall when God has
been on our side either directly or indirectly through others when we may have
been on the brink of disaster but managed to escape "like a bird from the snare
of the fowlers."

SECOND READING

ROMANS 12:1-8 (RCL)

Interpreting the Text

In an eloquent appeal to the Roman Christians of his day, Paul encourages them to live a life of holiness, to celebrate their unity in Christ, and to recognize and affirm their diversity based on a variety of gifts given to individual
members of the community. Paul's appeal is threefold. The Roman Christians

180

THE SEASON
OF PENTECOST
───────────

CAROL J.
DEMPSEY

should (1) offer themselves as a living sacrifice to God. In other words, their whole lives should be dedicated to God and God's ways. (2) They should shape the culture and not become entrapped by it. And (3) they should allow God to transform their lives (vv. 1-2). Paul lists seven gifts and suggests how each should be used for the common good of the community (vv. 6-8). The point here is that one's life is meant to be in union with God, and one's gifts are meant to assist others in their life-journey to God. All are gifted and none is to consider himself or herself better than another, since all gifts come from God and are given with grace for the sake of the community.

Responding to the Text

Paul sees the goodness and giftedness of the human person and pleads with his listeners then and now to dedicate themselves to God, to become single-minded, and to be transformed in and through God instead of getting caught up in and by the world around them. In Paul's message is an inherent theological dualism that favors the spirit over the flesh, the things of heaven over the things of the world. This dualism reflects the culture of his day and his own Hellenistic background. A better way of understanding his message is to hear it as a call to be and remain centered in God and to live life out of that center.

CHRISTIANS TODAY CAN FIND IN PAUL'S MESSAGE A RENEWED SENSE OF PURPOSE FOR THEIR LIVES, A CHALLENGE TO RECOGNIZE AND ACCEPT EACH OTHER'S GIFTS AND TALENTS, AND A SAFEGUARD AGAINST THE INSIDIOUSNESS OF PRIDE.

Paul's emphasis on humility complements his point about the diversity of gifts, a diversity that has to be recognized and celebrated, and a giftedness that has to be used for the common good. For Paul, all has been given through grace. Christians today can find in Paul's message a renewed sense of purpose for their lives, a challenge to recognize and accept each other's gifts and talents, and a safeguard against the insidiousness of pride.

ROMANS 11:33-36 (BCP, RC)

Paul's doxology summarizes the whole doctrinal section of his letter to the Romans (Rom. 1:16—11:36) and proclaims that God's ways are merciful and upright toward all humanity and thus "unsearchable" and "inscrutable." Paul marvels at and in God who is the creator, sustainer, and hope of all, and proclaims that to this God glory is due forever. For Paul, God's grace and goodness are beyond comprehension and given freely without merit.

The experience of God brings with it a feeling of awe and wonder that is almost inexpressible. One can sense this in Paul's comments about God: "O the depth of the riches and the wisdom and knowledge of God!" He touches on a truth known to the ancients and still true today: while we can know something about God and God's ways, we will never in this life have full comprehension. One thing, however, is certain, and Paul makes it clear: all creation is from God and through God, and God is the goal of all creation.

THE GOSPEL
MATTHEW 16:13-20

Interpreting the Text

One of the most dramatic stories in Matthew's Gospel is Peter's confession, which marks a turning point in Peter's life and clarifies what is meant by the term Messiah when used of Jesus. The main characters in Matthew's narrative are Jesus and Peter.

The story opens with Jesus and his disciples gathered at the district of Caesarea Philippi, a site located on the southern slope of Mount Hermon near one of the sources of the Jordan River (v. 13). Jesus' question about himself addressed to his disciples sparks a diverse response as to his identity. They tell Jesus what others are saying (v. 19). The phrase "Son of Man" is a typical Matthean way of speaking about Jesus. The fact that Jesus' identity is associated with John the Baptist, Elijah, and Jeremiah indicates that both Matthew and perhaps the people of Jesus' day understood Jesus in relation to the prophetic tradition.

The story becomes more personal and narrowly focused when Jesus' asks the disciples to voice their ideas about his identity (v. 15). Peter's response, "You are the Messiah, the Son of the living God" is the climax of the Matthean narrative (v. 16). The phrase "living God" appears throughout the Old and New Testaments (see, e.g., Pss. 42:2; 84:2; Hos. 1:10; Matt. 26:63; Acts 14:15; Rom. 9:26). For Matthew's community, such a statement represents a "high Christology," connecting the historical person of Jesus to the divinity of God. Peter's response receives an affirmative comment from Jesus. Jesus then proceeds to inform Peter of the divine plan and mission that is to be his lot. In Greek there is a play on words between the name Peter and the term for rock, *petra* (this is true also in Aramaic: Peter/Cephas and *kepha*, "rock"). Jesus' church will be stronger than any other existing powers, including death and evil. The motif of the "keys of the kingdom of heaven" harks back to Isaiah's prophecy to Shebna (Isa. 22:22).

Jesus' final command for the disciples to remain silent about his identity is meant to keep Jesus from being accused of blasphemy by his opponents and to safeguard his freedom for the mission to be accomplished (v. 20).

Matthew's story of Peter's confession pictures Jesus being knowingly curious about what people are saying about him. His disciples tell him "what the word on the street is," after which Jesus gets more specific and Peter blurts out the truth. His knowledge of Jesus' identity is revealed, intuited with divine inspiration, and intimate. Jesus knew that Peter knew who he was. Otherwise he would never have asked the question a second time, aimed directly at his disciples. Matthew's story is about knowledge. What Peter knows is not humanly acquired, as the text clearly states. It is revealed knowledge.

This story teaches two profound lessons to its first-century audience and to people today: first, God does empower human beings to know and understand what is in the realm of the divine and, second, Jesus allows himself and in fact wants himself to be known. Jesus understood as Messiah and Son of God has been the common faith of Christians for centuries, but the depth of one's personal understanding of Jesus as Messiah and Son of God is a gift and a grace. One final note is the trust that Jesus places in Peter. Jesus will build his church on Peter, the rock. Peter does become the first leader of the church, but today the question needs to be asked, "Was Peter chosen because he was a disciple and male, or was it because of his solid knowledge of Jesus, his relationship with God, and the holiness of his person?"

> GOD DOES EMPOWER HUMAN BEINGS TO KNOW AND UNDERSTAND WHAT IS IN THE REALM OF THE DIVINE.

Jesus asks the same question today, "But who do you say that I am?"

FIFTEENTH SUNDAY AFTER PENTECOST

Twenty-second Sunday in Ordinary Time
Proper 17
September 1, 2002

Revised Common	Episcopal (BCP)	Roman Catholic
Jer. 15:15-21 or Exod. 3:1-15	Jer. 15:15-21	Jer. 20:7-9
Ps. 26:1-8 or Ps. 105: 1-6, 23-26, 45c	Psalm 26 or 26:1-8	Ps. 63:1, 2-3, 4-5, 7-8 (Heb. Bible 63:2, 3-4, 5-6, 8-9)
Rom. 12:9-21	Rom. 12:1-8	Rom. 12:1-2
Matt. 16:21-28	Matt. 16:21-27	Matt. 16:21-27

Suffering is an experience of human life. For a variety of reasons all people have suffered or do suffer. Some suffering is redemptive, while other suffering is unjust. In today's readings we hear about different kinds of suffering. Jeremiah suffers insult from his own people because of his prophetic mission (Jer. 15:15-18; 20:7-9), and he is hurt deeply because he feels that God has deceived him (Jer. 15:18; 20:7). The Israelites' unjust suffering under Egyptian oppression leads to Moses' call and commission on their behalf (Exod. 3:7-12; Ps. 105:23-26). One psalmist cries out for divine vindication (Ps. 26:1); another longs for God (Ps. 63:1). Jesus reveals the suffering he must soon endure, and this causes the disciples pain (Matt. 16:21-22). The pain of injustice and unjust suffering can cause one to lash out in revenge, but Paul offers words of encouragement on how to handle one's enemies (Rom. 12:14-21). Collectively these readings are a source of comfort rooted in profound experience.

FIRST READING
JEREMIAH 15:15-21 (RCL, BCP)

Interpreting the Text

One of what are popularly known as Jeremiah's laments, this passage depicts the prophet speaking candidly yet reflectively to God (vv. 15-18). Jeremiah receives a response from God that offers the prophet hope for himself personally as well as hope for the community that he embodies in his person (vv. 19-21).

Jeremiah opens his lament in a prayerful tone but not devoid of frustration: he wants God to look favorably upon him and to bring divine retribution upon his persecutors (v. 15). Jeremiah's request reflects a theology prevalent in his day and embedded within the ancient Israelite world, namely, the deuteronomistic theology of retribution (see Deuteronomy 28). The just were worthy of divine blessing; the unjust deserved a divine curse. Jeremiah then reflects on his mission, rooted in the divine. Jeremiah's work is God's work and has caused the prophet much suffering. He has had to confront his people with unpleasant words and visions of events to come and has

> JEREMIAH RECEIVES A RESPONSE FROM GOD THAT OFFERS THE PROPHET HOPE FOR HIMSELF PERSONALLY AS WELL AS HOPE FOR THE COMMUNITY THAT HE EMBODIES IN HIS PERSON.

had to speak of divine judgment and the demise of Judah and Jerusalem. His people do not want to hear such things, and the utterances themselves surprise Jeremiah who, based on his early experience of having received God's word, had thought that his work was going to be pleasant (vv. 15b-16). His unpleasant experience confuses him, as does the suffering associated with his task. He declares his bewilderment and innocence to God and accuses God of deceiving him (vv. 17-18). In the ancient world, sin was associated with suffering. What Jeremiah does not realize is that he bears the pain of rejection not because of divine disfavor but because of his people's hostility and indifference toward him as he tries to make them see what is to befall them if they do not change their ways.

Finally God responds to Jeremiah with promises first established when he was called to mission (see Jer. 1:17-19). These words of hope foreshadow Jeremiah's future and the eventual redemption of the Judahites from exile.

Responding to the Text

As Jeremiah pours out his soul to God, listeners come face to face with his suffering as a prophet. In God he confides: "Know that on your account I suffer insult" (Jer. 15:15). Jeremiah had the arduous task of calling his people to repentance and urging them to return to God. What he thought was going to be a delightful task turns out to be unceasing pain, because his people do not want to hear what he has to say, nor are they going to change their ways. Yet Jeremiah is not without hope. God promises to be with him to deliver him.

Jeremiah's suffering recalls Elijah's experience when he fled from Jezebel and took refuge in a cave because the apostate Israelites of his day were killing the prophets with a sword and were seeking his life as well (1 Kings 19:10). Jeremiah's suffering is redemptive; some people will repent and be saved from the devastation about to befall the Southern Kingdom, but most will not. A prophet is called to be faithful, not successful.

EXODUS 3:1-15 (RCL, alt.)

Interpreting the Text

The story of Moses and the burning bush is full of wonder and surprise. It reflects Israel's understanding of Moses as not only a great lawgiver but also a great prophet. The narrative opens with Moses tending the flock of his father-in-law, Jethro (v. 1). In the midst of such a mundane task, the unexpected occurs. Moses has an encounter with God who reveals to him a mission that must be accomplished—the Israelites' liberation from Pharaoh's wretched grip (vv. 2-11). Such a task draws a reluctant response from Moses, who then receives a divine response: God will be with him (v. 12). As if that were not enough, Moses presses God further as to what he should say to the Israelites about this God who has commanded him to carry out such an extraordinary mission (v. 13). The last part of the narrative focuses on God revealing God's identity and name to Moses: God is the one who is, the God of Moses' ancestors, the God of the great patriarchs and matriarchs.

Quite probably what Moses saw was not a bush ablaze. In Israel there is a shrub known for its brilliant red blossoms. It is quite possible in the realm of religious experience that his type of bush may have been transfigured before Moses. The double call of Moses—the name and his response, "Here I am"—are two elements stereotypical of prophetic call narratives (see, e.g., 1 Samuel 3). Furthermore, Moses' encounter with God was not for his own self-

> GOD IS A GOD OF JUSTICE, COMPASSION, AND LIBERATION WHOSE PLAN OF SALVATION AND ITS REALIZATION HAS BEEN ENTRUSTED TO THE HUMAN COMMUNITY.

gratification but a twofold purpose: first, to empower Moses to lead the people out of oppression and, second, to reveal to the Israelites something about the person, wonder, and goodness of their God. The story attests to the fact that God is a God of justice, compassion, and liberation, whose plan of salvation and its realization have been entrusted to the human community—a plan whose revelation takes place in the natural world amid the ordinary.

Responding to the Text

The story of Moses and the burning bush is a fantastic one, laden with imagery and theological points of interest. As one reads and hears this story again and again, it becomes clear that Moses' experience at the bush was the foundation and cornerstone of his future life and ministry on behalf of his people, the Israelites. Several points come to the fore. First, Israel's God is attuned to unjust suffering and responds to it. Second, Moses' "religious" experience is a deeply personal and private one that leads to his being commissioned by God and thus putting him in the forefront of Egyptian-Israelite politics. Third, the work that

Moses has to do, namely, lead the Israelites out of oppression and begin moving them toward a new land, marks the beginning of the fulfillment of a covenant promise. Fourth, Israel's God is self-revelatory.

All the theological dimensions of this text have helped to shape not only Israel's religious history but also Jewish religious tradition which, in turn, has had an impact on the Christian religious tradition. Israel's God encountered in this narrative becomes embodied in Jesus in the New Testament, who takes God's response to the cry of the oppressed one step further: he lays down his own life, an event hinted at in today's Gospel.

JEREMIAH 20:7-9 (RC)

Interpreting the Text

In this poignant and candid lament the prophet Jeremiah confronts his God, who he thinks has tricked him. Jeremiah then proceeds to let God know the pain and struggles he is enduring because of the divine prophetic word and mission entrusted to him.

Earlier in the book of Jeremiah, one encounters the prophet being "set up" by God for the tasks ahead. God ensures Jeremiah that he has been made into a "fortified city," an "iron pillar," a "bronze wall" (Jer. 1:18). Anyone who would fight against Jeremiah would not prevail, because God would be there to deliver him (Jer. 1:19). Is it any wonder then that Jeremiah feels as though he has been duped? A better translation for the word "enticed" is "tricked" or "duped." God has tricked Jeremiah, who has become a laughingstock and a target of mockery because of what he proclaims, namely, the forthcoming demise of Judah, the fall of Jerusalem, and the exile of God's people. This sounds crazy to those among God's chosen ones who rest in smug confidence that because they are chosen and divinely blessed with land and a certain amount of power they are invincible. Jeremiah's cry of "violence" and "destruction" is a double entendre: it mirrors the internal strife of Judah and the chaos about to befall the Southern Kingdom at the hands of the Babylonians. His message is a disturbing one but, compelled by the Spirit of God within him, he has to proclaim his foreboding message, which would have been a moment of grace if heeded by his people.

Responding to the Text

Jeremiah has no fear about approaching God openly and honestly: "O Lord, you have enticed me, and I was enticed. . . ." Having been promised that he would be set up by God to be powerful and strong, he is bewildered by his experience of rejection. He suffers because he feels God has tricked him; he has become a laughingstock among his own people; and he has to proclaim a terrifying message. Moreover, he is unable to escape from being faithful to his prophetic mission to deliver God's word because when he tries not to speak out the word burns inside of him.

Jeremiah's suffering and dilemma of not being able to turn aside from his prophetic vocation are real experiences. In the global environment that we live in today, injustices and infidelities similar to and worse than those of Jeremiah's day present themselves daily. To what extent are we willing to exercise our prophetic vocations for the good of others? One's consolation rests in the fact that God is a prophet's best friend and will remain faithful through the struggles and the suffering for the sake of justice for the common good.

Responsive Reading

PSALM 26:1–8 (RCL; BCP, alt.); PSALM 26 (BCP)

The main theme of this "psalm of innocence" is the uprightness of one of Israel's community members who petitions God for vindication. Sincerely and confidently, the psalmist addresses God directly with a series of imperatives: "vindicate me," "prove me," "try me," "test my heart and my mind" (vv. 1–2).

This psalm is a lesson in expectation: If one is just and righteous before God and walks in God's ways, then one can anticipate divine favor in times of need, if such assistance is asked for with humility and faith.

PSALM 105:1–6, 23–26, 45c (RCL, alt.)

With enthusiasm the psalmist calls the Israelite community to give thanks to God and make known God's wonderful works (vv. 1–6). In the second part the psalmist recalls the early events of the exodus story (vv. 23–25) and then how God sent Moses and Aaron to assist the Israelites (v. 26). The psalm closes with an exhortation: "Praise the Lord" (v. 45c).

The art of retelling the history of a community in song helps to preserve the memory of that history. Interpreting the events from hindsight helps the singer to see the threads of the Divine at work in the tapestry of the human.

PSALM 63:1, 2–3, 4–5, 7–8, NRSV (RC)

The poet with great ardor expresses deep longing and thirst for God—a longing like that of a dry and weary land (v. 1–4). The psalm then moves from longing to satisfaction. No longer thirsting for God, the psalmist's soul is satiated as with a rich feast, a state that gives rise to further praise of God (vv. 5-8).

This psalm speaks of a different kind of suffering, one that is caused by a passionate yearning for God. For the psalmist the fullness of one's joy is God, who satisfies completely one's deepest hunger and trust. What a reflection for all of us who live in the midst of endless commercial consumerism and consumption!

SECOND READING

ROMANS 12:9-21 (RCL); ROMANS 12:1-8 (BCP); ROMANS 12:1-2 (RC)

Interpreting the Text

Having instructed the Roman Christians on their unity in Christ and the diversity of their gifts to be used for the common good of the community, Paul now offers his audience a series of counsels that will mark their lives as Christians. The counsels appear to be a random collection of maxims but when examined closely, two themes emerge: first, the ways that Christians are to manifest genuine love (vv. 10-13), and second, the obligations that one has towards one's enemies (vv. 14-20). The final verse summarizes Paul's comments: Christians are not to succumb to evil and evil's ways but are to deal with evil according to the ways of goodness. Implicit in Paul's final statement is the reversal of the *lex talionis* that advocated "an eye for an eye and a tooth for a tooth" mentality on the part of the people.

Responding to the Text

Paul's advice to his Roman Christian listeners calls them to a life of holiness marked by virtue, right relationships, and deep peace. Often common in any community is human strife, and this was no different in Paul's day than it is today. Paul's opening phrase, "Let your love be genuine" (v. 9), is central to the entire passage. It provides a context for his other exhortations. Genuine love is the foundation for being in right relationship with God and with others. It empowers and stirs up inner enthusiasm to accomplish the work of God, of which God's people have a part. Love enables one to be patient in suffering and persevering in prayer. Generosity and hospitality are love's fruits and the foundation out of which one must deal with one's opponents. Paul's message to his original hearers is profound and timeless and offers people today both a challenge and a vision.

GENUINE LOVE IS THE FOUNDATION FOR BEING IN RIGHT RELATIONSHIP WITH GOD AND WITH OTHERS.

MATTHEW 16:21-28 (RCL);
MATTHEW 16:21-27 (BCP, RC)

Interpreting the Text

In this passage Matthew features Jesus predicting his passion for the first time, a revelation that triggers an adverse response from Peter (vv. 21-23). Following the news of his forthcoming death, Jesus instructs his disciples on the role that suffering plays in the commitment to discipleship (vv. 24-26). In the final section Jesus describes the events surrounding his return in glory and what that will mean for humankind (vv. 27-28).

That Jesus had a sense of his fate is highly possible, given the political climate of Palestine and what he and others understood the lot of the prophets of old to be. There is good indication from Jesus' mission and ministry as attested by the evangelists that Jesus did understand himself and his work in the context of the prophetic tradition. Noteworthy is the point that Jesus would be made to suffer at the hands of the leaders of his day (v. 21). Matthew depicts Jesus being certain about the final outcome of his mission and, when tempted not to embrace it, he deals with the temptation head on (vv. 22-23).

Jesus' teaching on discipleship is paradoxical. Here the fate of the disciples becomes linked with Jesus' own fate. The work of God—bringing about the reign of justice, righteousness, and compassion—will cost nothing less than everything (vv. 24-26). The last part of the passage is somewhat apocalyptic in its tone and description. It echoes Mark 87:38, except that Matthew has added the idea of judgment to his own text.

JESUS' TEACHING ON DISCIPLESHIP IS PARADOXICAL. HERE THE FATE OF THE DISCIPLES BECOMES LINKED WITH JESUS' OWN FATE.

For Matthew's community, this passage adds further insight into the people's understanding of Jesus and offers them a bold challenge around which to focus their lives.

Responding to the Text

Perhaps nothing can be worse in life than knowing that you are soon going to die, or being a very close friend of someone who tells you that he or she is about to die soon. This is the situation of Matthew's Gospel—Jesus foreshadows his own death, and Peter responds negatively and with consternation. What anguish Jesus, Peter, and the other disciples must have felt in their hearts, knowing ahead of time what was to be a devastating and inevitable bend to one's mission, ministry, and life! In the Old Testament, the prophet Elijah fears for his life, especially since the Israelites are killing the prophets. His life is spared from the sword. In the New Testament, however, Jesus is put to death because of his mission and ministry, particularly to the outcasts, the poor, the unloved, and because of his teachings and reinterpretation of the Law. Jesus lived his whole life prophetically and with purpose and focus. Is it any wonder that he was put to death?

Today's Gospel leads into the final period of Jesus' life as we watch his single-mindedness confront temptation and move forward with his mission and ministry. As Christians called to live in union with Christ, this Gospel reminds everyone that the suffering endured as part of one's fidelity to God and God's liberating work is a redemptive suffering that may culminate in the loss of one's life for the sake of God's people and mission. Such is the story of modern-day martyrs like Oscar Romero.

Dare we fully embrace Jesus' life and journey with him to Jerusalem?

SIXTEENTH SUNDAY AFTER PENTECOST

Twenty-third Sunday in Ordinary Time
Proper 18
September 8, 2002

Revised Common	Episcopal (BCP)	Roman Catholic
Ezek. 33:7-11 or Exod. 12:1-14	Ezek. 33:(1-6), 7-11	Ezek. 33:7-9
Ps. 119:33-40 or Psalm 149	Ps. 119:33-48 or 119:33-40	Ps. 95:1-2, 6-7, 8-9
Rom. 13:8-14	Rom. 12:9-21	Rom. 13:8-10
Matt. 18:15-20	Matt. 18:15-20	Matt. 18:15-20

The biblical texts for this Sunday offer a potpourri of ideas. The writers try to paint a picture of their understanding of God while commenting on life as it was lived or meant to be lived in the ancient Israelite and early Christian communities. Ezekiel's proclamation depicts God warning both Ezekiel and his people what will happen to them if the right choices are not made by them and on their behalf (Ezek. 33:1-11). The reading from Exodus portrays God outlining for Moses and Aaron how the Passover feast is to be celebrated (Exod. 12:1-14). The psalms focus on the praise and worship of God and the ardent desire of the psalmist to know and keep God's law (Psalms 95, 119, 145). Matthew's Gospel provides a lesson on how to reprove one's brother or sister when an offense has been done (Matt. 18:15-20), and Paul's letter to the Romans picks up on the concept of law introduced in Psalm 119. Paul speaks of love as the law's fulfillment and reminds his listeners then and now of the essence of Christian life.

First Reading

EZEKIEL 33:7-11 (RCL); EZEKIEL 33: (1-6), 7-11 (BCP); EZEKIEL 33:7-9 (RC)

Interpreting the Text

God's message to Ezekiel is a warning that calls the people and Ezekiel to responsibility for their own future. The proclamation also sheds light on God's desire that all be saved, including the wicked. The community's fate rests in its own hands and is dependent upon the decisions it makes.

Ezekiel's proclamation has three segments. In the first, God commands Ezekiel to deliver a message to the Israelites. God sets up a hypothetical situation involving the people's "sentinel." The sentinel is to warn the people of approaching disaster, and if they respond positively they will be spared. If not, they will die. If the sentinel does not sound a warning at the sight of impending danger and people do die, then that will be the result of their own iniquity, with responsibility falling to the sentinel (vv. 1-6).

In the second part of the proclamation, God declares to Ezekiel that he is to be the sentinel described earlier. If he performs his task diligently, even if the so-called "wicked" people do not respond, then his life will be spared (vv. 7-9).

In the last part of the proclamation, Ezekiel receives a divine word that he must declare to his listeners. First he reflects back to members of his community the words of those who have acknowledged their sinfulness and their sense of apathy revealed by their rhetorical question, "How then can we live?" To this people in particular Ezekiel is to make known God's wishes: God desires that these people repent of their ways and live and thus avert death by the foreshadowed sword (vv. 10-11; cf. vv. 1-5).

Ezekiel's warnings are an attempt to help the people of his day see that Israel's God is a God of salvation who is ready to forgive if the people are willing to amend their wicked ways.

Responding to the Text

The word that Ezekiel receives from God is anything but pleasant and offers only a brief glimmer of hope. Like Israel's other prophets, Ezekiel has the task of declaring to the people their sins and injustices. He also alludes to God's forgiveness if the people are willing to repent and take responsibility for their transgressions. Although this seems somewhat foreboding, God's warnings to the people are all experiences of grace and part of the divine plan of salvation. The text makes clear that God's will is for reconciliation and not devastation, but Ezekiel's community members have to do their part at reforming their ways.

> ALTHOUGH THIS SEEMS SOMEWHAT FORE-
> BODING, GOD'S WARNINGS TO THE PEOPLE
> ARE ALL EXPERIENCES OF GRACE AND PART
> OF THE DIVINE PLAN OF SALVATION.

EXODUS 12:1-14 (RCL, alt.)

Interpreting the Text

One of the most important feasts for the Jewish people is Passover, a time of celebration commemorating their deliverance from Egyptian oppression. For ancient Israel, "passover" meant to spare, to protect, to deliver. Although the Passover ritual is a typically Jewish feast, its roots are much older than the ancient Israelite community itself. It probably dates back to the time of semi-nomadic shepherds in the ancient Near East and was understood as an offering by shepherds made to assure their flocks' welfare as shepherds and sheep set out for new pastures early each spring. This tradition was most likely known to the Israelites, who reinterpreted it in light of their relationship with God (vv. 1-11). The blood rite mentioned in the context of the Passover story links the Passover ritual to the tenth plague (see Exod. 11:4-5). The last portion of the narrative depicts Israel's God as a God of justice—Egypt will receive its just deserts, but at what cost to human and nonhuman life?

Responding to the Text

The story about the first Passover gives the details of how the feast was to be celebrated among the Israelites as they prepared to flee from Egypt. The main portion of the feast consisted of a whole, unblemished, one-year-old male lamb to be divided in proportion to the number of people who eat it. The figure of the lamb is a symbol of Israel in the book of Isaiah (40:11) and of the followers of Jesus in the Gospel of John (21:15). The prophet Jeremiah refers to himself as a lamb led to slaughter (Jer. 11:19), and John the Baptist calls Jesus the Lamb of God (John 1:29, 36). In keeping with the ancient ritual, Jesus used a lamb when celebrating the Passover meal with his disciples (Mark 14:12; Luke 22:7). The lamb is one of the primary symbols used in the book of Revelation to speak of hope to the persecuted Christians. In sum, the lamb is not only part of a sacred ritual but also integral to Israel's self-understanding throughout history.

The text raises an important theological issue: The image of God as a violent force that is about to strike down the firstborn of the land in Egypt—both humans and animals—is a troubling one. One can be sure that a certain amount of "theologizing" on the text has occurred. What kind of a God would do such a thing? Or is this the author's perception of God's ways? The text legitimates violence for the sake of the Israelites' liberation: innocent children and animals are killed. The way that the biblical tradition portrays God's justice is in need of further hermeneutical consideration.

RESPONSIVE READING
PSALM 119:33-40 (RCL);
PSALM 119:33-48 or 119:33-40 (BCP)

The focus of this psalm is Torah—God's law, commandments, decrees, and ways. For the poet God is the one who instructs in Torah. Hence the psalm speaks of the psalmists' intimate relationship with God, which becomes evident through a series of petitions in the first part of the psalm (vv. 33-40). The second part picks up on the theme of love, where the psalmist asks for God's steadfast love, which is salvific love (v. 41).

For the psalmist, God's word and decrees are a source of liberty and delight to be revered and meditated upon (vv. 42-48).

PSALM 149 (RCL, alt.)

Psalm 149 is a hymn of praise whose first and last lines form an *inclusio* that frames the entire poem: "Praise the Lord!" The psalmist beckons the Israelite community to exult in God the creator, especially God the creator of Israel (v. 2), with song, dancing, and musical instruments (vv. 1-5).

The imagery of this psalm captures the ancient people's delight in their God and invites communities today to reflect on God's goodness and celebrate it in a myriad of artistic ways.

PSALM 95: 1-2, 6-7, 8-9 (RC)

Psalm 95 is considered a New Year psalm that became part of the liturgy for an autumn festival. The psalmist calls the Israelite community to the festal praise of God, who is their rock of salvation, their maker, their God, and their shepherd (vv. 1-7a). The last part of the psalm is an exhortation in which the psalmist calls on the community not to harden their hearts, as their ancestors did at Meribah and at Massah in the wilderness (vv. 8-9; cf. Exod. 17:1-7; Num. 20:1-13; Ps. 81:7).

This psalm is a joy-filled and awe-filled expression of wonder at the marvel of God, the creator and sustainer of all.

SECOND READING
ROMANS 13:8-14 (RCL);
ROMANS 13:8-10 (RC)

Interpreting the Text

Paul's teaching to the Roman Christians on the topic of love, which he introduced already in Rom. 12:9-21, continues here, where Paul asserts that love fulfills the law (vv. 8-10). This assertion may be rooted in Paul's understanding of the deuteronomistic theology of love (see Deut. 10:12-14; cf. Lev. 19:17) and echoes the teachings ascribed to Jesus (see Matt. 22:34-40; cf. Mark 12:28-34;

Luke 10:25-28). The second half of Paul's message is an appeal. Here Paul urges Christians to be vigilant, for the time of their salvation is near. Paul uses a series of contrasting images to persuade his audience to live responsibly and in the image of Christ. Paul's reference to making no provision for the flesh and the gratification of its desires probably stems from his Hellenistic background. The inherent early Christian dualism between body and soul becomes apparent in Paul's preaching.

Responding to the Text

Paul's teaching about love goes right to the heart of the Law. If one truly understood and practiced the dynamics of love and the virtues of justice and righteousness inherent in it, then one would not need to be told not to commit adultery, not to murder, not to steal, and not to covet. Offenses against one's neighbor would be nonexistent if one understood love as being in right relationship with God and with the rest of creation.

> OFFENSES AGAINST ONE'S NEIGHBOR WOULD BE NONEXISTENT IF ONE UNDERSTOOD LOVE AS BEING IN RIGHT RELATIONSHIP WITH GOD AND WITH THE REST OF CREATION.

Paul's urgent appeal to watchfulness encourages all people to be vigilant. His advice to make no provision for the flesh and its desires cannot be taken literally. Today, the challenge is to move toward integration and away from subjugation. The whole person journeys to God.

THE GOSPEL
MATTHEW 18:15-20

Interpreting the Text

How to handle an injustice done by one member of the community against another had to be discerned wisely in the world of early Christianity. Matthew offers a view different from the traditional Old Testament "an eye for an eye and a tooth for a tooth." This discourse features Jesus instructing his disciples on how to deal with the situation when one member of the church community might sin against any of them. Jesus gives the disciples a three-step procedure for reconciliation (vv. 15-17). The Dead Sea Scrolls indicate that the Essenes at Qumran also practiced this procedure (see 1QS 5:24-25).

Following the outline for reproving a community member are three additional comments in which the Gospel writer depicts Jesus giving further advice to his disciples. These sayings about binding and loosing (v. 18), reaching a mutual agreement among themselves (v. 19), and Jesus' presence among two or three of

CAROL J.
DEMPSEY

them gathered in his name are sayings that probably refer to the community's power, ability, and decision to exclude members from it who refuse to refrain from injustice and thus choose not to be reconciled with one's brothers or sisters.

Responding to the Text

Matthew offers his community a compassionate way of dealing with a person who commits an offense against another. His suggested method of confrontation upholds the dignity and integrity of all persons involved. It also provides certain positive constraints and boundaries that leave the opportunity for reform in the hands of the offender, who has to exercise his or her free will and choose "the good." Recalcitrant members are subject to exclusion from the community. Matthew's Gospel illustrates to people today how they can be proactive against injustice, and how injustice can be dealt with nonviolently.

> MATTHEW OFFERS HIS COMMUNITY A COMPASSIONATE WAY OF DEALING WITH A PERSON WHO COMMITS AN OFFENSE AGAINST ANOTHER, ONE THAT UPHOLDS THE DIGNITY AND INTEGRITY OF ALL PERSONS INVOLVED.

Would that preachers and members of believing communities encourage people everywhere to settle disputes with honest dialogue instead of with verbal and physical abuse!

SEVENTEENTH SUNDAY AFTER PENTECOST

TWENTY-FOURTH SUNDAY IN ORDINARY TIME
PROPER 19
SEPTEMBER 15, 2002

REVISED COMMON	EPISCOPAL (BCP)	ROMAN CATHOLIC
Gen. 50:15-21 or	Sir. 27:30—28:7	Sir. 27:30—28:7
Exod. 14:19-31		
Ps. 103:(1-7), 8-13 or	Psalm 103 or 103:8-13	Ps. 103:1-2, 3-4,
Psalm 114 or Exod.		9-10, 11-12
15:1b-11, 20-21		
Rom. 14:1-12	Rom. 14:5-12	Rom. 14:7-9
Matt. 18:21-35	Matt. 18:21-35	Matt. 18:21-35

At the heart of Jewish and Christian life is reconciliation. Today's readings advocate forgiveness as a virtue and a way of life. Joseph forgives his brothers their past unkindness (Gen. 50:15-21). Ben Sira encourages one to forgive one's neighbor and extend mercy to all (Sir. 27:30—28:7). The psalmist proclaims that God is merciful and gracious and does not retain anger forever (Psalm 103). Paul calls his community not to judge one another (Rom. 14:1-12), and Matthew's Gospel depicts Jesus instructing Peter on forgiving others without measure (Matt. 18:21-35). In sum, this Sunday's readings call people to wholeness and holiness through the gift and virtue of forgiveness.

FIRST READING
GENESIS 50:15-21 (RCL)

Interpreting the Text

One of the final episodes in the story of Joseph and his encounter with his brothers involves the virtues of reconciliation and reassurance. The brothers, uncertain of Joseph's response toward them, approach him with their father's request that Jacob made before he died. It was Jacob's fervent desire that Joseph forgive his brothers the wrong they did to him in the past. When the brothers verbalize Jacob's wishes to Joseph, he is overcome with emotion, which initiates the same response from the brothers: they all weep. Joseph assures them that he has forgiven them and promises to care for them and their families. One other significant point in the story is Joseph telling his brothers not to be afraid and asking them the rhetorical question, "Am I in the place of God?" The goodness God has extended to Joseph, Joseph now offers to his brothers. Joseph's spirit of reconciliation and care is the living embodiment of the Spirit of God, who is quick to forgive and answer one's needs, especially when requested from a contrite heart. Jacob's desire that the brothers be reconciled one to another also sheds light on the importance of familial harmony, a primary virtue of Israelite and Jewish family life.

> JOSEPH'S SPIRIT OF RECONCILIATION AND CARE IS THE LIVING EMBODIMENT OF THE SPIRIT OF GOD, WHO IS QUICK TO FORGIVE AND ANSWER ONE'S NEEDS WHEN REQUESTED FROM A CONTRITE HEART.

Responding to the Text

Jacob's words given to his sons before he dies as well as Joseph's heartfelt forgiveness of his brothers accent the importance of family life and family unity in the ancient biblical and Near Eastern world. A father's plea moves the hearts of his sons, who are not afraid to express their emotions. This narrative, one of the last segments in the Joseph cycle, reminds people everywhere that the way to peace is through forgiveness. Reconciliation happens with risk and vulnerability, and sometimes by means of another's intercession.

EXODUS 14:19-31 (RCL, alt.)

Interpreting the Text

The crossing of the Red Sea, the climax of the Israelites' liberation from Egyptian oppression, occurs in this passage. This narrative contains material from both the Yahwist and Priestly traditions that have been woven together to dramatize the final events that led up to the Israelites' wilderness journey and their life-changing experience at Mount Sinai. The narrative of the crossing of the Red Sea is an example of God's active presence in the course of human history.

The story opens with various symbols which, according to the biblical tradition, are representative of God's presence. These symbols include the angel and the pillar of cloud, both of which assist the Israelites (vv. 19-20). The symbol of the cloud is associated with God's presence in the New Testament also (see, e.g., Matt. 17:1-13, especially v. 5). The cloud has a long history of interpretation in extrabiblical texts and early Christian writings as well.

The remainder of the narrative focuses on God and Moses. Moses' outstretched hand over the sea parts it and enables the Israelites to cross over to the other side, much to the dismay of the Egyptians, who experience calamity from God. The image of the outstretched hand is a sign of God's liberating power. Later, in the writings of the prophets, it becomes a sign of divine judgment against Israel (see, e.g., Ezek. 6:14). The Egyptians experience disaster by the exercise of divine power on Israel's behalf: The Red Sea swallows up Pharaoh and his entire army (vv. 26-29). The story closes with a brief comment by the narrator, who stresses Israel's belief in God and Moses because of what the people have heard, seen, and experienced.

The passage, fantastic in its description, is not meant to be taken literally. Theologically, it portrays a God who acts on behalf of the oppressed. Israel's God is a God of liberation, but how the author depicts this God of liberation is in need of further thought and comment.

Responding to the Text

The narrative about the crossing of the Red Sea depicts Moses having power over human and natural world forces. The symbol of his power is the outstretched hand. The story attests to God as a God of liberation who acts through humankind and the natural world to bring about justice. The text invites us to ponder God's ways of liberating grace made manifest through the human community and the created world.

SIRACH 27:30—28:7 (BCP, RC)

Interpreting the Text

The Wisdom of Ben Sira (Greek: Sirach) is known as one of the seven deuterocanonical books found in the Catholic canon of the Old Testament and considered part of the Apocrypha by Protestants. Known largely for its didactic style, Sirach contains much practical and speculative wisdom. This particular passage condemns anger and wrath. It points out both the folly of vengeance and also the need to forgive others if one expects to be pardoned (vv. 1-5). Four times the writer of the text calls for listeners "to remember" and then proceeds to highlight the importance and relevance of God's commandments and covenant, both of which need to be heeded. The wisdom contained within this passage echoes Lev. 19:17-18, which advises against revenge. The precepts to be followed that the writer sets down have as their goal peace with oneself, one's God, and one's neighbor.

200

THE SEASON
OF PENTECOST

CAROL J.
DEMPSEY

Responding to the Text

Sirach calls the people of his day to holiness by focusing on forgiveness and emphasizing that anger and wrath are abominations held in delight by sinners. Divine forgiveness is contingent upon a person's forgiveness of another. Hence for Sirach reconciliation involves mutuality, with forgiveness being the central factor in having a right relationship with others and with God.

RESPONSIVE READING
PSALM 103:(1-7), 8-13 (RCL);
PSALM 103: or 103:8-13 (BCP);
PSALM 103:1-2, 3-4, 9-10, 11-12 (RC)

The main theme of Psalm 103 is God's steadfast love, described in a variety of ways. The first part is a self-address: the psalmist calls upon his or her own soul not to forget all the goodness and graces that God has bestowed. "Soul" here does not imply immortality but denotes one's whole being as understood in the context of biblical tradition. In the second part the poet appeals to the exodus tradition (see Exod. 3; 34:6-7a-b), comparing God's compassion to that a father for his children. Human beings are like short-lived flowers, in complete contrast to God's everlasting steadfast love.

God's gift of compassion is at the heart of reconciliation. God's graciousness toward those who have sinned is an unearned grace. The challenge for believers today is to extend to one another God's forgiveness, compassion, and graciousness to those who have sinned against one's self or another.

PSALM 114 (RCL, alt.)

The original setting of Psalm 114 was most likely the covenant festival of Yahweh. In later Judaism, the psalm became known as a Passover hymn sung on the eighth day of the festival commemorating the exodus. The psalm opens with a direct reference to the exodus from Egypt (vv. 1-2), followed by four examples of the effects that the exodus had on the natural world (vv. 3-4).

One sees the gift of poetic imagination at work in this psalm, particularly the literary technique of personification. The psalm celebrates the power of God who is Lord of history and Lord of creation.

With joy and exuberance, the Israelite people celebrate their good fortune. Justice has been served; they have been liberated from Egyptian oppression; both they and their God have been victorious, and thus, there is great cause for singing. This reading consists of two songs that became part of Israel's collective history and tradition: the song of Moses (vv. 1b–11) and the song of Miriam (vv. 20–21).

After the ordeal of Egyptian oppression and God's liberating intercession, no response could be more appropriate than song. The two songs attributed to Moses and Miriam keep alive the Israelites' memory of salvation history and invite believers today to make up their own songs that commemorate God's wonderful deeds in their lives.

SECOND READING
ROMANS 14:1–12 (RCL);
ROMANS 14:5–12 (BCP);
ROMANS 14:7–9 (RC)

Interpreting the Text

Further developing his theme of love, Paul turns his attention to the "weak" members of the community who are to be welcomed and respected within the context of love. Whether or not Paul actually used the term "weak" with respect to specific people is uncertain. The term probably referred to the Jewish-Christian members of the Roman community, with the implied opposite group, the "strong," referring to Gentile-Christian members. Paul's immediate concern is with questions related to the eating of meat, the drinking of wine, and the observance of holy days. Within Judaism, some members practiced vegetarianism, though there was no formal prohibition against eating meat. Paul's point is clear: regardless of one's choices, mutual respect is to be the guiding principle. This principle extends to one's observation of holy days as well, for all choices are made with due respect to God (vv. 1–6).

PAUL MAKES THE POINT THAT THE LIVES OF ALL CHRISTIANS ARE INEXTRICABLY BOUND TO THE LIFE OF CHRIST AND THAT JUDGMENT BELONGS TO GOD AND NOT TO HUMAN BEINGS, ALL OF WHOM ARE ULTIMATELY ACCOUNTABLE TO GOD.

Paul makes the final point to all Christians that their lives are inextricably bound to the life of Christ and that judgment belongs to God and not to human beings, all of whom are ultimately accountable to God (vv. 10–12). In sum, Paul's message aims at promoting harmony among the various groups of people within the Christian community.

202

THE SEASON
OF PENTECOST

CAROL J.
DEMPSEY

Responding to the Text

Paul's message to the Romans indicates that there was strife in the Roman Christian community of his day. His exhortation to them and indirect admonishment of them highlights their problem of passing judgment. Paul refocuses their attention on God and reminds them that each person is responsible to God. Thus, to pass judgment against another is not within their purview. For those caught in the web of passing judgment unjustly on others, this reading offers some curt advice.

THE GOSPEL

MATTHEW 18:21-35

Interpreting the Text

The central focus of this Matthean text is forgiveness. Matthew here develops a theme introduced earlier, namely, the appropriate responses on the part of those church members who have been sinned against by other church members (see Matt. 18:15-20). Previously Jesus had been addressing his disciples. Now Peter responds to Jesus' teaching by asking a question, and thus begins a new episode in the conversation already begun by Jesus. Peter's concern is not about how to reprove unruly church members. He wants to know how many times he should forgive those who err against him. Jesus' response is straightforward: seventy-seven times (vv. 21-22). The point made is that there is to be no limit to one's willingness to forgive. A parable about an unforgiving servant illustrates the point further (vv. 23-35).

Following Jesus' comments to Peter, Matthew depicts Jesus telling Peter, and probably other listeners as well, a parable about an unforgiving servant (vv. 23-35). The crux of the lesson is that, just as God is merciful to sinners, so must human beings be merciful toward one another, especially when one has been wronged by another. The fact that the servant offers the king payment for what is owed is significant. Justice calls for willingness on the part of the offender to make restitution eventually. Justice complements mercy. The parable closes with Jesus disclosing its meaning: God desires people to forgive one another from the heart (v. 35). In turn, those who forgive will find favor with God.

> JUST AS GOD IS MERCIFUL TO SINNERS, SO MUST HUMAN BEINGS BE MERCIFUL TOWARD ONE ANOTHER.

Matthew's comments on forgiveness of sins emphasize not only the importance of this virtue but also the generosity with which this gift is to be given to others. The number of times one forgives another is to be without limit. The parable of the unforgiving servant drives home the message to the early Christian community and to believers today that as one has been forgiven, so must that person forgive others. The slave who demands repayment is a sign of how people should not act.

Give the gift of forgiveness from a hospitable heart.

EIGHTEENTH SUNDAY AFTER PENTECOST

TWENTY-FIFTH SUNDAY IN ORDINARY TIME
PROPER 20
SEPTEMBER 22, 2002

REVISED COMMON	EPISCOPAL (BCP)	ROMAN CATHOLIC
Jon. 3:10—4:11	Jon. 3:10—4:11	Isa. 55:6-9
or Exod. 16:2-15		
Ps. 145:1-8 or	Psalm 145 or 145:1-8	Ps. 145:2-3, 8-9, 17-18
Ps. 105:1-6, 37-45		
Phil. 1:21-30	Phil. 1:21-27	Phil. 1:20c-24; 27a
Matt. 20:1-16	Matt. 20:1-16	Matt. 20:1-16a

Two themes common to today's readings are God's graciousness and humankind's hunger for God. The passage from Jonah depicts God as having a sense a humor who cares for human and nonhuman life (Jon. 3:10—4:11), a theme picked up in Psalm 145. Trekking through the wilderness, the Israelites experience the twists and turns of their journey and begin groaning. God sends them manna from heaven (Exod. 16:2-15). Psalm 105:1-6, 37-45 recounts this event as well as others from the exodus experience. Paul reveals to the Philippians his insatiable desire for God (Phil. 1:20-30), a God whose wonderful kindness surpasses human expectations (Matt. 20:1-16).

FIRST READING
JONAH 3:10—4:11 (RCL, BCP)

Interpreting the Text

Divine compassion and comedy characterize this reading from the book of Jonah. The narrative opens with a description of God deciding not to bring calamity upon the Ninevites because they had changed from their wicked ways (3:10). This decision makes Jonah angry. He addresses God directly, acknowledging his feelings of the pointlessness of his mission to the Ninevites who, in the end, did repent and were forgiven by a compassionate God whose steadfast love Jonah knew existed long before it had to be proved to Nineveh (4:1-2).

Comic relief begins when Jonah goes out to sit in the shade of a booth he had made for himself after he vented his feelings to God and received God's challenging response (4:3-5). God first delights Jonah with a bush to give him shade, but the bush quickly withers from a worm attack planned by God (4:6-7). God next teases Jonah with a hot wind that makes him want to die, but God does not fulfill Jonah's death wish (4:8). A further confrontation between Jonah and God occurs, and Jonah learns further of God's great care for all life, inclusive of the natural world. God's plan of salvation includes both human life, as represented here by non-Judahites and Judahites, and nonhuman life. God's compassion embraces all of life.

Responding to the Text

One cannot help but be amused by Jonah's straightforwardness with God and God's comical acts that point to a wonderful sense of humor. The text illustrates to Jonah's community and to people today how elements of the natural world have a place in the sacred tradition and in the teaching of the prophets. The text also makes clear God's wonderful saving love for both people and the natural world. Read from an ecological perspective, the story could help lay the framework for a new environmental ethic.

> THE TEXT MAKES CLEAR GOD'S WONDERFUL SAVING LOVE FOR BOTH PEOPLE AND THE NATURAL WORLD.

EXODUS 16:2-15 (RCL, alt.)

Interpreting the Text

When the Israelites suffered under Egyptian oppression, they murmured (Exod. 2:23). According to the exodus tradition, God heard their groaning and, through Moses, God liberated the people from their struggles. Their journey from oppression to freedom entailed an arduous walk through the wilderness, a trek that demanded of them utmost trust in their God. Instead of embracing their new challenges with a sense of certitude and gratefulness to God who is leading them in a roundabout way to the Promised Land, they groan—they murmur—as in the land of Egypt (vv. 2-3). They were hungry, and wondered if their God would indeed provide for them. What follows is a story about quail and manna that attests to God's compassionate care and love for the Israelites whom God remembers even when they have their doubts about God's fidelity to them. Of interest is the fact that manna is the natural secretion of insects living on a tamarisk tree. At certain times of the year in the ancient world quail were readily captured and became part of the food chain. The narrative describes God's fidelity and graciousness to a people in spite of their doubts, groans, and trust in divine providence.

Responding to the Text

God's goodness to the Israelite people who moaned when they were oppressed and groaned when they were liberated is a striking example of divine compassion in the midst of the human condition that at times can give the impression of never being satisfied. Some people seem to be no different today than they were in Moses' day—they complain. Yet God listens to their complaints and responds. The story is a reminder that God does journey with us and does listen and respond to us, even when we grumble.

ISAIAH 55:6-9 (RC)

Interpreting the Text

Addressed to a people in exile, Third Isaiah beckons his listeners to seek God, who is indeed near. He exhorts the wicked to forsake their ways and to turn back to God, who wants to be merciful to them and extend pardon in abundance. The prophet's announcement presents a marvelous picture of God and offers a glimpse into God's heart wherein lies a great love for sinners and an ardent longing for them to live in righteousness. Such great love and willingness to forgive on God's part defies human reason and effort. Without such divine love and intention, humankind would have little, if any, hope.

Responding to the Text

Third Isaiah's heartening words invite all people into the welcoming embrace of God, who desires to be merciful, especially to sinners. Such divine hospitality and love can be disconcerting to those who have always been just and righteous. The prophet reminds us, though, that divine thought, intention, and action are all beyond human comprehension.

RESPONSIVE READING
PSALM 145:1-8 (RCL; BCP, alt.);
PSALM 145 (BCP);
PSALM 145:2-3, 8-9, 17-18 (RC)

Known as a liturgical hymn of the cultic community, this psalm depicts God as a regal king, great and glorious, whose dominion is caring, compassionate, gracious, and just. The psalm opens on a personal note with the psalmist pledging to extol God every day (vv. 1-3). Personal laud shifts to communal praise as the psalmist declares that one generation shall tell of God's great deeds to another generation, thus creating an atmosphere of continual praise rooted in past memory and present experience (vv. 4-7). The psalm closes with a pledge of personal and communal praise to the God of grandeur and grace.

207

EIGHTEENTH
SUNDAY
AFTER PENTECOST
───
SEPTEMBER 22

What a lovely psalm commemorating God's great love and care for all creation! The phrase, "The Lord is good to all, and his compassion is over all that he has made," captures the final thought of today's first reading, where God reminds Jonah of divine regard for humans and nonhumans alike. Looking at the condition of life on the planet today in relation to this psalm, one cannot help but ask what the human community must do to illustrate divine compassion and regard for all life.

PSALM 105:1-6, 37-45 (RCL, alt.)

In this song of thanksgiving the psalmist calls community members to sing praise to God and to remember all the good things God has done (vv. 1-6). The second part recaps parts of the exodus story, focusing on God's gracious acts of kindness done on behalf of the Israelites (vv. 37-45).

Psalm 105 ends with the exclamation "Praise the Lord!" God's ultimate desire is for all creation to be redeemed from whatever oppresses it. This desire and its fulfillment are a source of great joy, which finds its expression in exuberant song.

SECOND READING
PHILIPPIANS 1:20-30 (RCL);
PHILIPPIANS 1:21-27 (BCP);
PHILIPPIANS 1:20C-24, 27a (RC)

Interpreting the Text

One of the early Christian communities most dear to Paul's heart was the one at Philippi. The Philippians often sustained Paul's preaching ministry through intercessory prayers and gracious hospitality. Paul's message to them not only reveals his great love for and longing to be with Christ but also affirms his deep love for them. He pledges them his continuous labor on their behalf (vv. 20-26). With his heart set on their continued progress in faith and the Christian way of life, Paul exhorts the Philippians to live their lives in a manner worthy of the gospel of Christ and to stand in unity together—in one spirit and one mind—which will be their strength against any opposition that may come their way. Paul reminds them further that any

> SUFFERING HERE IMPLIES THE REWARD FOR BEING FAITHFUL TO GOD—A FIDELITY THAT ENCOMPASSES LOVE FOR ALL, HALLMARKED BY ACTS OF JUSTICE, RIGHTEOUSNESS, AND COMPASSION.

suffering to be endured on their part for the sake of the Gospel is to be seen as a privilege. Such suffering was Christ's lot and is Paul's also. Suffering here implies the reward for being faithful to God and God's ways—a fidelity that encompasses love for all, hallmarked by acts of justice, righteousness, and compassion.

Responding to the Text

Paul's passionate vacillation between (1) wanting to be fully alive and actively engaged in preaching and (2) wanting to die so that he could be with Christ in the fullest possible way is indicative of someone who is madly in love. And Paul is someone who is madly in love with God, with Jesus, and with the mission that has been entrusted to him—the preaching of the gospel. The resolution of his struggle comes in his realization that God is in the midst of his personal desires and in the midst of his work among the Philippians. Paul's message describes a "holy passion" at the root of authentic mission and portrays a heart fully committed to the divine.

THE GOSPEL

MATTHEW 20:1-16 (RCL, BCP); MATTHEW 10:1-16a (RC)

Interpreting the Text

The parable of the laborers in the vineyard is one of a group of eleven parables on the kingdom of heaven. Like Matthew's other parables, this one presents a situation in which the unexpected occurs. The parable sets up a stark contrast between the first and last laborers. At the same time, it establishes an unusual eschatological reversal (see Matt. 19:30—20:16). The parable as a whole proclaims the sovereign authority and freedom of God whose justice and mercy cannot be measured according to human standards. Furthermore it presents a vision of the kingdom of heaven that belongs not only to those who have been faithful followers of Jesus from the beginning but also to those who have come late into the faith tradition.

THE PARABLE AS A WHOLE PROCLAIMS THE SOVEREIGN AUTHORITY AND FREEDOM OF GOD WHOSE JUSTICE AND MERCY CANNOT BE MEASURED ACCORDING TO HUMAN STANDARDS.

The parable consists of two parts: vv. 1-7 and vv. 8-16. The first section opens with a simile: "The kingdom of heaven is like . . . ," followed by a series of narrative details in the second section that describe the landowner's method of payment and the workers' outrage at having been paid the same amount of money as those who came to work in the field at a much later time during the day. As a whole, the story celebrates the graciousness and generosity of God whose hospitality of heart far exceeds human calculation and expectation.

Responding to the Text

Matthew 20:1-16 proclaims the sovereign authority and freedom of God, whose justice and mercy cannot be measured according to human standards. The parable teaches that no one has a claim on God's choices and rewards, nor can one anticipate or calculate the actions of God who is a God of surprises. The parable assures Jesus' disciples, who have followed him from the beginning, of their reward, but reminds them that status and service do not guarantee them any special claims on God. To Matthew's church, the parable reinforces the ideas of eschatological reversal. Those who are last—the poor, those without rank and title, those who suffer and struggle—will indeed be first in the kingdom of heaven.

Come, participate in the work of the vineyard at any time and be among those whom God will reward most generously.

ST. MICHAEL
AND ALL ANGELS

SEPTEMBER 29, 2002

Dan. 10:10-14; 12:1-3
Ps. 103:1-5, 20-22
Rev. 12:7-12
Luke 10:17-20

FIRST LESSON
DANIEL 10:10-14; 12:1-3

Interpreting the Text

Daniel, mourning for three weeks and abstaining from rich food, meat, and wine, falls into a trance with his face to the ground. Suddenly he is startled and roused to his hands and knees and then to his feet by a divine intermediary who offers him comforting words and revelations of what is to happen to Israel in days to come (10:10-14). The divine intermediary sheds light on Daniel's character: he is "greatly beloved" (v. 11), and someone who has set his mind "to gain understanding" and "to humble himself" before his God (12). Thus he is one favored by God, worthy of divine visions and revelations, worthy of having his prayers answered, and worthy of knowing what is to befall his people at the end of days (v. 14). Israel's future unravels before Daniel in subsequent passages (11:2-45).

Daniel's experience concludes in 12:1-4. Here Daniel hears about Michael, who is revealed to be the great protector of the Israelites. Michael will arise to assist in Israel's redemption from the anguish that is to befall it. Then Daniel learns about the fate of his people: some who sleep in the dust —perhaps those who remained faithful under persecution—will awake to everlasting life; others—perhaps those who were unfaithful—will awake to shame and everlasting contempt (12:1-3).

The dualistic images of the passage's last few verses along with the fantastic visions involving the presence of angels throughout the passage indicate apocalyptic influences. The passage as a whole serves as a word of encouragement for people to remain faithful to God and God's ways even in the midst of persecution. The passage also

THE PASSAGE AS A WHOLE SERVES AS A WORD OF ENCOURAGEMENT FOR PEOPLE TO REMAIN FAITHFUL TO GOD AND GOD'S WAYS EVEN IN THE MIDST OF PERSECUTION.

hints at the notion of an afterlife, which becomes fully realized in the New Testament through the resurrection of Jesus.

Responding to the Text

This passage describes Daniel's strange yet wonderful encounter with a heavenly being who brought him words of comfort and woe. From the text, one can see that Daniel's experience seemed to have happened in the midst of daily events. Thus divine revelation becomes part of the fabric of ordinary life, helping to inform it and direct its present and future course.

Responsive Reading
PSALM 103:1-5, 20-22

The imperative and vocative, "Bless the Lord, O my soul," in the opening verses of this psalm begin the psalmist's prayer of thanksgiving that proclaims the goodness of God. This God whom the poet praises is a God of faithful and compassionate love whose care is life-sustaining and who is to be praised by all in heaven and on the earth.

Although the language of this psalm is in part hierarchical and monarchical, contemporary listeners and readers are reminded that God's dominion over heaven and earth is a beneficent one with power used to ensure care for all life (cf. Ps. 104:1-30).

Second Reading
REVELATION 12:7-12

Interpreting the Text

Daniel 10:10-14 and 12:1-3 allude to the angel Michael, who now takes center stage in this passage from the book of Revelation. It describes the archangel and the angels in his company waging battle against a dragon and the dragon's angels in which the latter are defeated (vv. 7-9). The second half of the passage shifts from prose to poetry (vv. 10-14). This poem, also known as a victory hymn, is both jubilant and foreboding in tone. It celebrates the defeat of evil, embodied in the devil and Satan, as the text indicates, and issues a warning to those on earth.

Written during a time of great persecution that the Christian community underwent during the first century after the time of Christ, this passage is meant to serve as a word of encouragement to those being persecuted. Indeed, God will assist them in their dire state; their enemies will be defeated, but they have to remain ever vigilant and guarded until the time when evil is defeated once and for all.

Responding to the Text

The setting for this passage is heaven, where a battle among divine beings has been waged. John, the presumed author of the text, describes the event with graphic language and images and then proceeds to outline what he hears in heaven after the archangel Michael, the victor, has defeated the dragon and his angels. Celebratory yet cryptic and somewhat foreboding, the heavenly message is informative and promises God's saving help. The text situates John in the prophetic tradition: he has a divine experience that he proclaims, and he also makes known God's ways and intentions revealed to him through his experience.

THE GOSPEL
LUKE 10:17-20

Interpreting the Text

In this brief passage Luke describes the return of the seventy disciples whom Jesus had sent out earlier to preach the good news pertaining to the reign of God (see 10:1-12). Filled with enthusiasm and excitement, the disciples relay to Jesus all of their experiences and their feelings of having been empowered (v. 17). Jesus is quick to remind them that the prize they seek is not human glory attained through marvelous feats. Rather, heavenly glory—the respect of God—has empowered them to perform such feats. The ultimate mission of the disciples is not so much the ability to deal with demons as it is their willingness to embrace and live out a way of life that, for some, will lead to the cross, which is the disciples' true boast.

> JESUS IS QUICK TO REMIND THEM THAT THE PRIZE THEY SEEK IS NOT HUMAN GLORY ATTAINED THROUGH MARVELOUS FEATS.

Responding to the Text

Today's Gospel teaches two lessons: first, power rests in Jesus' name and, second, while joy may come after having accomplished great feats, true and everlasting joy is in the assurance of an afterlife where one will enjoy the full presence of God. Jesus has empowered his disciples to defeat all negative and harmful forces, which is cause for great joy, but through him they will also overcome the power of death—their names are written in heaven.

Enjoy all successes, but keep your heart set on the ultimate goal: life with God forever.

NINETEENTH SUNDAY AFTER PENTECOST

TWENTY-SIXTH SUNDAY IN ORDINARY TIME
PROPER 21
SEPTEMBER 29, 2002

REVISED COMMON	EPISCOPAL (BCP)	ROMAN CATHOLIC
Ezek. 18:1-4, 25-32	Ezek. 18:1-4, 25-32	Ezek. 18:25-28
or Exod. 17:1-7		
Ps. 25:1-9 or	Ps. 25:1-14 or 25:3-9	Ps. 25:4-5, 6-7, 8-9
Ps. 78:1-4, 12-16		
Phil. 2:1-13	Phil. 2:1-13	Phil. 2:1-11 (2:1-5)
Matt. 21:23-32	Matt. 21:28-32	Matt. 21:28-32

Repent, reform, change, and turn away from sinfulness and toward God in order to live! We rely upon the mercy, kindness, and compassion of the God who gives us the time, the opportunities, and the examples we need to repent and change our lives. Jesus provides us with a stimulating attitude and stellar model of selfless humility.

FIRST READING
EZEKIEL 18:1-4, 25-32 (RCL, BCP);
EZEKIEL 18:25-28 (RC)

Interpreting the Text

The people of Israel are saying, "The way of the Lord is unfair!" But why? They think they are being punished with misfortune for the sins of their ancestors. They have applied to themselves the age-old but no longer relevant proverb: "The parents have eaten sour grapes, and the children's teeth are set on edge."

God, however, is dealing with them not according to this antiquated proverb but in accord with their own individual responsibility. They are not doomed because of the faults and failings of their ancestors. If they commit iniquity, they will suffer death for the iniquity that they—not their ancestors or anyone else— have committed. But if they turn away from all their transgressions, they shall surely not die but preserve their lives.

Therefore, God urges them: "Repent and turn from all your transgressions! Get yourselves a new heart and a new spirit!" God has no pleasure in the death of anyone. They are to turn their lives around and live anew.

Responding to the Text

It is perhaps human to want to blame others for our predicaments, misfortunes, or failings. Psychologists tell us that our personalities are formed from the earliest years of our lives. To what extent are we responsible? To what extent can we change? We may not be able to change everything about ourselves. But we all certainly have the opportunity to change those undesirable and sinful behaviors, attitudes, and habits for which we ourselves are responsible. With God internal renewal—the acquiring of a new heart and a new spirit in order to experience life anew—is always possible!

> WITH GOD INTERNAL RENEWAL—THE ACQUIRING OF A NEW HEART AND A NEW SPIRIT IN ORDER TO EXPERIENCE LIFE ANEW—IS ALWAYS POSSIBLE!

God is a God of life. God does not take pleasure in the death of any human being. Does not capital punishment usurp God's sovereignty over all human lives? By institutionally killing certain criminals, even in the name of justice, do we not deprive them of the opportunity to repent, reform, and renew themselves in order to live?

EXODUS 17:1-7 (RCL, alt.)

The setting is the wandering of the people of Israel in the wilderness after God has brought them out of slavery in Egypt. They think the God who once delivered them has now abandoned them and will allow them to die of thirst in the desert. They are complaining to and quarreling with God's chosen servant Moses and thus testing and finding fault with God.

But through the intercession of a threatened Moses, God wondrously produces the refreshing water the Israelites so desperately need. God commands Moses to strike a rock with his staff so that water will come out and the people may drink. After Moses does so, he calls the place Massah ("test") and Meribah ("find fault"), because the Israelites tested and found fault with God, wondering whether God was really with them or not.

The Israelites provide us with a double model. First, they serve as a negative example of unbelief, as they test and question the ongoing saving presence of the God who saved them in the exodus event and who has been with them ever since. Despite all the assurances we have that God is with us through his word and sacraments, have we nevertheless doubted the saving presence of God in our own lives, especially in times of crisis?

Second, the Israelites serve as a positive example of turning to God in prayer during a time of critical need. As God answered their complaining yet desperate pleas by fulfilling their need for water to sustain their lives, so God will answer our earnest prayers with the life-giving sustenance we need to persevere.

Moses likewise provides us with a double model. First, he demonstrates how pastoral leaders are to deal with complaining, quarreling, and threatening people by turning to God for help. Second, he demonstrates how pastoral leaders are to intercede with prayer to God on behalf of those who find themselves in desperate straits.

RESPONSIVE READING
PSALM 25:1-9 (RCL);
PSALM 25:1-14 or 25:3-9 (BCP);
PSALM 25:4-5, 6-7, 8-9 (RC)

Psalm 25 is a prayer of lament for deliverance from personal enemies. In it we pray that God be mindful of the mercy and steadfast love that have been God's hallmark from of old, and upon which our repentance depends: "Do not remember the sins of my youth or my transgressions; according to your steadfast love remember me, for your goodness' sake, O Lord!" (v. 7). Once we have had the humility to repent, this psalm assures us that God "leads the humble in what is right, and teaches the humble his way" (v. 9; and see today's Second Reading).

PSALM 78:1-4, 12-16 (RCL, alt.)

This psalm selection accompanies the alternative first reading from Exod. 17:1-7. It celebrates the wonders of God in providing the Israelites with abundant, life-giving water in the wilderness (vv. 15-16). It invites us to commemorate and celebrate with praise and thanksgiving the wonders God has performed for us in the past, with their promise of more to come in the future.

SECOND READING
PHILIPPIANS 2:1-13 (RCL and BCP);
PHILIPPIANS 2:1-11 or 2:1-5 (RC)

Interpreting the Text

The theme of joy runs like a refrain throughout Paul's letter to the Philippians. But it is a somewhat paradoxical joy, since Paul is sitting in prison. He

216

THE SEASON
OF PENTECOST
─────────────
JOHN PAUL
HEIL

may be at the point of a death he does not shun but actually looks forward to, because it means being with Christ (1:20-24). As Paul addresses a Philippian community that he holds in high regard as his close partner in advancing the gospel, he rejoices that the gospel of Christ is being proclaimed even while he is in prison (1:18). In today's reading Paul urges the Philippians to "make my joy complete" (2:2) by overcoming any divisiveness there may be within their community.

Paul holds up the ideal of a rather profound and provocative humility as the way for them to be of the same mind and heart. In humility they are to do nothing out of selfish ambition or conceit but to regard others as better or more important than themselves (2:3). Paul challenges them to have the humility to look out not for their own interests but for the interests of others in their community (2:4).

In hymnic fashion Paul presents them with the striking humility of Christ Jesus as the preeminent model for their own humble attitude. In contrast to Satan, the archangel who wanted to be equal to God in power (2 Enoch 29:4), and in contrast to Adam and Eve, who were made in the image and likeness of God (Gen. 1:26-27) yet, nevertheless, still desired to be like gods (Gen. 3:5-6), and in contrast to the earthly, tyrannical kings of old who arrogantly and boastfully strove for divine superiority (Isa. 14:12-14; Ezek. 28:2f.; 2 Macc. 9:12), Jesus, though in the form of God, did not regard equality with God as something to be exploited or grasped and held on to without relinquishing (2:6). Rather, he demonstrated an impressive, intensive threefold humility: (1) Though in the form of God, he "emptied" himself and took the form of a slave by being born in human likeness (2:7). (2) He further humbled himself by undergoing death as a human being. (3) But he suffered not a normal or ordinary death—he was put to death on a cross (2:8). He thus endured the most humiliating form of the public execution of criminals known to the Roman world in which he lived.

But, from the depths of his intense and total threefold humility God highly exalted him with a threefold universal homage (2:9-11): (1) homage from those in the heavenly realm from which he humbled himself by becoming human; (2) homage from those on the earth on which he humbled himself as a slave; and (3) homage from those under the earth, the realm of the dead to which he descended by his humiliating death. Through his totally selfless humility God established Jesus as our Lord—the Lord over all.

Responding to the Text

We can experience the paradoxical joy of Paul by adopting a Christ-like attitude of selfless humility. Paul provocatively challenges us to the selfless humility of regarding others and their interests as more important than ourselves and our interests. By such an altruistic humility we can overcome the differences that divide us and know the joy of living as a Christian community united by the same mind and heart. The stunning example of Jesus assures that such a total and selfless humility brings with it an exhilarating exaltation by God.

Today's selection from Philippians contributes to the theme of repentance that the other readings of the day present us. The impressive humility of Jesus provides us with the kind of humble attitude we need in order to truly repent and totally turn away from our sinfulness. After such a humble and complete repentance God's renowned mercy, compassion, and forgiveness will exalt us to newness of life.

PAUL PROVOCATIVELY CHALLENGES US TO THE SELFLESS HUMILITY OF REGARDING OTHERS AND THEIR INTERESTS AS MORE IMPORTANT THAN OURSELVES AND OUR INTERESTS.

THE GOSPEL
MATTHEW 21:23-32 (RCL);
MATTHEW 21:28-32 (BCP, RC)

Interpreting the Text

The Jewish leaders question by what authority Jesus conducts his ministry in the Jerusalem temple (21:23). By his clever counter-question Jesus ironically and masterfully manipulates them into undermining their own authority as leaders by admitting their ignorance about the heavenly origin of John's baptism (and thus of Jesus' authority) (21:24-27). Jesus has made his opponents painfully aware of their failure to repent, believe, and be baptized by John.

But by inviting them to ponder the parable of the man with two sons (21:28-32), Jesus opens for them the possibility of yet repenting. Jesus forces them to admit that the first son who said he would not work in the vineyard but later changed his mind and went, rather than the second son who said yes but did not go, is the one who did the will of the father (God). Not only do the Jewish leaders have the example of the first son in the parable, who first refused but later repented, they have the real-life, dramatic example of some very public sinners—the tax collectors and prostitutes—who repented and believed in John the Baptist, who prepared and pointed the way to Jesus.

Responding to the Text

In today's Gospel Jesus invites us to apply to ourselves the parable pointed at the unrepentant Jewish leaders. The example of the first son, who at first refused to work "but *later* he changed his mind and went" (21:29), provides us with a model for using the time God (the father) gives us to change our minds, repent, and turn away from our sinfulness. Initial refusal does not preclude later repentance when God gives us the time and opportunity.

The shocking example of the tax collectors and prostitutes reinforces that of the first son. They took advantage of the time and opportunity God gave them in the preaching of John the Baptist to repent and believe. What about us? Are we heeding the sometimes startling and stunning examples of repentance that others, even notorious public sinners, provide us? Are we like the second son of the parable, who said yes but failed to do the will of the Father? Do we talk a good game and make promises, but fail to fulfill them? Are we squandering the time God gives us to follow the lead of the first son by changing our minds, repenting, and doing the will of the Father?

Points to ponder:
- Regard others and their interests as more important than yourself.
- God exalts to new life those who selflessly and totally humble themselves like Jesus.
- It is never too late to change the undesirable and sinful elements that we can change in our lives in order to experience a new and more joyful way of living based upon God's renowned mercy and steadfast love.

TWENTIETH SUNDAY AFTER PENTECOST

TWENTY-SEVENTH SUNDAY IN ORDINARY TIME
PROPER 22
OCTOBER 6, 2002

REVISED COMMON	EPISCOPAL (BCP)	ROMAN CATHOLIC
Isa. 5:1-7 or Exod. 20:1-4, 7-9, 12-20	Isa. 5:1-7	Isa. 5:1-7
Ps. 80:7-15 or Psalm 19	Psalm 80 or 80:7-14	Ps. 80:8, 11, 12-13, 14-15, 18-19 (Heb. Bible 80:9, 12, 13-14, 15-16, 19-20)
Phil. 3:4b-14	Phil. 3:14-21	Phil. 4:6-9
Matt. 21:33-46	Matt. 21:33-43	Matt. 21:33-43

God takes loving care of us in the way that the owner of a vineyard lovingly and painstakingly provides everything necessary for his cherished vineyard to produce good fruit. Why then do we so often fail to produce the good fruit that God expects from us—social justice and peace? Paul exhorts us to imitate his total identification with and personal appropriation of the saving death and resurrection of Jesus Christ as the way to experience the transcendent peace that comes from God alone.

FIRST READING
ISAIAH 5:1-7

Interpreting the Text

In imitation of a vintage festival song, the prophet Isaiah sings a love song on behalf of his "beloved" or "friend"—the owner of a vineyard. Despite all of the favorable conditions that the owner has carefully provided—a very fertile hill, no stones, choice vines, a watchtower, and a dug-out wine vat, the vineyard yielded only wild grapes (5:1-2). The owner himself then invites the people of Israel to judge between him and his vineyard and thus vindicate him of any failure on his part to do everything possible for his vineyard. He invites them to ponder his lamenting query, "Why did it yield wild grapes?" (5:3-4).

After the perturbed owner's vehement threat to totally destroy his under-achieving vineyard (5:5-6) comes the shocking allegorical identifications: The owner and "beloved" friend of the prophet is the very God of Israel; the vineyard is God's chosen people of Israel; the wild grapes are the bloodshed and cry of the oppressed that the vineyard produced instead of the expected good fruit—social justice and righteousness (5:7).

Responding to the Text

Isaiah's provocative song of the vineyard invites us to consider all that God has done for us as the presently chosen people of God. We must admit that there is nothing we lack from God to produce the good fruit of social justice and righteousness in our day. Yet the bloodshed and cry of the oppressed that sprung up from the vineyard in Isaiah's day still seems to be with us today. We have the bloodshed of all of the innocent victims of violence, especially

THE BLOODSHED AND CRY OF THE OPPRESSED THAT SPRUNG UP FROM THE VINEYARD IN ISAIAH'S DAY STILL SEEMS TO BE WITH US TODAY.

violence from guns and assault rifles, because we lack the righteousness of effective gun control. The cries of those oppressed by racial, ethnic, and religious discrimination and prejudice are resounding throughout the land. The muted voices of the millions of human lives that have been aborted before they could open their mouths will be heard only if we cry out for them.

EXODUS 20:1-4, 7-9, 12-20 (RCL, alt.)

Seldom noticed and perhaps not fully appreciated about the familiar Ten Commandments is that they are intended to be the appropriate response to God's saving love for the chosen people of Israel. God introduces them by announcing, "I am the Lord your God, who brought you out of the land of Egypt, out of the house of slavery" (20:1-2).

The event of this saving activity demands imageless rather than idolatrous worship of the one and only invisible God (20:3-4). Since knowledge of the name imparted powerful dominance, there should be no misuse of God's name (20:7). One day a week is to be set aside for essential rest and worship of the only true and saving God (20:8-9). The remainder of the well-known commandments concern proper human relations in response to the saving love of God (20:12-17). Despite the awesome and fearful way in which God delivered the commandments, Moses assures the people that they need not be afraid, for the commandments represent the guides they need to avoid sin and appreciate the loving God of their salvation (20:18-20).

How often do we think of the Ten Commandments as the proper way of responding to God's saving love for us? Because they are so basic and fundamental they never seem to lose their contemporary relevance. We have our false gods today—money, power, prestige, success, even our very selves. The various names of God are routinely and commonly abused in everyday speech. Our intense, highly competitive, over-commercialized, consumer-obsessed culture threatens our need for proper rest and wholesome worship of God. Murder, stealing, adultery, lying, and coveting—far from being outmoded—have taken on modern and innovative forms. God has given us the Ten Commandments, not to burden us with oppressive rules and laws in order to earn God's love, but as a sure way to demonstrate our gratefulness for the God who has already chosen, loved, and saved us.

RESPONSIVE READING
PSALM 80:7–15 (RCL);
PSALM 80 or 80:7–14 (BCP);
PSALM 80:8, 11, 12–13, 14–15, 18–19 (RC)

Psalm 80, a communal lament for deliverance, quite fittingly accompanies today's first reading from Isaiah, the song of the vineyard. God's threat to destroy the vineyard (Israel) in that song has become reality in this psalm. We join the community of Israel in praying that the God who once so tenderly cared for the vine brought out of Egypt will once again extend a loving regard toward the cherished vine and thus deliver us from the calamitous and chaotic conditions we often experience due to our failure to produce the fruit of righteousness, justice, and peace.

PSALM 19 (RCL, alt.)

Psalm 19, a hymn to the Creator of nature and Giver of the Law, accompanies today's alternate first reading from Exodus, the giving of the Ten Commandments. A rhetorically powerful series describes the benefits of all of God's laws and commandments: They revive the soul, make wise the simple, rejoice the heart, enlighten the eyes, endure forever, and are more desirable than gold and sweeter than honey.

SECOND READING

PHILIPPIANS 3:4b-14 (RCL)

Interpreting the Text

Although in the past Paul, as a fully observant Jew, experienced "right-eousness," that is, a right and correct covenantal relationship with God (3:4-6), it does not compare to the new righteousness from God that he now experiences through faith in Christ (3:7-9). Paul, imprisoned and perhaps on the verge of being put to death as he writes to the Philippians, expresses an intense and earnest desire to fully identify with and totally appropriate in his own life the power of the death and resurrection of Christ by suffering like and for him (3:10-11).

In his ardent hope to attain the future resurrection from the dead like and along with Christ, Paul utilizes the athletic imagery of a Greco-Roman foot race. In striving for the finish line, the "goal," of future resurrection, Paul forgets what lies behind and "strains forward" in hope to what lies ahead. The "prize" of the heavenly call of God in Christ Jesus prompts Paul to persevere in hope (3:12-14).

Responding to the Text

Are we still trying to achieve our own righteousness based on what we have done and will do for God rather than accepting in faith the righteousness God freely gives us in the death and resurrection of Christ? As we experience the difficulties of life and our own sinfulness and weaknesses, do we, mindful of our mortality, need to forget what lies behind and strain forward in hopeful perse-verance of sharing in the future resurrection?

PHILIPPIANS 3:14-21 (BCP)

As the imprisoned Paul, employing the athletic imagery of a foot race, persistently presses on toward the "goal" of the heavenly call of God in Christ Jesus, he exhorts his community at Philippi to imitate his total identification with the death and resurrection of Jesus (3:14-17). Many live as enemies of the cross of Christ, as their minds are set on earthly things (3:18-19). But Paul assures the Philippians, who esteem their status as citizens of a Roman colony (Acts 16:12), that they have a citizenship in heaven from which they expect the return of the Lord Jesus, who will transform their earthly, mortal bodies into heavenly bodies of glory like his (3:20-21).

Our minds are often set firmly and resolutely on the pursuit of earthly things that can never satisfy our deepest human desires for a future, immortal life. This makes us, in effect, an enemy of the cross of Christ. Paul invites us to imitate his

complete orientation to the death and resurrection of Jesus by persevering through
present sufferings with confident hope of attaining our true heavenly home.

223

TWENTIETH
SUNDAY
AFTER PENTECOST

OCTOBER 6

PHILIPPIANS 4:6-9 (RC)

The imprisoned and thus "guarded" Paul assures his Philippian community that they have nothing to worry about as Christians if they make their concerns known to God in prayer (4:6). To the Philippians, familiar with their own military "guards" as a Roman colony (cf. Acts 16:12ff.), Paul promises that the profound peace of God that transcends all human understanding will "guard" their hearts and minds in Christ Jesus (4:7).

With a rhetorically powerful series of attributes Paul exhorts them to practice mental hygiene. They are to focus their thinking on whatever is true, honorable, just, pure, pleasing, commendable, excellent, and worthy of praise (4:8). By imitating the imprisoned Paul's total appropriation of the death and resurrection of Jesus, they will experience the presence of the God of peace (4:9).

Do we need to clean up our ways of thinking? Are our minds full of unedifying thoughts—judgmental, jealous, or lustful thoughts about others, negative thoughts about our own weaknesses and failures, or mundane and materialistic thoughts about earthly things? By imitating Paul's mental focus on what God has done for us in the death and resurrection of Christ, we practice Christian mental hygiene and experience the true peace of mind that comes from the profound peace that only the God of peace can give.

THE GOSPEL
MATTHEW 21:33-46 (RCL);
MATTHEW 21:33-43 (BCP, RC)

Interpreting the Text

The Isaian song of the vineyard from today's first reading offers background for the parable in today's Gospel. The landowner who planted the vineyard and provided everything necessary for it to produce thus represents God. The tenants represent the Jewish leaders entrusted by God to produce the good fruit of justice and righteousness from the vineyard, the people of Israel (21:33). The slaves sent by the landowner to the tenants to collect the produce represent the prophets God has repeatedly sent to the people of Israel, but whom their leaders have always rejected and killed (21:34-36; cf. Jer. 7:25-26; 2 Chron. 36:15-16; Neh. 9:26; Dan. 9:6).

When the owner (God) finally sends his own son (Jesus; cf. Matt. 3:17; 4:3, 6; 17:5), the tenants (leaders) kill him as well (21:37-39).

With his question of what the owner will do to his tenants, Jesus traps his audience of Jewish leaders ironically to condemn themselves: "He will put those wretches to a miserable death, and lease the vineyard to other tenants who will give him the produce at the harvest time" (21:40-41). Building upon their response, Jesus quotes Ps. 118:22-23, according to which the stone (Jesus) that the builders (Jewish leaders) rejected has become the cornerstone by God's wonderful doing (21:42). This points to God's ultimate vindication of Jesus as God's prophetic Son by resurrection after the religious and political leaders would unjustly put him to death. That the kingdom of God would be taken away from the leaders and given to a people that produces the fruits of the kingdom (21:43) refers to the Gospel audience, now entrusted with the prophetic task of producing the fruits of justice and righteousness God expects.

Although the religious leaders realize that Jesus is speaking about them, they fail to repent. Instead, they are ironically intent on playing the role of the tenants in the parable, as they seek to arrest Jesus but are prevented for now because they fear the crowds. That the crowds regard Jesus as a "prophet" confirms him as the prophetic Son of God who will be killed by the authorities but vindicated through resurrection to become "the cornerstone" (21:45-46).

Responding to the Text

This parable prompts us to repent of our failures to heed the prophets of today (e.g., Mother Teresa, Martin Luther King Jr., John Paul II), who show us the way to justice and peace by caring for the poorest of the poor, eliminating racial prejudice, and countering the culture of death that pervades our society with the practices of abortion, euthanasia, and the death penalty.

HEED THE PROPHETS OF TODAY WHO SHOW US THE WAY TO JUSTICE AND PEACE BY CARING FOR THE POOREST OF THE POOR, ELIMINATING RACIAL PREJUDICE, AND COUNTERING THE CULTURE OF DEATH THAT PERVADES OUR SOCIETY.

We are the parable's other people entrusted with the prophetic task of producing the fruits God expects. In carrying out that task we may encounter opposition, rejection, injury, even death—as Jesus did. We are not called necessarily to succeed, only to be faithful. If we remain faithful to our prophetic mission, we have the consoling promise that God will ultimately vindicate us like the prophetic Son who became the cornerstone.

Points to ponder:

- As the owner of the vineyard God has lovingly provided all we need to produce the fruits of social justice and peace.
- The commandments are our response to, not way of earning, God's love.
- Like Paul, forget what lies behind and strive forward in hope of what lies ahead.
- In Jesus, God's prophetic Son, we have a divinely vindicated cornerstone, a foundation for us to remain faithful despite failure in our prophetic calling.

TWENTY-FIRST SUNDAY AFTER PENTECOST

TWENTY-EIGHTH SUNDAY IN ORDINARY TIME
PROPER 23
OCTOBER 13, 2002

REVISED COMMON	EPISCOPAL (BCP)	ROMAN CATHOLIC
Isa. 25:1-9 or	Isa. 25:1-9	Isa. 25:6-10a
Exod. 32:1-14		
Psalm 23 or	Psalm 23	Ps. 23:1-3a, 3b-4, 5, 6
Ps. 106:1-6, 19-23		
Phil. 4:1-9	Phil. 4:4-13	Phil. 4:12-14, 19-20
Matt. 22:1-14	Matt. 22:1-14	Matt. 22:1-14 (22:1-10)

God, our shepherd, promises to feed us all with a rich banquet and to destroy the power of death forever. We are called to accept the invitation and demonstrate our worthiness to be chosen to participate in God's great feast in the kingdom of heaven. We rejoice in the God who provides all we need in answer to our prayers.

FIRST READING

ISAIAH 25:1-9 (RCL, BCP);
ISAIAH 25:6-10a (RC)

Interpreting the Text

Today's first reading from Isaiah begins with a hymn of thanksgiving for the wonderful things God has done (25:1). God has destroyed the fortified cities of the alien peoples who threaten God's people, so that "ruthless nations will fear you" (25:2-3). God has been a refuge for the poor and needy, sheltering them from both the "rainstorm" and blazing "heat" of aliens, so that "the song of the ruthless was stilled" (25:4-5).

DURING THIS GREAT, FINAL FEAST "ON THIS MOUN-TAIN" GOD WILL DESTROY FOREVER THE POWER OF DEATH THAT CASTS ITS SHADOW OVER ALL PEOPLES.

The prophet then promises that "on this mountain," that is, Mount Zion, the mountain of God's people, God will prepare a sumptuous banquet of the richest food and choicest wines for *all* peoples (25:6). During this great, final feast "on this mountain" God will destroy *forever* the power of death that casts its shadow over *all* peoples (25:7). After God eliminates all the mourning and sadness due to death, God's people will rejoice in the salvation for which they have patiently awaited from their God "on this mountain" (25:8-10).

Responding to the Text

God protects us from all the alien powers that threaten our lives and promises to destroy forever the greatest of those alien powers—death itself. We have all experienced the mourning and sadness that accompany the death of a loved one. We know that one day we too will succumb to the power of death. But Isaiah today invites us to rejoice, as we look forward to participating in God's sumptuous, final feast "on this mountain" in which we will celebrate with the richest of food and drink God's triumph over the power of death.

EXODUS 32:1-14 (RCL, alt.)

Thinking that Moses and the God of Moses, who brought them out of slavery in Egypt, has now abandoned them, the people of Israel wanted Aaron, the brother of Moses, to make "gods," visible symbols of divine presence that pagans worship, to go before them (32:1). Aaron took their gold and cast it into an image of a calf or young bull, a symbol of fertility and strength in the ancient Near East, declaring that these are the gods (not the God of the absent Moses) who brought them out of Egypt (32:2-4). The people then reveled in a festival of burnt offerings and sacrifices in worship to these gods (32:5-6).

After informing Moses of the people's rebellion and false worship, God makes known to Moses a plan to destroy them but make of Moses a great nation (32:7-10). Moses ardently intercedes on behalf of his people, praying to change God's mind. He brashly and bluntly points out that it would look very bad in the eyes of the Egyptians if God now killed the people he once rescued from slavery in Egypt. Furthermore, destroying the people of Israel would not be in accord with the promises to their patriarchs that God would greatly multiply their descendants and give them a land to inherit forever (32:11-13). God answered the intercessory prayer of Moses and "changed his mind about the disaster that he planned to bring on his people" (32:14).

Are we in effect worshiping false gods when we focus too much upon or expect too much in terms of happiness and fulfillment from money, material things, prestige, our jobs, other people, or even ourselves? Like the people of Israel we are deluding ourselves if we think anything or anyone can be made into a substitute for the one and only true God who created and saved us.

Moses serves as a stellar model of the power of intercessory prayer. In their desperate delusion the people were unable to pray for themselves. They would have been destroyed if Moses had not prayed and changed God's mind. That is how critical our prayers of intercession can be. Some people—the sick, the incapacitated, the deluded, the depressed—cannot or will not pray for themselves. The example of Moses reminds us how powerful our prayers of intercession can be in prompting God to change the lives of those for whom we pray.

RESPONSIVE READING

PSALM 23 (RCL, BCP); PSALM 23:1-3a, 3b-4, 5, 6 (RC)

The renowned Psalm 23, a prayer of trust in God's protection, appropriately accompanies today's first reading from Isaiah. That God is the shepherd who leads us through the "darkest valley" or the "valley of the shadow of death" corresponds to God's promise to destroy the power of death forever. And that the shepherd God will "prepare a table before me in the presence of my enemies" corresponds to God's promise of a great banquet after protecting from alien powers.

PSALM 106:1-6, 19-23 (RCL, alt.)

Psalm 106, which recounts Israel's continual unfaithfulness, accompanies today's alternate first reading from Exodus. The first unit climaxes in the admission that "we and our ancestors have sinned" and the second unit acknowledges the power of Moses' prayer of intercession.

SECOND READING

PHILIPPIANS 4:1-9 (RCL); PHILIPPIANS 4:4-13 (BCP); PHILIPPIANS 4:12-14, 19-20 (RC)

Interpreting the Text

The imprisoned Paul urges one of his loyal companions at Philippi to help two women who are his co-workers in the gospel, Euodia and Syntyche, to resolve their differences so that they may be of the same mind in the Lord (4:1-3). The Philippian church is to rejoice exceedingly in expectation of the imminent coming of the Lord (4:4-5).

They have nothing to worry about as Christians if they make their concerns known to God in prayer (4:6). To the Philippians, familiar with their own military "guards" as a Roman colony (cf. Acts 16:12ff.), Paul promises that the profound peace of God that transcends all human understanding will "guard" their hearts and minds in Christ Jesus (4:7).

With a rhetorically powerful series of attributes Paul exhorts them to practice mental hygiene. They are to focus their thinking on whatever is true, honorable, just, pure, pleasing, commendable, excellent, and worthy of praise (4:8). By imitating the imprisoned Paul's total appropriation of the death and resurrection of Jesus, they will experience the presence of the God of peace (4:9).

> PAUL EXHORTS THE PHILIPPIANS TO PRACTICE
> MENTAL HYGIENE.

Paul rejoices in the Lord for the concern the Philippians have shown him in prison by sending Epaphroditus, a co-worker, from Philippi with gifts for him (4:10; cf. 2:25; 4:18). Although grateful for their kindness in his distress, Paul is quick to point out that he has "learned the secret" of being content in whatever circumstances he finds himself and of making do with whatever amount of material sustenance he has. The secret of his own contentment comes from his deep trust in God: "I can do all things through him who strengthens me" (4:11-14).

Paul glorifies the God who satisfied him and who will likewise fully satisfy every need of the Christians at Philippi in accord with his riches in Christ Jesus (4:19-20).

Responding to the Text

Are we able to resolve our differences as Christians in order to be of the same mind in the Lord? Do we need to clear and cleanse our minds? Are our minds full of unedifying thoughts—judgmental, jealous, or lustful thoughts about others, negative thoughts about our own weaknesses and failures, or mundane and materialistic thoughts about earthly things? By imitating Paul's mental focus on what God has done for us in the death and resurrection of Christ, we practice Christian mental hygiene and experience the true peace of mind that comes from the profound peace that only the God of peace can give.

Paul presents us with a model of being fully satisfied and content in whatever circumstances we find ourselves through our faith in what God has done for us in the death and resurrection of Jesus. We can do all things through the God who strengthens us with the riches of Christ. This Pauline "secret" contradicts our consumer-obsessed culture that tries to convince us that we can never have enough money or material things.

THE GOSPEL

MATTHEW 22:1-14;
MATTHEW 22:1-10 (RC, alt.)

Interpreting the Text

Jesus addresses yet another allegorical parable to the national leaders (22:1; cf. 21:23, 28, 33, 45). This one is about a marriage feast and brings to expression yet another dimension of the kingdom of heaven that is now arriving in and through the person and ministry of Jesus. A king, representing God, gave a wedding banquet for his son, representing Jesus (22:2; cf. 3:17; 17:5; 21:37-39), who has already referred to himself as the "bridegroom" (9:15) of God's awaited messianic wedding banquet that would climactically culminate God's covenantal nuptial relationship with God's people (Hos. 1-3; Jer. 2:2-3; 3:1-10; Ezek. 16:8-63) in a rich and sumptuous festival of food and drink (see today's First Reading).

The slaves sent by the king to call those invited to the wedding banquet represent the prophets sent by God to Israel and their leaders (cf. 21:34-36; cf. Jer. 7:25-26; 2 Chron. 36:15-16; Neh. 9:26; Dan. 9:6). That those invited refuse to come characterizes how the leaders are refusing to recognize Jesus as the messianic bridegroom (22:3). The king's instructions to the second group of slaves he sends out ("my oxen and my fat calves have been slaughtered, and everything is ready") underlines the sumptuous richness and therefore end-time, messianic quality (see Isa. 25:6 in today's first reading) of this wedding banquet (22:4). This time those invited not only dismiss God's gracious invitation, but kill the slaves, reenacting how the leaders kill God's prophets (22:5-6). In Matthew's perspective, the king's enraged destruction of the murderers and their city with his troops (22:7) ominously prefigures the Roman destruction of Jerusalem and her religious leaders for the failure to recognize Jesus, God's prophetic Son, as the messianic bridegroom.

After those invited demonstrated their unworthiness the king told his slaves to invite anyone and everyone to the wedding banquet, so that the wedding hall was filled with guests both good and bad (22:8-10). That one of the guests was found without a proper *wedding* robe indicates his failure to recognize that this is a *wedding* banquet for God's messianic bridegroom, Jesus (22:11-12). Despite his acceptance of the invitation in contrast to those originally invited (Jewish leaders), he nevertheless, like them, demonstrates his unworthiness. He thus suffers the stereotypical Matthean punishment of exclusion from God's kingdom—"throw him into the outer darkness, where there will be weeping and gnashing of teeth" (22:13; cf. Matt. 8:12; 13:42, 50; 24:51; 25:30). Jesus concludes the parable with a slogan serving as both a warning and a challenge: Although many (= all) are invited to the messianic wedding banquet of the kingdom of heaven, only a few demonstrate that they are worthy of being chosen (22:14).

Responding to the Text

Are we too preoccupied with our own concerns and business to accept God's gracious invitation to participate in the great messianic wedding banquet that has arrived in the person and ministry of Jesus? Are we failing to heed or rejecting the invitation as it comes to us through the prophets of today? Even accepting the freely given invitation offered to all is not enough. We must be clothed with a proper wedding garment—by recognizing and accepting Jesus as God's messianic bridegroom. To be called *and* chosen means to do God's will as Jesus, God's prophetic Son and messianic bridegroom, teaches and embodies it. Then we are assured of being properly clothed with a "wedding robe" to participate in God's great messianic wedding banquet in the kingdom of heaven.

> TO BE CALLED AND CHOSEN MEANS TO DO GOD'S WILL AS JESUS TEACHES AND EMBODIES IT.

Points to ponder:
- God has promised to destroy the power of death forever.
- As our Shepherd, God guides and amply nourishes us through lives threatened by the darkness of death.
- There is no substitute for worshiping the one and only God.
- Our prayers of intercession, like those of Moses, can be both critical and powerful.
- Like Paul we can learn the secret of being content in any circumstances through the God who strengthens us and satisfies our every need.
- We must demonstrate that we are worthy of having been chosen by God to share in the final messianic wedding feast in the kingdom of heaven.

TWENTY-SECOND SUNDAY AFTER PENTECOST

TWENTY-NINTH SUNDAY IN ORDINARY TIME
PROPER 24
OCTOBER 20, 2002

REVISED COMMON	EPISCOPAL (BCP)	ROMAN CATHOLIC
Isa. 45:1-7 or	Isa. 45:1-7	Isa. 45:1, 4-6
Exod. 33:12-23		
Ps. 96:1-9, (10-13) or	Psalm 96 or 96:1-9	Ps. 96:1, 3, 4-5, 7-8, 9-10
Psalm 99		
1 Thess. 1:1-10	1 Thess. 1:1-10	1 Thess. 1:1-5b
Matt. 22:15-22	Matt. 22:15-22	Matt. 22:15-21

God achieves salvation for all peoples by working through present governmental leaders and political powers. Total allegiance to the one and only saving God of all transcends allegiance to earthly rulers and institutions. We manifest our allegiance to God by Christ-centered lives of faith, hope, and love.

FIRST READING

ISAIAH 45:1-7 (RCL, BCP);
ISAIAH 45:1, 4-6 (RC)

Interpreting the Text

The setting for today's first reading from so-called Second Isaiah (Isa. 40–55) is the return of the people of Israel from their exile in Babylon in 538 B.C.E. after the destruction of Jerusalem in 587 B.C.E. Astoundingly God addresses the non-Israelite Cyrus—the king of Persia who conquered Babylon, liberating the Jews and permitting them to return to their native land to rebuild the Temple and Jerusalem—as God's "anointed," that is, "messiah" (45:1). God makes it clear that Cyrus is able to "subdue nations" and "strip kings" only because "it is I, the Lord, the God of Israel, who calls you by your name" (45:2-3). Although Cyrus does not know the God of Israel, he has derived his name and thus his power from the God of Israel to

ALTHOUGH CYRUS DOES NOT KNOW THE GOD OF ISRAEL, HE HAS DERIVED HIS NAME AND THUS HIS POWER FROM THE GOD OF ISRAEL TO SAVE THE CHOSEN PEOPLE.

save the chosen people (45:4). Cyrus is merely the subordinate agent and instrument of the God who creates light and darkness, weal and woe, so that all peoples may know of the God of Israel that "I am the Lord, and there is no other" (45:5-7).

Responding to the Text

God can work through the governing reigns and political regimes of today's world to accomplish his salvific purposes for all peoples. Do present earthly rulers realize that their power and authority derive ultimately from the one and only God who desires the salvation of all peoples? Can we see how today's world governments and rulers are furthering God's plan of universal salvation? Are national governments interested in the welfare not only of their own nations but of all the peoples of the world? Are the nations of the first world doing enough for the nations of the third world in terms of sharing their resources, forgiving debts, and assisting them in meeting the needs of their people?

EXODUS 33:12-23 (RCL, alt.)

The context of this reading is Israel's wandering in the wilderness after Moses brought them up from Egypt. Although God commissioned Moses to bring Israel out of Egypt, God has not yet revealed who will help Moses to lead the people to rest in the promised land (33:12). After Moses prays that God make known God's ways to him, God promises, "My presence will go with you, and I will give you rest" (33:13-14). That God will accompany Israel on their pilgrimage to the promised land distinguishes them from all the other peoples on the earth (33:15-16).

Since Moses has found favor with God, he asks God to reveal to him God's glory (33:17-18). God promises to proclaim to Moses the name, "The LORD" (YHWH), which discloses the character and identity of God in terms of God's sovereign freedom to extend compassion: "I will be gracious to whom I will be gracious, and will show mercy on whom I will show mercy" (33:19). No one can see the "face" of God and live; by placing Moses in the cleft of a rock, God protects him from the passing by of God's glory and thus allows him to see only the "back" not the "face" of God (33:20-23).

Moses provides us with a model of praying for God's accompanying presence as we struggle and strive to make our way from our earthly to our heavenly home. Are we able to see how God reveals God's glory to us indirectly and invisibly through God's word, the sacraments, and the events of our daily lives?

RESPONSIVE READING

PSALM 96:1-9, (10-13) (RCL); PSALM 96 or 96:1-9 (BCP); PSALM 96:1, 3, 4-5, 7-8, 9-10 (RC)

Psalm 96, one of the royal psalms that celebrates God's universal kingship, appropriately accompanies today's first reading from Isaiah. It invites all the peoples of the world to acknowledge, worship, and praise the God of Israel as the heavenly King (v. 10) whose greatness, glory, majesty, and strength transcends all earthly kings and gods (vv. 4-5).

PSALM 99 (RCL, alt.)

Psalm 99 is another royal psalm celebrating God's universal kingship. In accord with today's alternate reading from Exodus it recounts how God answered the prayers of an obedient Moses when he called upon the name of the forgiving God.

SECOND READING

1 THESSALONIANS 1:1-10 (RCL and BCP); 1 THESSALONIANS 1:1-5b (RC)

Interpreting the Text

In typical Pauline fashion the first letter to the Thessalonians opens with a salutation from the senders to the recipients of the letter. Paul, along with his co-workers in the gospel, Silvanus (Silas) and Timothy, are addressing "the church," the assembly of Christians in the city of Thessalonica, the capital of Macedonia, who are characterized as being under the fatherhood of God and lordship of Jesus Christ. They extend the usual Pauline greeting of "grace," which refers to the freely given gift of God's salvation now available in the death and resurrection of Christ, and "peace," which corresponds to the Hebrew concept of *shalom*, an overall situation of harmony and well-being in relation to God and one's fellow human beings (1:1)

They thank God for the Thessalonians, remembering always in their prayers their "work of faith and labor of love and steadfastness of hope in our Lord Jesus Christ" (1:2-3). This introduces the renowned Pauline triad of faith, love, and hope. Faith is submission in obedience and trust to the saving activity of God initiated by the life, death, and resurrection of Jesus Christ. Love is the sincere, mutual, and active care and concern for one's fellow Christian in response to God's love for us manifested in the death and resurrection of Jesus Christ. Hope is an absolutely firm and assured expectation of participating in the future and final salvation of God based on faith.

The senders continue to build a bond with the recipients as they acknowledge that the Thessalonians not only received the gospel from them with full conviction but imitated them in receiving it with joy in spite of persecution (1:4-6). The Thessalonians have thus proved to be good examples to the other Christians not only in their own region of Macedonia (northern Greece) but also in the region of Achaia (southern Greece), where the community of Corinth is located (1:7). Indeed, their faith has become well known everywhere after they welcomed Paul and his co-workers in love and turned away from idols to serve the true God, and to wait in hope for the return from heaven of the Jesus who "rescues us from the wrath that is coming" (1:8-10).

Responding to the Text

The faith of the Thessalonians provides a model for us also to place our trust in the saving activity of God manifested in the death and resurrection of Jesus Christ, in order paradoxically to experience joy despite the difficulties that threaten our faith. The love of the Thessalonians in welcoming Paul and his co-workers prompts us to extend hospitality to and support for Christian missionaries. And we are invited to share in the Thessalonians' hope for the return from heaven of Jesus to complete for us the salvation initiated by his death and resurrection.

THE GOSPEL
MATTHEW 22:15-22 (RCL, BCP);
MATTHEW 22:15-21 (RC)

Interpreting the Text

The setting of today's Gospel is Jesus' controversial teaching in the Jerusalem temple. The literary genre is that of a pronouncement story, which begins with the raising of a controversial issue by opponents, is met by a counter-argument by Jesus, and climaxes with a new, often poignant and provocative revelatory pronouncement.

Unable to arrest Jesus because the crowd held him to be a prophet (21:46), the Pharisees plot to entrap him in his speech (22:15). That they send their own disciples along with the Herodians, presumably a group aligned with the Roman regime of Herod Antipas, suggests that the verbal trap may have religious as well as political ramifications. Their sarcastically exaggerated compliment that Jesus teaches the way of God in truth without deference or partiality to any person intimates that their trap will involve a conflict between his lack of concern for human opinion or status and his sincere teaching of the way of God (22:16). They set the trap by raising the issue of whether it is lawful, that is, in accord with the way of God, for Jews to pay taxes to the Roman emperor (22:17).

Aware of their malicious and devious test, Jesus begins the counter argument by commanding them to bring him a denarius, the Roman coin used in paying the tax. Jesus thus asserts his own authoritative control over his opponents. Ironically, they rather than he possess and readily produce the coin connected to the Roman regime (22:18-19). Jesus then acts as the masterful teacher they have complimented as he forces them to state whose "head" or "image" and whose "title" or "inscription" is on the Roman coin (22:20). After their correct and obvious answer, "the emperor's," comes the climactic pronouncement: "Give therefore to the emperor the things that are the emperor's, and to God the things that are God's!" (22:21).

The aphoristic form and parallel construction of this forceful pronouncement, which concisely contrasts "the things that are the emperor's" with "the things that are God's," directs the audience to consider the danger and difficulty of relating life to both the emperor and God. The pronouncement prevents thinking of either separately. Political life cannot be separated from the claims of God and the religious dimension of life cannot ignore the political dimension and problems of society. The powerful pronouncement thus reminds its audience of the possible conflict between the claims of political government and of God.

Answering his opponents' question about the dilemma of paying the tax, Jesus deftly commands them to give to the emperor the things that are the emperor's—the coins bearing his image and inscription. Thus devaluing the concern to pay the tax, Jesus, with an astute variation on the same words, issues the overriding command to repay to God the things that are God's, that is, to give to God what in accord with the biblical tradition bears his "image" and "likeness," namely, the totality of the human person (Gen. 1:26-27). Whereas the emperor's claims are limited to the coins that belong to him, the claims of God are not so limited. Every human being created by God belongs to God and so Jesus' powerful pronouncement appeals for all human beings to give to God their complete allegiance.

> WHEREAS THE EMPEROR'S CLAIMS ARE LIMITED TO THE COINS THAT BELONG TO HIM, THE CLAIMS OF GOD ARE NOT SO LIMITED. EVERY HUMAN BEING CREATED BY GOD BELONGS TO GOD.

Jesus' brilliant pronouncement extricated him from the verbal trap. By teaching the payment of the tax, Jesus cannot be delivered to the Roman authorities as a political rebel. But neither can he thereby be accused by his fellow Jews of respecting human and political status over the religious authority of God, for he indeed truly teaches the "way of God" by urging his audience to submit the totality of their persons to the absolute claim of the sovereign God, which embraces and surpasses the claim of political government. Confounded by Jesus' response, the opponents left him and went away in amazement (22:22), failing to repent and submit to the way of God Jesus truly teaches.

Responding to the Text

Jesus' powerful and provocative pronouncement in the Jerusalem temple exhorts us to submit ourselves totally and unreservedly to the sovereign dominion of God, an absolute dominion which embraces and exceeds all other claims for our allegiance, even those of ruling political authorities. Sovereignty over the life of every human being—the unborn child, the death row inmate, the aged and terminally ill—belongs exclusively to God. No political power or ruling government can give us the right to take the life of another human being.

By teaching complete dedication to the sovereign claim of God over us and the world as the true way of God, Jesus reveals his own attitude of total submission to the will of God. It is his attitude of complete trust in God that enables him to accomplish the salvific will of God by undergoing suffering, death, and resurrection. We are called to adopt that attitude.

Points to ponder:
- God can work through political powers and governments to achieve God's salvific purposes.
- God promises, "I will be gracious to whom I will be gracious, and will show mercy on whom I will show mercy."
- We can experience joy in the midst of life's troubles and tribulations by living the fundamental Pauline triad of faith, love, and hope.
- "Give therefore to the emperor the things that are the emperor's, and to God the things that are God's!"

TWENTY-THIRD SUNDAY AFTER PENTECOST

THIRTIETH SUNDAY IN ORDINARY TIME
PROPER 25
OCTOBER 27, 2002

REVISED COMMON	EPISCOPAL (BCP)	ROMAN CATHOLIC
Lev. 19:1-2, 15-18 or Deut. 34:1-12	Exod. 22:21-27	Exod. 22:20-26
Psalm 1 or Ps. 90:1-6, 13-17	Psalm 1	Ps. 18:1-2, 2-3, 46, 50 (Heb. Bible 18:2-3, 3-4, 47, 51)
1 Thess. 2:1-8	1 Thess. 2:1-8	1 Thess. 1:5c-10
Matt. 22:34-46	Matt. 22:34-46	Matt. 22:34-40

We are called to lives of a holiness that derives not from ourselves but from the holiness of a compassionate God. This involves living in accord with the double commandment of loving God with the totality of our beings and of loving our neighbors as ourselves. Loving God and neighbor entails courageously sharing not only the gospel of God but even our very selves.

FIRST READING
LEVITICUS 19:1-2, 15-18 (RCL)

"You shall be holy, for I the Lord your God am holy" expresses the keynote for the whole of the so-called Holiness Code (Leviticus 17–26). To be holy means to be separate from the ordinary. God, who brought the Israelites out of slavery in Egypt, separated them from the other peoples of the world for a special covenant relationship with God. This relationship with the holy God rather than any intrinsic attributes gives the people of Israel their holiness (19:1-2). This holiness involves loving their neighbor, their fellow Israelites, as themselves by not judging, slandering or taking revenge upon them (19:15-18).

It seems to be ordinary, normal, and accepted practice for human beings to judge one another, to gossip about and slander one another, and, especially, to take revenge upon and pay back when we are harmed by another. Our relation-

ship with the "holy" God demands that we be "holy," that is, that we separate ourselves from this ordinary behavior by loving our fellow human beings
as ourselves.

EXODUS 22:21-27 (BCP); EXODUS 22:20-26 (RC)

Doing God's commandments is the way that the people of Israel are to
live in the covenantal relationship for which God chose and saved them. Among
those commandments is protecting and caring for those who otherwise have no
means of support—the resident alien, widows, orphans, the poor (22:21-24).
When lending to the poor the Israelites are to extend God's compassion to them
by not exacting interest and by not taking essential possessions as collateral
(22:25-28).

Like Israel, we are called to manifest our appreciation of God's love for us by
extending that love to those who are most needy among us. It is somewhat surprising that the United States, which was founded by immigrants, is not more
welcoming to its immigrants and resident aliens of today. Does our nation as well
as the other wealthy nations of the world need to be more forgiving of the debil-
itating debts of the poorer nations?

DEUTERONOMY 34:1-12 (RCL, alt.)

This reading comprises the final, climactic chapter of the book of
Deuteronomy, which brings the people of Israel to the point of entering the
promised land. Although God shows to Moses the full extent of the spacious land
that fulfills the promise God swore to the patriarchs, Moses will not enter it (34:1-
4). Since Moses has completed his role in God's plan by bringing Israel to this
point, he died and was buried in the land of Moab. That his burial place remains
unknown hints that God secretly buried him, adding to his status as a revered
prophet (34:5-6). Indeed, the Israelites mourned for thirty days the death of their
leader, who lived a full and vigorous life (34:7-8). Although the leadership and
authority of Moses now passes to Joshua, Moses, because of all of the marvelous
mighty deeds God worked through him, was Israel's greatest prophet (34:9-12).

The great prophet Moses provides us a model for obediently fulfilling our roles
in God's plan of salvation. Like Moses, we will be revered and rewarded by
enabling God to accomplish great deeds through our obedient faithfulness to our
Christian calling.

RESPONSIVE READING

PSALM 1 (RCL and BCP)

The promise of God's happiness and prosperity to those who delight "in the law of the Lord, and on his law they meditate day and night" (1:2), relates this psalm to today's first readings, which call for obeying God's law of loving our neighbors and the needy as ourselves.

PSALM 18:1-2, 2-3, 46, 50 (RC)

This selection's praise of God as "my rock" of refuge, strength, and deliverance connects with today's first reading from Exodus, in which a compassionate God promises to be a "rock" for the poor and needy by hearing their cries for help.

PSALM 90:1-6, 13-17 (RCL, alt.)

Psalm 90, subtitled "a prayer of Moses, the man of God," relates to today's alternate first reading, which recounts the end of Moses' career. The first unit (vv. 1-6), which expresses the transience of human life in contrast to the eternity of God, serves as a fitting comment on the end of Moses' life. And the second unit (vv. 13-17), a prayer for deliverance from difficulties, characterizes the many prayers of intercession by Moses on behalf of Israel.

SECOND READING

1 THESSALONIANS 2:1-8 (RCL and BCP)

Interpreting the Text

The senders of this letter to the Thessalonians—Paul, Silvanus, and Timothy—recount how they, after being mistreated in Philippi, brought the gospel of God to the Thessalonians in spite of great opposition (2:1-2). Part of the opposition presumably involved accusations that they were preaching the gospel from deceit or impure motives or trickery, just to win the favor of their audience. The implication is that they were like the many wandering philosophers of the day, who attracted audiences with impressive preaching, only "to pass the hat" and take their money. But Paul and his companions insist that their aim is to please the God who approved them and entrusted them with the message of the gospel. They are not interested in the flattery, praise, or money of the Thessalonians (2:3-6).

Although, as authorized apostles of Christ, they could expect some financial support from the Thessalonians, they never made any such demands. Rather, they related to the Thessalonians in the manner of a gentle nurse "tenderly caring for her own children" (2:7). So dear were the Thessalonians to Paul and his co-workers that they took a deep personal interest in them and their well-being. They shared with them not only the gospel of God, but their very selves (2:8).

Responding to the Text

Paul and his companions provide us a model of deep personal involvement in bringing the gospel to others. We must not merely relay the message of the gospel but demonstrate a sincere care and concern for the personal lives and well-being of those who hear it. Sharing ourselves is an essential part of the endeavor to spread the good news of Christ. We preach, bear witness to, and live the gospel not to win praise, adulation, or awards from people but to please the God who calls us to relate and apply the gospel of God to people's lives.

1 THESSALONIANS 1:5c-10 (RC)

Interpreting the Text

The senders of the letter, Paul, Silvanus, and Timothy, continue to build a bond with the recipients as they acknowledge that the Thessalonians not only received the gospel from them with full conviction, but imitated them in receiving it with joy in spite of persecution (1:4-6). The Thessalonians have thus proven to be good examples to the other Christians not only in their own region of Macedonia (northern Greece) but also in the region of Achaia (southern Greece), where the community of Corinth is located (1:7). Indeed, their faith has become well known everywhere after they welcomed Paul and his co-workers in love and turned away from idols to serve the true God, and to wait in hope for the return from heaven of the Jesus who "rescues us from the wrath that is coming" (1:8-10).

Responding to the Text

The faith of the Thessalonians provides a model for us to likewise place our trust in the saving activity of God manifested in the death and resurrection of Jesus Christ, in order paradoxically to experience joy despite the difficulties that threaten our faith. The love of the Thessalonians in welcoming Paul and his co-workers prompts us to extend hospitality toward and support for Christian missionaries. And we are invited to share in the Thessalonians' hope for the return from heaven of Jesus to complete for us the salvation initiated by his death and resurrection.

THE GOSPEL

MATTHEW 22:34-46 (RCL and BCP); MATTHEW 22:34-40 (RC)

Interpreting the Text

Jesus has just silenced the Sadducees in their attempt to entrap him over the question of resurrection from the dead (22:23-33). He had previously thwarted the scheme of the Pharisees, who were unable to arrest him because the crowd revered him as a prophet (21:46), to trap him on the issue of paying taxes to the Roman emperor (22:15-22). And so the Pharisees gather together for yet another confrontation with Jesus that might lead to his arrest in the Jerusalem temple (22:34).

The test begins as a lawyer from among the Pharisees asks Jesus which of all the many and diverse commandments in the Jewish law, the Torah, is the greatest (22:35-36). The lawyer thus dares Jesus to choose which of the vast number of various commandments epitomizes the very essence and spirit of God's will and is therefore the most important to perform. Surely Jesus will neglect something of significance, surmises the lawyer, and leave himself open to accusation and arrest.

Jesus answers the menacing question by quoting from the familiar *Shema* found in Deuteronomy, which Jews recited regularly in their daily worship, "You shall the love the Lord your God with all your heart, and with all your soul, and with all your mind" (Deut. 6:5). Jesus claims that this commandment, which requires that the love of God be a matter of the total personal commitment and devotion of one's whole being, is the greatest and first of all the commandments (22:38). But before the lawyer can reply, Jesus quickly adds a second commandment that is found in Leviticus, "You shall love your neighbor as yourself" (Lev. 19:18, cited in Matt. 22:39). On both of these commandments, Jesus authoritatively announces, "hang all the law and the prophets" (22:40). In other words, a complete, personally committed love of both God and neighbor embodies the will of God that is contained in the scriptural law and prophets of the Jewish people.

Having deftly defended himself against the lawyer's test, Jesus goes on the offensive. To the gathered Pharisees Jesus asks a question of his own—whose son is the messiah? They immediately offer an answer obvious from the biblical tradition (2 Sam. 7:12-16, etc.), "the son of David" (22:41-42). Jesus is asking not just a theoretical question about the messiah but whether he himself, whom the audience has already heard affirmed as the messiah (16:16), is "the son of David."

Continuing his provocative inquiry, Jesus explains that David himself, the traditional author of the Psalms, spoke under the inspiration of God's Spirit when he said that "the Lord," that is, God himself, commanded "my Lord," that is, the Messiah, that he should sit enthroned at the authoritative "right hand" of God, while God himself gives him a triumphant victory over his "enemies" by placing them in submission "under your feet" (Ps. 110:1). Jesus thus not only subtly implies that as the Messiah he is the one David calls "Lord," but also indirectly proclaims his future enthronement at God's right hand in heavenly triumph over the enemies who are presently plotting against him.

Jesus then brings his penetrating query to a pointed climax by asking that if David himself calls the Messiah "Lord," then "how" or in what sense is the Messiah David's Son? (22:45). Jesus' question projects a double meaning: How can one whom David calls "Lord" be David's *son*? And how can one whom David calls "Lord" be *David's* son? This double-edged question invites the audience to reflect on both the lordship and the sonship of Jesus, It leads to the conclusion that "the Messiah," and therefore Jesus himself, is more appropriately understood as the "Lord" rather than the "Son" of David, but also to the realization that as "Lord" Jesus is more than the Son of David, namely, the beloved Son of God (3:17; 14:33; 17:5). Jesus has thus silenced all of the questioners seeking to entrap him (22:46).

> A COMPLETE, PERSONALLY COMMITTED LOVE OF BOTH GOD AND NEIGHBOR EMBODIES THE WILL OF GOD THAT IS CONTAINED IN THE SCRIPTURAL LAW AND PROPHETS OF THE JEWISH PEOPLE.

Responding to the Text

Loving God in a completely committed way but neglecting the needs of our fellow human beings fails to accomplish God's will. To be able to love our neighbor as ourselves, we must first realize and respond to God's love for all of us. Once we realize that God's love for us is also meant for all other human beings, we can love our fellow human beings as ourselves, as those who love and are loved by God.

We are invited to submit ourselves to the messianic lordship and divine sonship of Jesus as part of our total love of God and neighbor. As followers of Jesus, we may look forward to participating in the glorious triumph and heavenly exaltation over all opposition and enemies that God has granted Jesus as our messianic "Lord" and God's beloved "Son" enthroned at God's right hand with divine power and authority.

Points to ponder:
• God calls and enables us to be "holy" as God is "holy."
• God wants us to extend God's compassion to immigrants, the poor, and the most needy among us.
• Moses provides us a model for obedient and faithful service of God and God's people.
• Preaching the gospel entails sharing our very selves.
• We can love our neighbor as ourselves by loving in a completely committed way the God who created, saved, and loves both us and our neighbor.

REFORMATION DAY

OCTOBER 31, 2002
(OR TRANSFERRED TO OCTOBER 27, 2002)

Jer. 31:31-34
Psalm 46
Rom. 3:19-28
John 8:31-36

Rather than a triumphalistic celebration of the Protestant movement, Reformation Day provides the opportunity not only to affirm the distinctive contributions to Christianity of Protestantism but to reflect upon the need for all who profess faith in Jesus Christ to respect and work with one another for peace and unity. The fragmentation of Christianity into various rites, denominations, and factions is a scandal that has been with us so long that we have sadly taken it for granted. There is a positive side in that such diversity often adds a richness to the expression and manifestation of Christianity. Although the gospel does not necessarily call us as Christians to uniformity, it definitely calls us to unity. The signing of the joint declaration on justification on October 21, 1999, at Augsburg, Germany, by representatives of the Roman Catholic Church and the Lutheran World Federation as well as recent collaboration and sharing of resources by Episcopalians and Lutherans signal hope for a somewhat stalled ecumenical movement.

Today's readings provide themes pertinent to the need that all Christians have for the ongoing reform and renewal that is possible only with God's grace and assistance: God promises to establish a new covenantal relationship with God's people characterized by internal renewal and forgiveness. We trust in God's presence among us as a refuge against all adversity. We are justified and in a right relationship with God only because of God's grace revealed in the death and resurrection of Jesus Christ. As God's Son, Jesus offers us true freedom from slavery to the sinfulness of our failure to grow in faith.

FIRST READING

JEREMIAH 31:31–34

245

REFORMATION

DAY

OCTOBER 31

Interpreting the Text

In the biblical tradition "covenant" referred to the fundamental relationship uniting God to Israel as God's specially chosen people, the pledge of mutual fidelity and loyalty according to which God would be their saving and loving God and they would be his grateful and obedient people. But Israel often failed to uphold their role in God's covenant with them. Consequently, God, through prophecies such as that pronounced by Jeremiah, promised to establish a new, permanent, and definitive covenant with God's people.

The prophet Jeremiah uttered this great oracle of the "new covenant" about the time of the destruction of Jerusalem by Nebuchadnezzar in 587 B.C.E. when its leading citizens were led into exile in Babylon. In the oracle God promises to establish an entirely new and different kind of covenant with the whole of God's chosen people of Israel—with both "the house of Israel" (northern kingdom) and "the house of Judah" (southern kingdom) (31:31). It will be unlike the Sinai covenant God made with their ancestors when he brought them out of Egypt. Even though through Moses God provided the laws and commandments for them to fulfill the requirements and obligations of their part of the covenant— to be God's own specially chosen people, they continually failed to keep the commandments and broke that covenant (31:32).

In this new covenant a proactive God takes an even greater role in assuring that the people of Israel will be able to uphold their side of the covenant. There are three essential elements that make this covenant radically new: (1) Unlike the old covenant, in which the law was external to the people and written on tablets of stone, in the new covenant God himself will make God's law completely internal to the people—God "will write it on

> IN THIS NEW COVENANT A PROACTIVE GOD TAKES AN EVEN GREATER ROLE IN ASSURING THAT THE PEOPLE OF ISRAEL WILL BE ABLE TO UPHOLD THEIR SIDE OF THE COVENANT.

their hearts" (31:33). (2) Whereas under the old covenant they had to teach the external laws to one another in order to know God and what God wanted from them in fulfillment of the covenant, in the new covenant, because the laws will be internal to them, everyone without exception will know God and God's will. (3) Since they broke the old covenant through their sin and iniquity, divine forgiveness is necessary for a new covenant—"I will forgive their iniquity and remember their sin no more" (31:34).

Responding to the Text

To be a truly unified people of God as Christians, we cannot allow God's saving will to remain external and unknown to us. We pray that God may fulfill for us the promise of a new covenant by placing a knowledge of God's saving will and a desire to carry it out deep within our inner beings. As Christians who have failed to achieve the unity God desires of us, we need the forgiveness God promises in the new covenant.

Jesus established this new covenant at his last supper, which anticipated his sacrificial death (Matt. 26:28; Mark 14:24; Luke 22:20). By referring to his blood as the blood of the (new) covenant, Jesus indicated that the blood of his death will effect the fulfillment of the definitive covenant according to which God pledges a permanent and profound presence with God's people in a salvific and liberating relationship. Jesus thus transformed the Jewish Passover meal into a covenant meal, whereby those who drink the wine designated as his blood of the (new) covenant are sacramentally and profoundly united into this new and final covenantal relationship God establishes with God's people through the salvific death of Jesus.

RESPONSIVE READING
PSALM 46

This psalm is one of the songs of Zion that proclaims confidence in God's ultimate triumph over all opposing powers. Verse 1 inspired Luther's hymn, "A Mighty Fortress." The psalm reverberates with the theme that God is a secure and ever present refuge for us in the midst of the world's trials, troubles, and tribulations—"the Lord of hosts is with us; the God of Jacob is our refuge" (vv. 7, 11). The psalm's keynote thus appropriately accords with today's first reading from Jeremiah in which God promises a new covenantal relationship of internal and intimate presence with God's specially chosen people.

SECOND READING
ROMANS 3:19-28

Interpreting the Text

With his emphasis on the universal (every mouth/whole world/no human being) failure to observe the law of God, Paul has imparted to his implied audience at Rome the utter hopelessness of universal sinfulness—all human beings without exception are under the devastating power of sin (3:19-20). This demonstrates Paul's strategy of inducing his audience to identify with various sinful groups in a dramatically progressive fashion: the totally unrighteous, ungodly (1:18-32), the supposedly morally upright (2:1-16), the supposedly upright Jew (2:17-3:8), and finally, all sinners (3:9-20), including Paul's audience!

But Paul immediately begins to revive the hope of his audience with the announcement that the marvelous "righteousness of God" has now been fortuitously manifested "apart from the law," that is, independently and outside of the previous principle whereby one was declared to be in a righteous or proper relationship with God by faithfully performing the works of the Mosaic law. Yet this new "righteousness of God" represents that righteousness to which the scriptural "Law and the Prophets" originally bore witness. This new "righteousness of God" is received and appropriated through faith in Jesus Christ and it extends to all who so believe, and are thus justified by the "redemption," the liberation from slavery to the overwhelming power of sinfulness, that is in Christ Jesus (3:21-24).

God has openly and publicly "put forward" Christ Jesus to the world as a "sacrifice of atonement," a means of expiation for sins, which is acquired through faith. Christ has become such an atonement for sins not by pouring out the blood of an animal sacrifice but by pouring out his very own blood in death. By this public manifestation God quite effectively demonstrates God's very own "righteousness" in forgiving sins from the past down to the present through God's enduring forbearance. All of this proves beyond any doubt that God is truly "righteous" or "just" and that he generously "justifies" any person who believes in Jesus (3:25-26). Paul is thus convincing his audience to realize the full significance of their faith. That they are now freely justified by their faith in Jesus Christ means they now have liberation from, atonement for, and forgiveness of the devastating sinfulness that has engulfed them and all of humanity in absolute hopelessness.

Paul employs a clever play on words to assert that now a whole new situation involving "righteousness" is operative. Whereas he previously used the word "law" (nomos) to refer to God's Law or Torah primarily as the instructions and commandments for doing God's will, he now adduces it in a more general yet perhaps purposely ambivalent sense to signify primarily "principle" or "system." The radically new "law" or "principle" of faith has now abolished any "boasting" (2:17, 23) based upon the righteousness that one might establish for oneself through accomplishing the works of the Law. For, as Paul boldly insists with emphasis on the words "by faith," a person is now justified solely *by faith* and not by the performance of the works of the Law (3:27-28).

We are part of the utter hopelessness of universal sinfulness. We do not seem to be able to achieve the moral perfection that God's laws and commandments intend for us. We continually and repeatedly fail in one way or another. We simply cannot make ourselves "righteous" before God, we cannot earn our own salvation, we cannot forgive ourselves of sins against God. Part of our sinfulness as Christians has been the failure to achieve reconciliation and unity among the various Christian denominations. Is Christian unity a hopeless endeavor because of our human weaknesses and sinfulness?

> WE ARE PART OF THE UTTER HOPELESSNESS OF UNIVERSAL SINFULNESS. BUT THE GOOD NEWS IS THAT GOD MORE THAN COMPENSATES FOR OUR HUMAN FAILINGS.

But the good news is that God more than compensates for our human failings. God has publicly manifested for all God's very own "righteousness" in the sacrificial death of Jesus Christ, which effects the expiation for all of our human sinfulness. We can become righteous before God not on our own but only by faith in what God has done for us in the death of Jesus. The grace of God's forgiveness for our sins is available to all who believe. There is hope for Christian unity if we acknowledge our past failures and seek God's reconciling and rectifying forgiveness. We pray that this fundamental Christian doctrine of the freely given grace of God's justification of all sinners by their faith in Christ may unite rather than divide us as Christians.

THE GOSPEL
JOHN 8:31-36

Interpreting the Text

The context is Jesus' teaching in the Jerusalem temple during the pilgrimage festival of Booths or Tabernacles, which commemorate Israel's wandering in the wilderness and living in booths or tents after God brought them out of Egyptian slavery in the exodus event. This feast, then, provides background and motivation for the theme of slavery and freedom in today's Gospel.

Although most Jews rejected Jesus, many did believe in him (8:30). In the Gospel of John, however, faith is not a static but an ongoing and progressive phenomenon. There are various levels and degrees of belief. Jesus thus challenges those Jews who do believe to develop and grow in their faith. If they continue or remain in Jesus' "word," his revelatory teaching, they can move from the level of an initial believer to a true disciple (8:31-32). Then they will "know," that is, personally experience the "truth" that will make them free (8:33). "Truth" in

John refers to Jesus' revelation of the Father's saving love. The person of Jesus himself embodies this "truth" (see 14:6). That the truth will make them free means, then, that Jesus will make them free. By growing in faith and coming to know the truth that is Jesus they will experience true freedom.

But these believing Jews object that they are descendants of Abraham and have never been slaves to anyone! What is this "freedom" of which Jesus speaks? (8:33). Here is a fine example of Johannine irony. In the context of the Feast of Tabernacles, which reminds them of their slavery in Egypt, how can they claim they have never been enslaved?

Jesus explains that the freedom of which he is speaking is freedom from the slavery of sin, which in John means *the* sin of unbelief (8:34). The ironic implication is that they are slaves to their refusal to grow in faith (sin) by recognizing their need for the true freedom Jesus offers. Jesus can offer this true freedom because he is the Son of God. Unlike a slave who does not have a permanent place in the household (cf. Ishmael in Gen. 21:9f.; Exod. 21:2; Deut. 15:12), Jesus as God's Son has a permanent place in God's heavenly household (8:35-36). Jesus is thus offering them the freedom of an eternal life, of living forever in the heavenly household of God.

Responding to the Text

Are we blind to our need for Jesus to free us from the slavery of our refusal to grow in our Christian faith? We can never be satisfied with achieving a certain level of faith and then merely maintaining that level. We must continually deepen, develop, and grow in our faith of Jesus by more fully knowing and experiencing him as the Son of God who can free us for an eternal life in his Father's heavenly household.

Part of our slavery to sin is being satisfied with the current state of ecumenical relations among the various Christian denominations. We need to be freed from a narrow focus on our own particular brand of Christianity. We need to experience the freedom of appreciating the distinctive and unique charisms of the rich and varied expressions of Christianity throughout the world. Our own faith can be enriched by knowledge of and exposure to different yet legitimate manifestations of Christianity. Before we as Christians can achieve true unity we must respect, appreciate, and learn from our differences.

> WE NEED TO BE FREED FROM A NARROW FOCUS ON OUR OWN PARTICULAR BRAND OF CHRISTIANITY. WE NEED TO EXPERIENCE THE FREEDOM OF APPRECIATING THE DISTINCTIVE AND UNIQUE CHARISMS OF THE RICH AND VARIED EXPRESSIONS OF CHRISTIANITY THROUGHOUT THE WORLD.

Points to ponder:

- God promises us a new covenant in which God's forgiveness of our sinfulness enables God's saving will to be written in our hearts.
- God is an ever-present refuge from life's difficulties.
- God makes us righteous and forgives our sins by our faith in the saving death of Jesus.
- As the Son of God Jesus offers us the true freedom of growing in our faith and living eternally in the heavenly household of God.

ALL SAINTS DAY

NOVEMBER 1, 2002
(OR TRANSFERRED TO NOVEMBER 3, 2002)

REVISED COMMON	EPISCOPAL (BCP)	ROMAN CATHOLIC
Rev. 7:9-17	Sir. 44:1-10, 13-14	Rev. 7:2-4, 9-14
Ps. 34:1-10, 22	Psalm 149	Ps. 24:1-2, 3-4, 5-6
1 John 3:1-13	Rev. 7:2-4, 9-17	1 John 3:1-3
Matt. 5:1-12	Matt. 5:1-12	Matt. 5:1-12a

Many of the canonized Christian saints have their own special feast days. Today is the feast for remembering and celebrating the vast array of saints, canonized or uncanonized, of every time and place. Today we pray that we may imitate their exemplary Christian lives and that they may intercede for us from their heavenly home to which we are still journeying.

Today's readings challenge us to be the saints of today by reminding us that we are God's children called to live in accord with the beatitudes from Jesus' great Sermon on the Mount. As God's children we look forward to joining the saints that have gone before us in their heavenly worship of God.

FIRST READING
REVELATION 7:9-17 (RCL);
REVELATION 7:2-4, 9-14 (RC)

Interpreting the Text

In the interlude between the opening of the sixth and seventh seals, John has two heavenly visions. In the first vision (7:1-8), John sees that the complete number (144,000) of those sealed from every tribe of the people of Israel are now in heaven. The angels of God had sealed them to protect and preserve them throughout the persecutions that plagued them on earth (7:2-4).

The second vision (7:9-17) outdoes the first. Now there is a countless great multitude not just from Israel but "from every nation, from all tribes and peoples and languages." Clothed with heavenly white robes and with palm branches signaling victory, they praise God and the Lamb (risen Christ) for salvation, thus sharing in the heavenly worship of the angels, the elders, and the four living creatures (7:9-12). After one of the elders asks John about the identity and origin of those clothed in white, he answers his own question. They are the Christians who endured persecution and martyrdom on earth. They have shared in the sacrificial death of Jesus as "they have washed their robes and made them white in the blood of the Lamb" (7:13-14). Consequently, they now share in the Lamb's triumph over death, as the "Lamb" paradoxically "shepherds" them to the waters of eternal life (7:15-17).

JOHN'S VISION OF HEAVENLY WORSHIP ENCOURAGES US TO ENDURE THE TRIALS, TROUBLES, AND TRIBULATIONS OF BEARING WITNESS TO THE GOSPEL AND LIVING THE CHRISTIAN LIFE IN TODAY'S SECULAR AND MATERIALISTIC WORLD.

Responding to the Text

John's vision of heavenly worship encourages us to endure the trials, troubles, and tribulations of bearing witness to the gospel and living the Christian life in today's secular and materialistic world. The many martyrs now in heaven inspire us to proclaim and bear witness to the gospel of life in the midst of a culture of violence and death.

SIRACH 44:1-10, 13-14 (BCP)

God's wisdom is revealed through the history of God's people as seen in the lives of Israel's great ancestors. Sirach first praises those ancestors who by their great deeds have "made a name for themselves"—rulers, counselors, prophets, teachers, musicians, peacemakers (44:1-8). Then he mentions those whose names have been forgotten but not their righteous deeds (44:9-10). Although buried, their memory and "glory will never be blotted out" (44:13-14).

This reading fits today's feast of all the saints, in which we remember not only all of those Christians who have made names for themselves but also those whose names may not be famous or widely known. Today we can remember and thank God for the saints we have known in our own personal lives—relatives and friends whose names may not be renowned in the world, but whom we remember as the Christians who most influenced and helped us.

RESPONSIVE READING
PSALM 34:1-10, 22 (RCL)

As a thanksgiving for deliverance from trouble, Psalm 34 accompanies today's first reading from Revelation with its vision of the martyrs God has delivered from death. After repeated praise of God for deliverance, today's selection reaches its climax: "The Lord redeems the life of his servants; none of those who take refuge in him will be condemned" (34:22).

PSALM 149 (BCP)

Psalm 149 is a hymn calling for the praise of God in song and festive dance. Verse 4 connects with today's first reading from Sirach, which remembers the humble, unnamed saints of old: "For the Lord takes pleasure in his people; he adorns the humble with victory."

PSALM 24:1-2, 3-4, 5-6 (RC)

Psalm 24 is a processional song of entrance into the temple for worship. It fittingly accompanies today's first reading from Revelation with its scene of the heavenly worship of the martyred saints. They are "those who have clean hands and pure hearts, who do not lift up their souls to what is false; and do not swear deceitfully" (24:4).

SECOND READING
1 JOHN 3:1-13 (RCL); 1 JOHN 3:1-3 (RC)

Interpreting the Text

The author of 1 John informs his audience that they are even now children of God, because of the love the Father has given us. The Father demonstrated that love in sending his Son, Jesus, into the world (cf. John 3:16). Jesus reveals the love of the Father to the world. The reason the world does not know us Christians as children of God is that it did not recognize Jesus as the Son who reveals the love of the Father (3:1). Not knowing Jesus as the Son means not knowing God as the Father. That we are God's children now gives us the hope of being like "him"—either the Father or the Son who will fully and finally reveal God at the end of time, when we "see him as he is," that is, see God revealed in the Son (3:2). All who have this hope are purified of the uncleanness of sinfulness, just as "he" (God or Christ) is pure and sinless (3:3).

The sinless Son of God was revealed to take away the sins of which we are guilty (3:4-5). By remaining with the Son we avoid sin and do what is righteous (3:6-7). Every sinner is a child of the devil, but the Son of God destroyed the works of the devil (3:8). Love for our fellow Christians demonstrates that we are children of God rather than of the devil (3:9-10). Since Cain killed Abel because he was righteous, we should not be astonished if the world hates us for the righteousness of loving one another (3:11-13).

This reading challenges us to be the saints of today, the holy ones who, as God's children, are separate and different from the world. What distinguishes us as children of God from the world is our love for one another—"See how they love one another" and "They will know we are Christians by our love." What enables us to love one another is God's love for us in sending us his Son to take away our sinfulness and make us children of God. That we are already children of God and thus already living the eternal life of God gives us the sure hope that when our lives in the world have come to an end "we will be like him, for we will see him as he is."

REVELATION 7:2-4, 9-17 (BCP)

See today's First Reading (RCL, RC), above.

THE GOSPEL

MATTHEW 5:1-12 (RCL, BCP); MATTHEW 5:1-12a (RC)

Interpreting the Text

Matthew's version of the beatitudes introduces and sets the tone for Jesus' great Sermon on the Mount (Matthew 5–7), which he addresses to both the crowds ("Jesus saw the crowds") and his disciples ("his disciples came to him"). The sermon is thus not elitist teaching for the disciples only but is intended for all. The sermon takes place on a mountain—a place of closeness to the divine realm and a special place of revelation in the biblical tradition (cf. God's giving of the Law to Moses on Mt. Sinai). That Jesus "sat down" (5:1) as well as the otherwise redundant notice that "he began to speak" (literally, "he opened his mouth") prepares the audience for an especially solemn teaching with divine authority (5:2).

The first eight beatitudes divide themselves into two stanzas of four each. The first four beatitudes (5:3-6) promise God's reversal for those who find themselves in unfortunate, socially oppressive situations, while the next four beatitudes (5:7-10) promise God's reward for those who exhibit virtuous behavior on behalf of the unfortunate mentioned in the first four beatitudes. The climactic ninth beatitude (5:11-12) invites the audience to identify with all of those described in the first eight beatitudes.

The first beatitude pronounces God's favor ("blessed") to those who are "poor in spirit," those dispossessed and abandoned by society who feel hopeless or dispirited because of their lack of material possessions. The beatitude promises that "theirs is the kingdom of heaven" (5:3), that is, that God's kingship is presently ruling over them. The kingship or reign of God now present in the person and ministry of Jesus is already reversing their misfortune.

In the second beatitude "those who mourn," that is, those who are miserable and unhappy as they lament the oppression and unjust violence they have received from society, are "blessed" because "they will be comforted" (by God, divine passive). This beatitude thus promises that God's comfort and encouragement will surely in the future reverse the lot of those who are presently mourning misfortune (5:4).

The third beatitude pronounces God's blessing upon "the meek," that is, those whom the wicked of the world have humiliated and rendered powerless by denying them access to their share of God's creation (cf. Ps. 37). In this beatitude God promises that the world's meek "will inherit the earth," that is, that in the future God will depose the world's wicked elite so that all those who presently find themselves in the unfortunate situation of "meekness" will experience a reversal and thus will enjoy their "inheritance" of God's creation meant to be shared by all (5:5).

> THE FIRST FOUR BEATITUDES (5:3–6) PROMISE GOD'S REVERSAL FOR THOSE WHO FIND THEM- SELVES IN UNFORTUNATE, SOCIALLY OPPRESSIVE SITUATIONS, WHILE THE NEXT FOUR BEATITUDES (5:7-10) PROMISE GOD'S REWARD FOR THOSE WHO EXHIBIT VIRTUOUS BEHAVIOR ON BEHALF OF THE UNFORTUNATE MENTIONED IN THE FIRST FOUR BEATITUDES.

The fourth beatitude climactically sums up the first three. It pronounces God's blessing upon "those who hunger and thirst for righteousness," that is, those who long for God to make present social injustices right and just. They "will be filled" (by God, divine passive). Through Jesus, who is bringing about the kingdom of heaven, God will satisfy those who are hungering and thirsting for a reversal of social injustices (5:6).

Introducing the second stanza, the fifth beatitude pronounces God's blessing upon those who manifest mercy and have compassion for the unfortunate described in the first stanza. The beatitude assures them that they in turn will receive mercy from God not only for themselves but also for those unfortunate and oppressed for whom they have sought mercy (5:7)

In the sixth beatitude God's favor is upon "the pure in heart," that is, those who demonstrate sincere integrity and truthfulness in human relations rather than behaving falsely and deceitfully (Ps. 24:4). As those who have sought to make God's righteousness and justice visible in the world, thus furthering the cause of the socially oppressed, they are promised that "they will see God" (see today's Second Reading from 1 John) in the kingdom of heaven (5:8).

The seventh beatitude assures God's blessing upon "the peacemakers," those who work to bring about *shalom*, a situation of overall harmony and well-being among human beings and between human beings and their creator. As those striving to make God's peace a reality in the world, especially on behalf of the unfortunate who most lack that peace, they are promised future familial intimacy with God, as "they will be called (by God) children of God" (5:9).

In the eighth beatitude God's favor is upon those who experience persecution as they try to bring about God's righteousness and thus reverse social injustices. Like the "poor in spirit" in the first beatitude they are already experiencing God's kingship in their lives (5:10).

Whereas the first eight beatitudes employ a distancing third person address ("blessed are *those*"), the climactic ninth beatitude engages the audience directly and emphatically: "Blessed are *you* when people revile *you* and persecute *you* and utter all kinds of evil against *you* falsely on my account" (5:11). This beatitude thus invites the audience to become those who, along with and for the sake of Jesus, work for God's reversal of the social injustices experienced by the unfortunate. Although they can expect to be persecuted like the prophets before them, they may rejoice and be glad, because God will reward them greatly in heaven (5:12).

Responding to the Text

Many of the saints of the past have provided us with stellar examples of living the beatitudes. But the beatitudes are not ideals that only elite "saints" can ever hope to actualize. They are directed to all of us. They urge us to be "saints," holy and separate ones, by participating in God's reversal of the oppressive social injustices of today, such as the unfortunate plight of the hungry, the homeless, the poor, the underpaid, immigrants, those unjustly imprisoned, victims of racial discrimination, victims of violence, and so on. Although we can expect adversity like the prophets (and saints) of old, Jesus' powerful beatitudes promise us not only God's present blessedness but a future great reward in God's heavenly kingdom.

> THE BEATITUDES URGE US TO BE "SAINTS," HOLY AND SEPARATE ONES, BY PARTICIPATING IN GOD'S REVERSAL OF THE OPPRESSIVE SOCIAL INJUSTICES OF TODAY.

Points to ponder:

- The lives of the martyred saints of the past, who are now part of the heavenly liturgy, encourage us to bear witness to the gospel despite difficulties.
- We remember, thank God for, and strive to imitate those unnamed saints who have been part of our lives.
- As children of God now, we look forward to seeing God in heaven after we have loved one another because of God's great love for us in sending us Jesus.
- The beatitudes both comfort and challenge us to be saints in the kingdom of heaven by being part of God's reversal of social injustices along with and for the sake of Jesus.

TWENTY-FOURTH SUNDAY AFTER PENTECOST

Thirty-first Sunday in Ordinary Time
Proper 26
November 3, 2002

Revised Common	Episcopal (BCP)	Roman Catholic
Mic. 3:5-12 or	Mic. 3:5-12	Mal. 1:14b—2:2b, 8-10
Josh. 3:7-17		
Psalm 43 or	Psalm 43	Ps. 131:1, 2, 3
Ps. 107:1-7, 33-37		
1 Thess. 2:9-13	1 Thess. 2:9-13, 17-20	1 Thess. 2:7b-9, 13
Matt. 23:1-12	Matt. 23:1-12	Matt. 23:1-12

Beware of false prophets who lead astray by speaking self-serving messages rather than the authentic and authoritative word of God. Jesus calls us to a leadership of humble service of one another rather than a pursuit for human recognition, honors, and adulation. Paul models for us a selfless leadership of parental care and concern as he delivers to us the gospel of God, a truly divine rather than merely human word.

FIRST READING
MICAH 3:5-12 (RCL, BCP)

Regarding those "seers" who prophesy according to what they are paid rather than according to the divine revelation that they "see," the prophet Micah warns that God ironically will deprive them of the light to "see" God's revelation (3:5-7). In contrast, with the power and spirit of God, Micah himself has the courage to point out to the people of Israel their sinfulness (3:8). Because Israel's leaders ignore the demands of social justices and allow themselves to be bribed and corrupted, Jerusalem and the temple will be destroyed (3:9-12).

Like Micah we are called to have the courage to proclaim not just what we think people want to hear but the authentic word of God, even when it accuses them of sinfulness and injustice.

We must not allow our own sinfulness to prevent us from hearing and communicating the authentic word of God and devoting ourselves to the cause of social justice.

MALACHI 1:14b-2:2b, 8-10 (RC)

Speaking the word of God, the prophet Malachi castigates the levitical priests who are offering unacceptable sacrifices in the Jerusalem temple in ironic contrast to the Gentiles throughout the world who are properly revering God's name with their offerings (1:14b—2:1). Consequently, God will transform the blessings these priests offer their people into curses (2:1-2b)! Instead of properly leading the people by instructing them in the ways of God in accord with the covenant God made with their priestly ancestor Levi, they have made the people stumble (2:8). Instead of instructing in accord with the authentic word of God, they have shown partiality to human beings in their instruction (2:9). Despite their unity under the one Father and God who created them, their faithlessness to one another has brought about destructive divisions (2:10).

Malachi calls us to seek from our religious leaders not the human words of partiality that may benefit us personally but the actual word of God that challenges us to be faithful and unified. We can properly lead people to God by instructing them in accord with God's word rather than the words of human beings.

JOSHUA 3:7-17 (RCL, alt.)

The crossing of the Jordan River marks an important point in the salvation history of Israel, as it begins to fulfill God's promise to Abraham of a land for his descendants. The miraculous way that God brings Israel through the swollen waters of the Jordan recalls the miraculous way that God brought Israel through the Red Sea in the exodus event. The same God who was with them under the leadership of Moses is now leading them through Moses' successor, Joshua. The crossing has the character of a solemn liturgical procession.

After receiving instruction from God, Joshua, as a true and proper leader, directs the people to "hear the words of the Lord your God" (3:7-9). He gives them God's word that God will drive out the foreign peoples now occupying the land (3:10). God himself, whose presence is represented by the Ark of the Covenant carried by the priests, will lead them across by stopping the flow of the river (3:11-13). It happens just as God said it would; they crossed over opposite Jericho (3:14-16). That the priests bearing the ark of the covenant stood on dry ground in the middle of the Jordan until all the people crossed over underlines how the crossing is God's salvific activity (3:17).

Joshua serves as a model of a true and faithful leader who instructs people in accord with the word of God. It is God himself who enables us to cross the obstacles we encounter in life and to ultimately enter into the promised heavenly land God has prepared for us.

RESPONSIVE READING
PSALM 43 (RCL, BCP)

259

TWENTY-FOURTH
SUNDAY
AFTER PENTECOST
───
NOVEMBER 3

Psalm 43 prays for deliverance "from those who are deceitful and unjust" (43:1), like the corrupt leaders Micah is warning us about in today's first reading. God is our refuge in whom we place our hope; God is ultimately the one who will truly lead us.

PSALM 131:1, 2, 3 (RC)

In contrast to the self-service, arrogance, and partiality of the priestly leaders in today's first reading from Malachi, Psalm 131 expresses humble submission to God's rule and leadership. Unlike false leaders, who often occupy themselves "with things too great and too marvelous" (131:1), the psalmist possesses a infant-like contentment with the will and guidance of God.

PSALM 107:1-7, 33-37 (RCL, alt.)

The climax of the first unit from this hymn of pilgrimage thanksgiving, "he (the Lord) led them by a straight way, until they reached an inhabited town" (107:7), correlates with today's alternate first reading from Joshua, in which God leads Israel by a straight way across the Jordan to a point opposite the inhabited town of Jericho. The second unit (107:33-37) mentions God's transformation of nature ("springs of water into thirsty ground," v. 33), which connects with God's miraculous stopping of the waters of the Jordan river so that Israel can cross and "establish a town to live in" (v. 36).

SECOND READING
1 THESSALONIANS 2:9-13 (RCL);
1 THESSALONIANS 2:9-13, 17-20 (BCP);
1 THESSALONIANS 2:7b-9, 13 (RC)

Interpreting the Text

Rather than seeking human praise or financial support for their preaching, when Paul and his companions Silvanus and Timothy brought the gospel of God to the Thessalonians, they related to them very gently, in the parental manner of a mother nurturing and tenderly caring for them (2:7). They were leaders who shared with the Thessalonians not only the gospel about Jesus Christ but their very selves (2:8).

Paul and his co-workers supported themselves by working very hard, so as not to burden the Thessalonians (2:9). As a complement to the maternal way in which they related to the Thessalonians, Paul and his associates also related to each one of them purely, blamelessly, and uprightly in a paternal fashion by urging, encouraging, and pleading that their conduct be worthy of the God who graciously calls them through the gospel about Jesus Christ into the glory of God's kingdom (2:10-12). They are most grateful that the Thessalonians received their preaching of the gospel not as a merely human word but as the very word of God already at work within them (2:13).

Completing the parental imagery, Paul expresses regret for being absent and separated from the Thessalonians, in which "we were made orphans" or, more appropriately in this context, "we made you orphans" (2:17). Although Paul had a deep parental longing to return to them as those who will be his glory and joy at the final coming of the Lord Jesus, the power of evil, Satan, thwarted his plans (2:18-20).

Responding to the Text

The truly Christian leadership exhibited by Paul and his co-workers stands in sharp contrast to the false and hypocritical leadership depicted in today's first reading and gospel selection. Their preaching of the gospel is not just a profession by which they earn their living. They support themselves instead of burdening their fellow Christians. Rather than self-serving mongers of adulation, they are deeply interested, like parents, in the personal lives of those to whom they bring the gospel. Instead of seeking praise or money, they share their very selves. But, most important, they are instruments for delivering not mere human words but the very word of God in the gospel about Jesus Christ.

PAUL AND HIS COMPANIONS THUS PROVIDE US WITH MODELS OF THE DEEP, PERSONAL CARE AND CONCERN WE SHOULD HAVE FOR THOSE TO WHOM WE MINISTER AS CHRISTIANS. THE PERSONAL SHARING OF OURSELVES IS PART OF SHARING THE WORD OF GOD.

Paul and his companions thus provide us with models of the deep, personal care and concern we should have for those to whom we minister as Christians. The personal sharing of ourselves is part of sharing the word of God. We must make sure that we are sharing the true and authentic word of God rather than our own merely human words. We must be more interested in what we can do for others in sharing with them ourselves and the gospel as the very word of God rather than in what they can do for us.

MATTHEW 23:1-12

Interpreting the Text

During his teaching in the Jerusalem temple Jesus warns both the crowds and his disciples about the woefully inadequate leadership of the scribes and Pharisees. Jesus' acknowledgment that they "sit on Moses' seat" (whether literally, on a piece of synagogue furniture, or metaphorically, as an expression of the authority of their leadership) does not endorse their authority to teach and interpret the Mosaic law, but only indicates that they are the ones who quote and make the law known. For Matthew, only Jesus has authentic divine authority to teach (cf. 7:28-29). Therefore, Jesus urges the doing of whatever the scribes and Pharisees "tell" (not "teach," as in the NRSV) you, but not the doing of what they do, because they do not practice the very law that they quote to the people (23:1-3).

Their refusal to lighten or remove the heavy burdens they arrogantly lay upon people by adding their own rules and regulations to the law (23:4) sharply contrasts the humble leadership of Jesus: "Come to me, all you that are weary and are carrying heavy burdens, and I will give you rest. Take my yoke upon you, and learn from me; for I am gentle and humble in heart, and you will find rest for your souls. For my yoke is easy, and my burden is light" (11:28-30).

Rather than sincerely seeking to please God through the authority of their leadership, they desire human adulation, recognition, and honor. Thus, they ostentatiously widen their phylacteries—the leather boxes containing bits of scriptural texts worn on the left arm and forehead, and lengthen the "fringes" or "tassels" of their garments, in order to be noticed for their piety. They seek seats of honor at banquets and in synagogues, and pompously want people to call them "rabbi" (which literally means "my great one") (23:5-7).

But Jesus urges his audience not to seek the human honor of being called rabbi. Furthermore, their respect for human fathers and instructors should not prevent them from acknowledging God as the one Father and the Messiah as the one instructor of all (23:8-10). For Jesus the true greatness of leadership lies in selfless service: "The greatest among you will be your servant" (23:11). All

> FOR JESUS THE TRUE GREATNESS OF LEADERSHIP LIES IN SELFLESS SERVICE: "THE GREATEST AMONG YOU WILL BE YOUR SERVANT."

who arrogantly and pompously exalt themselves will be humbled by God, but all who selflessly humble themselves like Jesus will be exalted by God (23:12).

262

THE SEASON
OF PENTECOST

JOHN PAUL
HEIL

Responding to the Text

Jesus not only taught but embodied the humble, selfless style of leadership he advocates for us. Rather than burdening people with excessive rules and regulations, Jesus pointed to the essence and epitome of all of the commandments—loving God with our whole being and loving our neighbor as ourselves (22:34-40). Rather than looking for human honor and praise, Jesus sought to serve the needs of others throughout his ministry. His life and leadership of humble and selfless service climaxed in his sacrificial death for all of us. But after his humiliating death by crucifixion God exalted him, and thus vindicated his humble, selfless leadership, by raising him from the dead.

Jesus calls us to take up the cross, deny our selfishness, and follow his way of leadership. We are to live the paradox of losing our lives in selfless service of others in order to save our lives. We serve as true leaders when we practice the authentic will of God that we teach and are taught by others, even by those who do not practice it. Does our need for human recognition and affirmation prevent us from the kind of humble and selfless service that truly brings the very word of God into the lives of others?

Points to ponder:
- "I am filled with power, with the spirit of the Lord, and with justice and might, to declare to Jacob his transgression and to Israel his sin" (Mic. 3:8).
- "You have caused many to stumble by your instruction . . . inasmuch as you have not kept my ways but have shown partiality in your instruction" (Mal. 2:8-9).
- As God through the leadership of Joshua enabled Israel to cross the Jordan River, so God can enable us to lead others across the obstacles and difficulties of a life on pilgrimage to the promised land of heaven.
- The gospel about Jesus Christ is not a mere human word but the very word of God at work in those who believe.
- "The greatest among you will be your servant" (Matt. 23:11).

TWENTY-FIFTH SUNDAY AFTER PENTECOST

THIRTY-SECOND SUNDAY IN ORDINARY TIME
PROPER 27
NOVEMBER 10, 2002

REVISED COMMON	EPISCOPAL (BCP)	ROMAN CATHOLIC
Josh. 24:1-3a, 14-25	Amos 5:18-24	Wisd. of Sol. 6:12-16
or Amos 5:18-24 or		
Wisd. of Sol. 6:12-16		
Psalm 70 or Ps. 78:1-7	Psalm 70	Ps. 63:1, 2-3, 4-5, 6-7
or Wisd. of		(Heb. Bible 63:2, 3-4,
Sol. 6:17-20		5-6, 7-8)
1 Thess. 4:13-18	1 Thess. 4:13-18	1 Thess. 4:13-18 (4:13-14)
Matt. 25:1-13	Matt. 25:1-13	Matt. 25:1-13

As we approach the conclusion of the liturgical year, the focus becomes readiness for the final coming of our Lord Jesus Christ—whether at the end of time or the end of our lives. The scriptures urge us to be prepared by eliminating any false gods from our lives and re-committing ourselves to the one and only God, by working for social justice, and by pursuing the instruction of God's wisdom. Paul encourages us with the hope of sharing, together with our deceased loved ones, in the culmination of the salvation initiated by the death and resurrection of Jesus.

FIRST READING
JOSHUA 24:1-3a, 14-25 (RCL)

Joshua gathered all the tribes of Israel, who at that time were rather disparate and unrelated groups, to one of the major cities that the Israelites had not destroyed in the land of Canaan, Shechem, where they presented themselves before God (24:1). Joshua then reminds them of what unites them. In Abraham they have a common ancestor, whom God took from serving other gods and began to fulfill his promise of land and descendants, as he led him through the land of Canaan and made his offspring many (24:2-3). Eventually Joshua exhorts them to follow the example of him and his household by putting away the gods that their ancestors served beyond the Euphrates river and in Egypt and serve the Lord (24:14-15). The people assure Joshua that they will serve the Lord who brought them out of slavery in Egypt and gave them the land of the Amorites (24:16-18). After Joshua warns them that the Lord is a holy, jealous, and unforgiving God, they nevertheless choose to serve the Lord and thus agree to the solemn covenant that Joshua made between them and God that day at Shechem (24:19-25).

What are the false gods that we need to eliminate from our lives in order to serve the one and only God who saved us in the death and resurrection of Jesus? We can often find ourselves serving the false gods of our material possessions, our jobs and professions, the pursuit of more money, even our own self-absorbed lives. Joshua challenges us to re-commit ourselves to the covenant with God that we agreed to in our baptismal promises.

AMOS 5:18-24 (BCP; RCL, alt.)

The prophet Amos shockingly redefines the popular Israelite concept of "the Day of the Lord." Rather than a time to which Israel could look forward, when God would powerfully intervene on their behalf and triumphantly vindicate them over their enemies, now "the Day of the Lord" will bring them only darkness and gloom. It will be a nightmare of seeming to escape one danger ("a lion") only to meet another ("a bear"), of unexpectedly being bitten by a snake (5:18-20). God takes no pleasure in the abundance and variety of the sacrifices and offerings of their festive worship (5:21-23). Rather, God wants them to work for and bring about an abundance of social justice and right relationships among them: "But let justice roll down like waters, and righteousness like an ever-flowing stream" (5:24).

"BUT LET JUSTICE ROLL DOWN LIKE WATERS, AND RIGHTEOUSNESS LIKE AN EVER-FLOWING STREAM" (AMOS 5:24). OUR WORSHIP IS USELESS AND MAY LEAD TO DISASTER RATHER THAN GOD'S SALVIFIC INTERVENTION IN OUR LIVES IF WE DO NOT WORK FOR SOCIAL JUSTICE.

Our worship is useless and may lead to disaster rather than God's salvific intervention in our lives, if we do not work for social justice. We cannot go to church and worship God and then ignore the social problems that surround us outside of church. Worship is not an escape from or substitute for working for today's abundant and burning social justice issues—abortion, the death penalty, euthanasia, gun control, racial prejudice and profiling, criminal justice reform, refugees, world hunger, poverty, homelessness, human rights, and so on.

WISDOM OF SOLOMON
6:12-16 (RC; RCL, alt.)

As often in the biblical tradition the wisdom of God is here personified as a woman—Lady Wisdom. The wisdom of God is synonymous with God's will, instruction, laws. When we ardently desire to align our lives with the will and instruction of God, we easily and readily find Lady Wisdom (6:12-13). When we rise early in pursuit of God's will, Lady Wisdom is there to meet us (6:14). When our thoughts are focused on the wisdom of being vigilant for ways to do God's will, we will be free from cares and worthy to have Lady Wisdom accompany us throughout our lives (6:15-16).

This reading exhorts us to experience the wisdom of being vigilant in seeking out and doing God's will in our lives. When we desire what God wants for our lives, we are living in accord with God's wisdom and Lady Wisdom will meet and accompany us. When we focus our mind and thoughts on what God wants for us and from us rather than on what we want or on what other people and our society tell us to want, we will experience the wisdom of being free from life's cares and worries.

RESPONSIVE READING
PSALM 70 (RCL and BCP)

Psalm 70 is a prayer for God's deliverance from enemies. Verse 4 fits today's first reading from Joshua that calls for turning away from false gods to serve the God of salvation: "Let all who seek you rejoice and be glad in you. Let those who love your salvation say evermore, 'God is great!'" Verse 5 fits today's first reading from Amos, as it pleads for God's help in bringing about social justice: "But I am poor and needy, hasten to me, O God! You are my help and my deliverer; O Lord, do not delay!"

PSALM 63:1, 2-3, 4-5, 6-7 (RC)

With its expression of deep desire and devotion to God's presence and love, this selection accompanies today's first reading from the Wisdom of Solomon, which advocates that our desires and thoughts be focused on God's wisdom. Especially relevant is the psalmist's expression of satisfaction and joy when he meditates on God through the night (63:5-6).

PSALM 78:1-7 (RCL, alt.)

With its exhortation to listen to and to do God's commandments, this selection fits today's alternate first reading from Amos, in which God exhorts the doing of justice and righteousness.

WISDOM OF SOLOMON 6:17-20 (RCL, alt.)

This selection is the continuation of today's alternate first reading from the Wisdom of Solomon. It describes a process that begins with the desire for the instruction of Lady Wisdom, moves through the keeping of her laws, and culminates with the attainment of immortality in the eternal kingdom of God.

SECOND READING
1 THESSALONIANS 4:13-18

Interpreting the Text

Although Paul congratulated the Thessalonians for exhibiting the fundamental Christian triad of faith, love, and hope (1:3), he later hinted that there is something lacking in their faith (3:10). Indeed, their faith is lacking a proper hope for their loved ones who have already died. Since they were expecting the final coming of Christ during their lifetimes, they are worried that their deceased loved ones will be left out when Christ comes again.

Paul exhorts the Thessalonians not to grieve for their deceased loved ones in the manner of non-Christians who have no hope (4:13). Our Christian hope is based on our faith in the death and resurrection of Jesus. The resurrection of Jesus implies and assures the resurrection of those loved ones who have already died. God will bring back along with Jesus at his final coming those who have already died (4:14). In fact, those who are still living at the final coming will have no advantage or precedence over those who have already died (4:15).

Indeed, those who have already died in Christ will rise first at the final coming, which Paul depicts with traditional biblical and apocalyptic stage props. It will begin with the Lord's cry of command, with the archangel's call, and with the sound of God's trumpet. When the Lord descends from heaven, those who have died will rise first (4:16). Then those who are still alive will follow them. With an imaginative, apocalyptic description of an event that transcends our human knowledge, Paul depicts how those who are still alive "will be caught up in the clouds" along with those who have already died to meet the Lord in the heavens. Then we will all—those who have died and those still alive—be with the Lord forever (4:17). By adding this essential element of hope to their Christian faith, the Thessalonians can comfort and console one another with regard to their departed loved ones (4:18).

Responding to the Text

We all wonder what happens when we die. We all miss our departed loved ones. This reading does not take away the mystery that surrounds death, the afterlife, and the second coming of Christ. These are mysteries that will always elude our human understanding. As a transhistorical, superterrestrial event, the final coming of Christ can only be imagined not scientifically delineated. How it will happen we do not know; that it will happen is assured. Indeed, Paul assures us that our faith in the death and resurrection of Jesus gives us the confident and consoling hope of somehow being reunited with our departed loved ones. Our faith allows us to look forward to being together with both our loved ones and the risen Lord forever. With such hope we cannot only be encouraged but also encourage others.

> PAUL DOES NOT TAKE AWAY THE MYSTERY THAT SURROUNDS DEATH, THE AFTERLIFE, AND THE SECOND COMING OF CHRIST. HOW THESE WILL HAPPEN WE DO NOT KNOW; THAT THEY WILL HAPPEN IS ASSURED.

THE GOSPEL
MATTHEW 25:1-13

Interpreting the Text

The cultural custom of a bridegroom festively leading his bride from her parents' home to his own provides a backdrop for today's parable. When Jesus comes as the Son of Man at the end of the age, the kingdom of heaven will be like the case of ten bridesmaids or virgins who took their lamps and went out to meet the bridegroom (25:1). The meeting of the bridegroom depicts the return of Jesus, the "bridegroom," after he is taken away from his disciples by his death (9:15). The comparison of the ten bridesmaids to what the kingdom of heaven will be like include five who are foolish and five who are wise (25:2).

As the foolish man built his house on sand (7:26) and as the wicked and foolish servant beat his fellow servants and ate and drank with drunkards (24:49), so the foolish bridesmaids did not take with them oil for their lamps (25:3). But as the wise man built his house on rock (7:24) and as the faithful and wise servant gave his fellow servants their food at the proper time (24:45), so the wise bridesmaids took flasks of oil with their lamps (25:4). Whereas the wicked servant thought his lord would be delayed (24:48) but was not (24:50), the bridegroom is actually delayed so that all the bridesmaids became drowsy and slept (25:5).

When at midnight came the cry to go out and meet the bridegroom (25:6), all the bridesmaids arose and trimmed their lamps (25:7). When the foolish bridesmaids ask their fellow bridesmaids to give them some of their oil (25:8), the wise bridesmaids recognize that there is not enough oil for all and direct their foolish fellow bridesmaids to procure oil for themselves (25:9). The foolish bridesmaids expect their wise fellow bridesmaids to compensate for their own lack of preparation.

Those bridesmaids who were "ready," who thus fulfilled Jesus' command to the disciples to be "ready" for the unknowable time of his coming (24:44), entered with the bridegroom into the wedding feast, representative of entering the kingdom of heaven (25:1; 22:1-14), and the door was closed (25:10). The disciples will be as ready and prepared as the wise bridesmaids if each, like the wise man, hears and does the words of Jesus (7:24), which reveal the will of his Father that each is to do in order to enter the kingdom of heaven (7:21).

> THE DISCIPLES WILL BE AS READY AND PREPARED AS THE WISE BRIDESMAIDS IF EACH HEARS AND DOES THE WORDS OF JESUS, WHICH REVEAL THE WILL OF HIS FATHER.

When the foolish bridesmaids cry, "Lord, Lord, open to us!" (25:11), the bridegroom can only reply, "I do not know you" (25:12). This recalls Jesus' reply, "I never knew you; go away from me, you evildoers" (7:23), to those who will cry on the day of his coming, "Lord, Lord," and point to their prophesying, exorcising, and working wonders in his name (7:22). But only the one who does the will of Jesus' Father (7:21), in order to become a member of the family known to Jesus (12:50), will enter the kingdom of heaven. Jesus, the bridegroom, does not know the foolish bridesmaids because they are not members of his family who do the will of his Father.

Applying the parable directly to his disciples, Jesus warns, "Keep awake therefore, for you know neither the day nor the hour" (25:13). The disciples and the audience must be constantly ready and prepared whether Jesus' final coming is delayed (25:1-13) or not (24:45-51).

Responding to the Text

This parable warns us to reckon with a possible delay of unknown duration for Jesus' final coming. Like the wise bridesmaids we must be prepared to enter the wedding feast of the kingdom of heaven whenever Jesus comes as the bridegroom. We will be ready and enter with Jesus if he knows us as members of his family, as those who hear and do the words of Jesus that reveal the will of his heavenly Father. Unlike the foolish bridesmaids, we must not foolishly expect our fellow Christians to be able to help us if we ourselves are not personally prepared and ready for the unknown day and hour of Jesus' final coming.

Points to ponder:

- Are we serving false gods or the true God of our salvation?
- Does our worship inspire us to work for social justice?
- Do we desire the conventional wisdom of the world or the wisdom of God?
- Does our faith include the consoling and confident hope of being reunited with loved ones forever with the risen Jesus?
- "Keep awake therefore, for you know neither the day nor the hour" (Matt. 25:13).

TWENTY-SIXTH SUNDAY AFTER PENTECOST

THIRTY-THIRD SUNDAY IN ORDINARY TIME
PROPER 28
NOVEMBER 17, 2002

REVISED COMMON	EPISCOPAL (BCP)	ROMAN CATHOLIC
Zeph. 1:7, 12-18 or Judg. 4:1-7	Zeph. 1:7, 12-18	Prov. 31:10-13, 19-20, 30-31
Ps. 90:1-8, (9-11),12 or Psalm 123	Psalm 90 or 90:1-8, 12	Ps. 128:1-2, 3, 4-5
1 Thess. 5:1-11	1 Thess. 5:1-10	1 Thess. 5:1-6
Matt. 25:14-30	Matt. 25:14-15, 19-29	Matt. 25:14-30 (25:14-15, 19-21)

Are we ready for the end—either the end of our lives or the end of the world when Christ comes again? Either may happen at any time. We will be ready and "awake" by being reliable, industrious, and enterprising stewards of all that God has given us.

FIRST READING
ZEPHANIAH 1:7, 12-18 (RCL, BCP)

The prophet Zephaniah places a surprisingly negative and threatening twist on the otherwise positive and beneficial "Day of the Lord." The Lord God is preparing a festive sacrifice for that day, but it will be a slaughter of sinners!" (1:7). God promises to punish those "who rest complacently on their dregs," that is, those who have become "thick" or lazy, like the inert sediment at the bottom of a bottle of wine. They overconfidently think God is indifferent to their behavior (1:12). God will not allow sinners to enjoy the wealth they have accumulated, the houses they have built, or the vineyards they have planted (1:13). The imminent Day of the Lord will bring utter disaster and devastation, "because they have sinned against the Lord" (1:14-17). All of their wealth and material possessions will not be able to save them (1:18).

Have we become overconfident and complacent in our relationship to God? Do we think that God does not care if we simply become part of the materialistic, affluent, consumer-obsessed culture in which we live? If the accumulation of wealth and material things rather than the doing of God's will is the priority of our lives, what will the final Day of the Lord bring for us?

PROVERBS 31:10-13, 19-20, 30-31 (RC)

In the biblical tradition the wisdom of God is often personified as a woman. Today's reading from Proverbs extols the wisdom of acquiring a capable wife. The praise of the ideal wife in the first excerpt (31:10-13) culminates in the industriousness of working well with her hands (see today's Gospel). The focus on her hands continues in the second excerpt (31:19-20), in which she admirably extends her diligent hands to the poor and needy. The third excerpt (31:30-31) praises her reverence for God, who is requested to reward the labor of her hard-working hands.

The diligence of a wise wife provides a model for all of us to imitate. She prompts us not only to work well with what we have to provide for ourselves and our families, but also to extend our hands to the poor and needy in the world. Today's reading provides an opportunity not only for husbands and children but for all of us to thank God for the good example of the many industrious, generous, and loving wives and mothers among us.

JUDGES 4:1-7 (RCL, alt.)

This reading exhibits a typical pattern in the book of Judges: God punishes the Israelites for their sinfulness by allowing enemies to oppress them; they cry out to God for deliverance; and God wonderfully delivers them through one of the judges. In this case the enemy is King Jabin of Canaan, who ruled in Hazor. His exceptionally high number of "nine hundred chariots of iron" intensifies the hopelessness of this situation of oppression for the Israelites (4:1-3). The judge in this case is the prophetess Deborah, through whom God promises the Israelites that they will prevail over their enemies (4:4-7).

We always have the opportunity to overcome the pain and oppression our sinfulness causes us by crying out to God for help. With the help of God we can correct our own faults and failings and, like Deborah, help others in our common struggle against the power of evil and sin in our lives.

RESPONSIVE READING

PSALM 90:1-8, (9-11), 12 (RCL);
PSALM 90 or 90:1-8, 12 (BCP)

This group lament pleads for God's merciful compassion on us mortal, wicked, and weak humans. It responds to today's first reading from Zephaniah with an acknowledgment of God's punishment for our sinfulness: "For we are consumed by your anger; by your wrath we are overwhelmed. You have set our iniquities before you, our secret sins in the light of your countenance" (90:7-8). There is wisdom in the realization that our opportunities for repenting are numbered (90:12).

PSALM 128:1-2, 3, 4-5 (RC)

This wisdom psalm correlates with today's first reading from Proverbs about the ideal wife. God's promise of reward for the good stewardship of hard-working hands in verse 2 echoes the climax of the selection from Proverbs (31:31). Reverence for and devotion to God promises that "your wife will be like a fruitful vine" (128:3).

PSALM 123 (RCL, alt.)

This communal plea for God's merciful deliverance from enemies cor-relates with today's alternate first reading from Judges, in which the Israelites cry out to God for help in their oppression by enemies. In the distress and difficul-ties of life our focus is on God: "our eyes look to the Lord our God, until he has mercy upon us" (123:2).

SECOND READING
1 THESSALONIANS 5:1-11 (RCL);
1 THESSALONIANS 5:1-10 (BCP);
1 THESSALONIANS 5:1-6 (RC)

Interpreting the Text

Paul warns his Thessalonian audience that the Day of the Lord, that is, the final coming of Christ, will come unexpectedly "like a thief in the night" (5:2), so that those unprepared for its coming will surely not escape sudden dis-aster (5:3). But Paul assures the Thessalonians that they are not in spiritual "darkness" for the Day to overcome them like a thief (5:4). With regard to the apocalyptic, dualistic worldview of that time, they and all Christians are in the realm of "light" and of "day," not of "night" or "darkness" (5:5). This indicative of their present status, however, carries with it an urgent imperative, expressed with a series of three verbs of exhortation in 5:6: "So then, let us not fall asleep" like others do but "let us keep awake" and "be sober"—metaphorical language for moral vigilance. In 5:7-8a Paul reiterates the imperative that corresponds to the indicative: Since we Christians are of the day, not sleeping or getting drunk at night, "let us be sober"—by living in moral uprightness.

We Christians are able not to fall asleep but to be awake and sober because in becoming believers at our baptism we have already "put on the breastplate of faith and love, and for a helmet the hope of salvation" (5:8b). In other words, the fundamental Christian triad of faith, love, and hope has given the Thessalonians the spiritual "armor" of God they need to be vigilant "soldiers" or "guards" who do not fall asleep. Paul's previous prayer indicated how, by increasing their love,

THE FUNDAMENTAL CHRISTIAN TRIAD OF FAITH, LOVE, AND HOPE HAS GIVEN THE THESSALONIANS THE SPIRITUAL "ARMOR" OF GOD THEY NEED TO BE VIGILANT "SOLDIERS" OR "GUARDS" WHO DO NOT FALL ASLEEP.

the Thessalonians can be vigilant for Christ's final coming: "May the Lord make you increase and abound in love for one another and for all, just as we abound in love for you. And may he so strengthen your hearts in holiness that you may be blameless before our God and Father at the coming of our Lord Jesus with all his saints" (3:12-13).

Paul further grounds the imperatives of not being asleep but awake and sober (5:6-8) in the indicative of God's grace: "For God has destined us not for wrath but for obtaining salvation through our Lord Jesus Christ, who died for us" (5:9-10a). The exhortation not to be asleep but awake and sober in 5:6-8 is the main purpose of 5:1-11. Paul's exhortation, "let us not fall asleep," implied the possibility of the Thessalonians falling asleep "as others do" (5:6), that is, non-believers, "the others who have no hope" (4:13), those who are not ready for the Day of the Lord (5:2-3). But in the case that some Thessalonians may be spiritually or morally "asleep" before the Day of the Lord, Paul's previous powerful exhortation, "let us *not* fall asleep" (5:6) still holds. The implication is that if some are now "asleep," they must be "awakened" by the others, so that together—as those awake and those awakened, "we may live with him" (5:10b) when the Day of the Lord arrives. Paul thus exhorts his audience to encourage, build up, and "awaken" one another to be ready for the final coming of Christ.

273

TWENTY-SIXTH
SUNDAY
AFTER PENTECOST

NOVEMBER 17

Responding to the Text

Will our preoccupation with mundane cares and concerns cause us to be caught off guard when the Lord comes, either at the end of our lives or at the end of time? The fundamental Christian triad of our faith in what God has done for us in the death and resurrection of Jesus, our hope that we will share in that resurrection, and our love for one another based on that faith and hope give us the spiritual armor we need to be awake and alert for the end. We all have the responsibility of "awakening" one another to moral and spiritual vigilance so that we will all be ready for final salvation.

THE GOSPEL

MATTHEW 25:14-30 (RCL);
MATTHEW 25:14-15, 19-29 (BCP);
MATTHEW 25:14-30 (25:14-15, 19-21) (RC)

Interpreting the Text

In this parable the kingdom of heaven will be like the case of a man who, going on a journey, called his own servants and entrusted to them his possessions (25:14). The "talents" that he distributed to three different servants according to their ability (25:15) refer to units of coinage of very high value, but symbolically embrace what we currently understand by "talents"—native, God-given abilities. The man represents Jesus, his journey represents the absence of Jesus after his resurrection and before his final coming, and his servants represent the disciples.

That the servant who received five talents and the one who received two talents gained another five and two respectively (25:16-17) resonates with how the disciples, as "sowers" who are to "sow" the word of the gospel, can expect to yield a remarkably abundant harvest of people for the kingdom of heaven (13:8, 23). But the servant who received only one talent hid "his master's money" (25:18). The emphasis on the man as "master" of the servant underlines that the money still belongs to the master and has only been entrusted to the servant to be a steward of it. That the master comes after a long time represents how Jesus comes as Lord and Son of Man at an unknown day and unexpected hour (25:19; 24:42, 44).

Both the servant who received five talents as well as the one who received two are rewarded with entrance into the joy of the master—the kingdom of heaven (25:20-23). Despite their very high value, the talents are designated as "a few things" in comparison with "the many things" (v. 21), the heavenly reward for the faithful stewardship of earthly gifts. Important is not the amount one is given but whether one is a productive steward in accord with one's ability (v. 15) of whatever amount has been entrusted.

In contrast to the two servants who took the risk of doing business with the talents given them, the servant who received the one talent is still holding it (25:24). That he hid "your" talent in the ground and declared to his master, "Here you have what is yours" (25:25), underscores his failure to be a productive steward of the talent entrusted to him by his master. But this wicked and lazy servant should have at least taken the minimum risk of depositing his master's money with the bankers to earn some interest (25:26-27). The master then shockingly commands that the talent be taken away from him and given to the one who has the ten (25:28). The one talent has been taken away from the servant because he did not risk working aggressively with it to know and experience the mystery of the kingdom of heaven, as did the servant who earned the ten talents, so that he is given even more in abundance (25:29; cf. 13:11-12).

The master finally commands that the useless servant be thrown into "the outer darkness, where there will be weeping and gnashing of teeth" (25:30)—an expression of the extreme anguish of final exclusion from the kingdom of heaven (see 8:12; 13:42, 50; 22:13; 24:51). His punishment serves as a dramatic warning for the disciples to be watchful for the unknown day and hour of Jesus' final coming by taking the risk to be productive stewards with whatever they have been entrusted.

Responding to the Text

We value our individual rights of private ownership of what we have often worked so hard to acquire. Although we may not be as talented as some, we have all been blessed with natural gifts and talents that we often do not use and develop. Yet whatever amount of natural talent and ability we have, and whatever amount of money and material possessions those abilities have enabled us to earn, ultimately belongs to the Master. We are merely stewards of all that God has given us. Jesus warns us to be like those servants who took the risk of being productive stewards by aggressively and energetically working with whatever amount of talents were entrusted to them for promoting and thus experiencing the kingdom of heaven. If we cautiously conserve the talents, money, and material things entrusted to us like the lazy and useless servant paralyzed by fear, we will not be prepared and qualified to enter into the final joy of the kingdom of heaven at the unknown day and hour of Jesus' final coming.

Points to ponder:

- "Neither their silver nor their gold will be able to save them on the day of the Lord's wrath" (Zeph. 1:18).
- "She opens her hand to the poor, and reaches out her hands to the needy" (Prov. 31:20).
- "Then the Israelites cried out to the Lord for help" (Judg. 4:3).
- "Encourage one another and build up each other" (1 Thess. 5:11).
- "For to all those who have, more will be given, and they will have an abundance; but from those who have nothing, even what they have will be taken away" (Matt. 25:29).

LAST SUNDAY AFTER PENTECOST, CHRIST THE KING

THIRTY-FOURTH SUNDAY IN ORDINARY TIME
PROPER 29
NOVEMBER 24, 2002

REVISED COMMON	EPISCOPAL (BCP)	ROMAN CATHOLIC
Ezek. 34:11-16, 20-24	Ezek. 34:11-17	Ezek. 34:11-12, 15-17
Ps. 95:1-7a or Psalm 100	Ps. 95:1-7	Ps. 23:1-2, 2-3, 5-6
Eph. 1:15-23	1 Cor. 15:20-28	1 Cor. 15:20-26, 28
Matt. 25:31-46	Matt. 25:31-46	Matt. 25:31-46

God expected the kings of Israel to be like shepherds to their people, leading, feeding, healing, finding, and uniting their people. But these kings failed miserably, so that God himself promised to be the Shepherd-King. In Matthew 25, Jesus is the Shepherd-King who fulfills God's promise. When he comes again in glory as the King, Jesus will judge all people, separating them as a shepherd separates the sheep from the goats. At the end of time, Christ the King, who became the heavenly head of the church, his earthly body, through his death and resurrection, will hand over the kingdom to God the Father, "so that God may be all in all."

FIRST READING
EZEKIEL 34:11-16, 20-24 (RCL);
EZEKIEL 34:11-17 (BCP);
EZEKIEL 34:11-12, 15-17 (RC)

Interpreting the Text

Since the kings of Israel have failed to be shepherds who feed, clothe, and care for the sheep, their people, but instead have scattered them (34:1-10), God promises to be the Shepherd who will search out, find, and bring back the people from all the places they have been scattered in various exiles and dispersions throughout their history (34:11-12). God will bring them back and feed them richly on the mountain heights of their own land of Israel (34:13-15). But God will make distinctions among the sheep. Although God will seek the lost, bring back the strayed, bind up the injured, and strengthen the weak, God will destroy the fat and strong among the sheep, "feeding" them with justice (34:16-17).

God promises to "judge between sheep and sheep," between the "fat" sheep, who feed only themselves and push the others aside until they are scattered, and the "lean" sheep, who have been neglected and oppressed (34:20-22). God will set up over the people a new Davidic shepherd-king who will feed and truly shepherd them (34:23-24).

Responding to the Text

For Christians, Jesus fulfills God's promise for a new Davidic shepherd-king. He gathered huge crowds of "sheep" and miraculously—from a few loaves and fishes—fed them to overabundance, to the point that they had to collect the many leftovers. Jesus thus empowered his disciples to feed the people with enough left over to continue feeding others. In the Eucharist Jesus feeds us with his own body and blood in a spiritually overabundant way, so that we in turn can feed and nourish others. Are we "fat" sheep who feed only ourselves?

RESPONSIVE READING
PSALM 95:1-7a (RCL); PSALM 95:1-7 (BCP)

This psalm invites us to celebrate God's kingship as the creator over all—"a great King above all gods" (95:3). The selection climaxes with the acknowledgment that God is our Shepherd-King: "For he is our God, and we are the people of his pasture, and the sheep of his hand" (95:7).

PSALM 23:1-2, 2-3, 5-6 (RC)

The familiar Psalm 23 contains the classic description of God as our Shepherd. The psalm invites us to place our confidence in the goodness and mercy of the God who, like a shepherd, feeds, refreshes, leads, guides through danger, comforts, and vindicates us over oppressive enemies.

PSALM 100 (RCL, alt.)

Although this psalm does not specifically mention God as "king," it serves as a concluding doxology to the preceding royal psalms celebrating God's kingship (Psalms 93 and 95–99). In accord with today's first reading from Ezekiel this psalm acknowledges God as our Shepherd: "Know that the Lord is God. It is he that made us, and we are his people, and the sheep of his pasture" (100:3).

EPHESIANS 1:15-23 (RCL)

Interpreting the Text

In this thanksgiving section from the letter to the Ephesians an idealized Paul functions as a mystagogue—one who initiates into and imparts the experience of a mystery. In this case the mystery is the cosmic and universal dimensions of Christ and his church. In antiquity the image of "head" and "body" often portrayed the relationship between the visible and invisible dimensions of the universe as a cosmic human person—the "head" representing the spiritual, heavenly realms and the "body" the material, earthly realms. The "head" was considered to be not only the origin and source of power for the "body" but also its goal or final destiny. The "body" is growing and flowing both from and back to the "head," until the "head" embraces, unifies, and fills the entire cosmos.

> PAUL FUNCTIONS AS A MYSTAGOGUE; IN THIS CASE THE MYSTERY IS THE COSMIC AND UNIVERSAL DIMENSIONS OF CHRIST AND HIS CHURCH.

Paul thanks God for the faith that his Ephesian audience has in the Lord Jesus and the love they have for one another (1:15-16). Faith and love are the basis of the mystery that Paul as mystagogue wants to impart. He prays that God may give them the wisdom to "know," that is, "experience" in a mystical way as part of the "body" the great hope to which God has called them together with all of their fellow Christians (1:17-18). As part of the "body" they can experience the immeasurable greatness of the power (1:19) that comes from the "head"—the risen Christ. "God put this power to work in Christ when he raised him from the dead and seated him at his right hand in the heavenly places" (1:20). Thus, Christ is the heavenly "head" exalted and enthroned over all of the invisible and spiritual powers, past and present, in the universe (1:21). This, then, is the mystery: God has made the risen Christ the "head" over the entire cosmos with the church as his "body"—"the fullness of him who fills all in all" (1:22-23). As heavenly "head," Christ is both the source of power and final destiny of the "body," the church.

Responding to the Text

When we look up at the sky on a clear night and see the myriads of stars and planets, we realize how vast is the universe and how we are just a small part of it. But where is everything in the universe headed and how are we part of it? The mystery of Christ as "head" and his church as "body" embraces the totality of the cosmos. There is nothing over which the risen Christ, enthroned as heavenly king, does not have power. Through the "body" of the church of which we are a part the risen Christ is working to reconcile and unify everything in the universe under his headship. We pray that we may play our part in this great mystery by opening our lives to the power of the risen Christ to reconcile and unify us with one another and with God.

1 CORINTHIANS 15:20-28 (BCP); 1 CORINTHIANS 15:20-26, 28 (RC)

Interpreting the Text

Although the Corinthian Christians believed in the resurrection of Jesus, they did not realize its ramifications for the general resurrection of the dead (15:12) and thus for their own resurrection. But Paul explains that as the "first fruits"—the first portion of a harvest offered to God in thanksgiving that guaranteed the rest of the harvest—the resurrection of Jesus guarantees the general resurrection of the dead (15:20). Just as the first human being, Adam, was the prototypical representative of all human beings, so that his death meant that all would die, so also the resurrection of Christ, as a second Adam, means that all will be raised (15:21-22).

But the general resurrection of the dead will not take place until Christ comes again at the end of time, when he will hand over the kingdom to God the Father. Until then the risen Christ is reigning as king in heaven, still in the process of destroying all the demonic powers of evil on earth (15:23-24). The last power that Christ the king will destroy is the power of death (15:25-26). But this is sure to happen since "God has put all thing in subjection under his feet." After God has subjected all things to Christ the king, then Christ himself will be subjected to God, "so that God may be all in all" (15:27-28).

Responding to the Text

The kingship of Jesus Christ is a kingship in progress. It will not be complete until God destroys for us the power of death that God began to destroy in raising Jesus from the dead. Although death still has power over us in that we all will one day die, it is just a matter of time until God destroys the power of death completely and for everyone in and through the kingship of Christ. Today we look forward in hope to our future resurrection from the dead, a sure hope guaranteed by the resurrection that enthroned and exalted Christ as our heavenly king.

MATTHEW 25:31-46

Interpreting the Text

In this dramatic scene of the Last Judgment, Jesus, the new-born king of the Jews (2:2), who entered Jerusalem as her king (21:5), now represents *the king*, the Son of Man who will judge all the peoples of the world in the manner of a shepherd separating sheep from goats (25:31-33). The reason the sheep on the right are blessed with *the kingdom* is that they served Jesus himself in accord with the way that Jesus not only served those in need but taught and empowered his disciples to serve those in need.

THE REASON THE SHEEP ON THE RIGHT ARE BLESSED WITH THE KINGDOM IS THAT THEY SERVED JESUS HIMSELF IN ACCORD WITH THE WAY THAT JESUS NOT ONLY SERVED THOSE IN NEED BUT TAUGHT AND EMPOWERED HIS DISCIPLES TO SERVE THOSE IN NEED.

1. That "I was hungry and you gave me food" (25:35) means the sheep have done for Jesus what Jesus himself commanded his disciples to do for the hungry crowds (14:16). After he miraculously increased an insufficient amount of food twice (14:17; 15:34), he empowered his disciples to feed those who were hungry as he gave the food to his disciples who in turn gave it to the crowds.

2. That the sheep received the reward of the kingdom because "I was thirsty and you gave me something to drink" (25:35) accords with Jesus' teaching the disciples that whoever gives a drink of cold water to one of these little ones simply because he is a disciple will surely not lose his reward (10:42), the everlasting reward of the kingdom.

3. That "I was a stranger and you welcomed me" (25:35) means the sheep have imitated Jesus, who welcomed strangers with mercy (9:13) when he shared the hospitality of meal fellowship with estranged public sinners (9:9-13; 11:19) and when he healed foreigners (8:5-13; 15:21-28). Jesus' teaching of love of enemies (5:43-48) embraces the hospitable welcoming of strangers.

4. That "I was naked and you gave me clothing" (25:36) means the sheep have served Jesus by emulating his compassion in accord with his teaching to love one's neighbor as oneself (22:39), especially as it is expressed in Isa. 58:7: "If you see someone naked, clothe him."

5. That "I was sick and you took care of me" (25:36) means the sheep have ministered to Jesus in accord with his authoritative command and empowerment for the disciples to heal the sick (10:8). They thus share in and extend the compassionate healing ministry of Jesus himself.

6. That "I was in prison and you visited me" (25:36) means the sheep assisted Jesus not only as one in critical need but in the way that disciples should assist their master, as exemplified by the disciples of John the Baptist, who assisted him after he was put in prison (14:3, 10).

But the righteous are surprised that it was Jesus himself whom they had served. Their three questions, each introduced with the same words of incredulous astonishment that it was "you," repeat the compassionate conduct that gained them the kingdom (25:37-39). Jesus as "the king" adds to the surprise not only by identifying himself with the needy whom the righteous have helped but by designating the needy as members of his new family (25:40). Not only are the disciples who do the will of the Father in heaven members of his new family (12:49-50), but now even the lowliest among the needy belong to the new family of Jesus.

Furthermore, the disciples may find themselves in the position of the needy "least" ones. Since they are to take no money on their mission (10:9), disciples may find themselves in need of food or drink like the least ones. Like the least ones they will be strangers seeking to be welcomed into the homes of others (10:11-13) and persecuted refugees fleeing from city to city (10:23). Like the naked least ones they may be in need of clothing, since they are not to take a traveling bag, second tunic, or sandals with them (10:10). Like the least ones they may find themselves sick or imprisoned because of the expected hardship and persecution of their mission (10:16-23). But as needy least ones the disciples can be encouraged that those who take care of them will be rewarded with the kingdom (25:34).

> JESUS AS "THE KING" ADDS TO THE SURPRISE NOT ONLY BY IDENTIFYING HIMSELF WITH THE NEEDY WHOM THE RIGHTEOUS HAVE HELPED BUT BY DESIGNATING THE NEEDY AS MEMBERS OF HIS NEW FAMILY.

The reason the goats are cursed for the eternal fire is that their behavior toward Jesus was precisely the opposite of that of the sheep. For the third time the audience experiences the criteria of judgment, but this time negatively (25:41-43). Like the righteous sheep the goats are surprised that it was Jesus himself whom they had failed to serve. Their query quickly and powerfully brings the audience once again through the list of criteria for judgment climaxed by their self-condemning failure: "And we did *not* take care of *you*" (25:44). Once again the audience experiences the shock of Jesus identifying himself with the least ones (25:45). After the negative experience of the goats and their eternal punishment, the parable concludes on a positive note with the reward of eternal life for the righteous (25:46).

Responding to the Text

Jesus' shocking identification of himself with the needy least ones adds a new twist to the theme of being prepared for the unknown time of his final coming as king. There is a sense in which Jesus is not really absent at all. The parable urges us to be the righteous sheep who must take care of the neediest, the least ones, in the world as a way of serving Jesus himself until his final coming. By doing so we will be blessed at the last judgment by inheriting the eternal life of the kingdom God has prepared for us. But it also encourages us to become needy least ones in our Christian mission of bringing the kingdom to the world. As least ones we can be assured of Jesus' presence with us as members of his own family. We can take the risk of becoming needy least ones because the righteous must and will take care of us.

Points to ponder:
- God is the Shepherd-King who not only takes care of but judges between the sheep.
- As part of the "body" that is the church we can experience the immeasurable greatness of the power that comes from the "head"—the risen Christ enthroned as king in heaven.
- Christ the King is reigning in heaven until he destroys the power of death.
- The words of Christ the King: "just as you did it to one of the least of these who are members of my family, you did it to me" (Matt. 25:40).

APRIL 2002

Sunday	Monday	Tuesday	Wednesday	Thursday	Friday	Saturday
March 31 Easter Day	1 Easter Monday	2	3	4	5	6
7 2 Easter	8	9	10	11	12	13
14 3 Easter	15	16	17	18	19	20
21 4 Easter	22	23	24	25	26	27
28 5 Easter	29	30				

MAY 2002

Sunday	Monday	Tuesday	Wednesday	Thursday	Friday	Saturday
			1	2	3	4
5	6	7	8	9 Ascension Day	10	11
12	13	14	15	16	17	18
7 Easter Mother's Day						
19	20	21	22	23	24	25
Pentecost						
26	27 Memorial Day	28	29	30	31	
1 Pentecost Holy Trinity Sunday						

JUNE 2002

Sunday	Monday	Tuesday	Wednesday	Thursday	Friday	Saturday
						1
2 Pentecost Body and Blood of Christ	3	4	5	6	7	8
3 Pentecost	10	11	12	13	14	15
16	17	18	19	20	21	22
4 Pentecost Father's Day						
23	24	25	26	27	28	29
5 Pentecost						
30						
6 Pentecost						

JULY 2002

Sunday	Monday	Tuesday	Wednesday	Thursday	Friday	Saturday
	1	2	3	4 Independence Day	5	6
7 7 Pentecost	8	9	10	11	12	13
14 8 Pentecost	15	16	17	18	19	20
21 9 Pentecost	22	23	24	25	26	27
28 10 Pentecost	29	30	31			

AUGUST 2002

Sunday	Monday	Tuesday	Wednesday	Thursday	Friday	Saturday
				1	2	3
4 11 Pentecost	5	6	7	8	9	10
11 12 Pentecost	12	13	14	15	16	17
18 13 Pentecost	19	20	21	22	23	24
25 14 Pentecost	26	27	28	29	30	31

SEPTEMBER 2002

Sunday	Monday	Tuesday	Wednesday	Thursday	Friday	Saturday
1 15 Pentecost	2 Labor Day	3	4	5	6	7
8 16 Pentecost	9	10	11	12	13	14
15 17 Pentecost	16	17	18	19	20	21
22 18 Pentecost	23	24	25	26	27	28
29 19 Pentecost St. Michael and All Angels	30					

OCTOBER 2002

Sunday	Monday	Tuesday	Wednesday	Thursday	Friday	Saturday
		1	2	3	4	5
6 20 Pentecost	7	8	9	10	11	12
13 21 Pentecost	14	15	16	17	18	19
20 22 Pentecost	21	22	23	24	25	26
27 23 Pentecost	28	29	30	31 Reformation Day		

NOVEMBER 2002

Sunday	Monday	Tuesday	Wednesday	Thursday	Friday	Saturday
					1 All Saints Day	2
3 24 Pentecost	4	5	6	7	8	9
10 25 Pentecost	11	12	13	14	15	16
17 26 Pentecost	18	19	20	21	22	23
24 27 Pentecost/Christ the King	25	26	27	28 Thanksgiving Day	29	30